To Cathy, Koji, Andrea, and Lynda

Foreword

ABOUT THE SERIES

These case studies in cultural anthropology are designed to bring to students, in beginning and intermediate courses in the social sciences, insights into the richness and complexity of human life as it is lived in different ways and in different places. They are written by men and women who have lived in the societies they write about and who are professionally trained as observers and interpreters of human behavior. The authors are also teachers and, in writing their books, they have kept the students who will read them foremost in their minds. It is our belief that when an understanding of ways of life very different from one's own is gained, abstractions and generalizations about social structure, cultural values, subsistence techniques, and the other universal categories of human social behavior become meaningful.

These case studies are concerned not only with the description and analysis of distinctive cultures, but also with the ways in which they have been affected by momentous global and regional changes that have occurred particularly during the post–World War II period. The case studies include attention to intercultural conflicts and adaptive processes, the struggle for survival as habitat and hegemony are destroyed, and the struggle for identity as cherished beliefs and values are challenged and often degraded by outside forces.

ABOUT THE AUTHOR

Leo Chavez was born in Alamogordo, New Mexico. His family has a long history in New Mexico. Leo is a thirteenth-generation New Mexican on his father's side, and fourth-generation on his mother's side. His parents moved to the Los Angeles area in the early 1950s.

He studied anthropology at the University of California, Santa Cruz, receiving his B.A. in 1974. He then moved to Stanford University, conducted dissertation research among the Otavalo Indians of Ecuador, and received his Ph.D. in anthropology in 1982.

His work on immigration began in 1980, when he was hired as the Coordinator of Field Research at the newly created Center for U.S.– Mexican Studies at the University of California, San Diego. For the next three years he was involved in the center's activities, including research that involved interviewing more than 2,000 legal and undocumented Mexican immigrants. From 1984 to 1987, he continued his relationship with the center, but as a research associate, having won a National Science Foundation research grant and a Rockefeller Foundation fellowship to continue his research on immigration. Between 1984 and 1986, he was also a research associate with El Colegio de la Frontera Norte (located in Tijuana), Mexico's leading research institute focusing on issues important to the U.S.–Mexico border region. This experience allowed him to see first-hand the Mexican perspective on the migration of Mexicans to the United States. In 1986, Chavez undertook another research project on the integration of undocumented immigrants into American society, this one comparing the experiences of Mexicans with those of Central Americans.

Chavez has published widely on various aspects of the immigrant experience, including problems in access to health services, domestic group organization, and the effects of immigration policy on immigrants, lives. He also spends a great deal of time addressing public concerns about immigration. He has written numerous opinion articles for newspapers, given many public talks, and assisted in the production of documentaries that have aired on the Public Broadcasting System.

ABOUT THIS CASE STUDY

In *Shadowed Lives* Leo Chavez provides a telling description and analysis of the lives of undocumented workers in southern California, particularly San Diego County. The analysis goes beyond their lives to the antecedent conditions and needs that have caused many thousands of workers to risk arrest and worse as they cross the border between Mexico and the United States.

The hardship and ambiguity of the undocumented workers' situation is portrayed in the objective, yet somehow passionate, detail of individual lives, some of it told in the author's words and some in the words of the workers and their families. Their situation is also analyzed in the more abstract vernacular of anthropology. Chavez has the ability, not as widely distributed in our profession as one might wish, to combine analysis with portrayal, and include himself, though not obtrusively, in the picture.

Undocumented workers are essential to agriculture, industry, and tourism in southern California and elsewhere in the United States. Nevertheless they are feared, even loathed, in some quarters by those who see them as dirty, disease ridden, amoral, and capable of any desperate or disgusting act. Though documentation shows that they are none of these in disproportion to their numbers, the mythology persists and is constantly elaborated upon.

The workers have no secure place to eat or sleep. Some sleep under bushes, some in cardboard shelters in the canyons near the fields where they work. The shantytowns are periodically destroyed—bulldozed away—and no alternatives are provided. The Immigration and Naturalization Service picks them up, sends them back to Mexico, apprehends them again as they attempt to cross the border . . . and again, and again . . . as they attempt to return. They are harassed, and sometimes seriously hurt or murdered, by vandals and marauders, including their own brethren, the Cholos. They are often vilified and treated as vermin, but they are needed. The work has to be done and American citizens will not do it—at least not for the minimal wages paid.

The undocumented workers, or "illegal aliens" in more popular terms, somehow survive the ambiguity, ambivalence, and danger of their situation; some eventually become citizens. But most go back to Mexico, and many return more than once. Their objective is to survive, not to become rich or even happy. Most would prefer to remain in their own country, but worsening conditions there have made survival at home virtually impossible for many.

The author also writes of those Central Americans who have fled the terror and "disappearances" of their situation at home. Particularly notable in this case study is the inclusion of women's voices—as wives, mothers, and workers. The majority of undocumented workers have traditionally been male, but the number of women has increased lately. Some live in the canyon shantytowns, suffering the same vicissitudes as the men.

Leo Chavez's own family has resided for about four centuries in that area of the Southwest now part of the United States, but he has not lost identity as a Latino. He speaks Spanish and has maintained old ties with the people and culture. And he has developed new links that have permitted him to enter the lives of the people he is researching. He interprets the workers' lives with both empathy and enough intellectual detachment to produce sound interpretations and analyses.

For this already rich case study Leo Chavez has written a new introduction and an epilogue for the second edition. In the introduction he provides a historical overview of Mexican immigration to the United States that shows how the present-day patterns of immigration were established over the past century and even longer. It is easy to forget that the history of immigration includes the movement of United States citizens into Mexican territory. This movement resulted finally in the Mexican-American War of 1846-48. The spoils of war were what is now the Southwest of the United States. The immigration of Mexicans into what became U.S. territory began shortly thereafter but did not assume the proportions of a major movement until the 20th century. The author explains how the separation of Mexican peasants from their land consequent to a modernization program implemented by the President of Mexico, Porfirio Diaz, coincided with the development of industrialized agriculture on the desert lands of the Central and Imperial Valleys in the United States and a building boom in the cities of the Southwest. Both created a heavy demand for cheap labor. This demand continued to the present, particularly as represented in the "Bracero Program." Hundreds of thousands of Mexicans were recruited. The twists and turns of U.S. policy concerning Mexican immigration are touched upon by Chavez as a commentary on the presently negative attitude toward immigration and immigrants expressed in politicians' speeches and voters' sentiments and incorporated in legislation.

The epilogue carries the discussion of policy concerning immigration to the United States further. The present anti-immigrant sentiment, which has grown so much recently, is seen in the context of the larger society. The illogic of immigration policy in the United States becomes abundantly clear. The discussion began with candidates for political office taking up the widespread anti-"illegal alien" rhetoric but then broadened to include all immigrants. Problems in the U.S. economy, education, health care, and even the relations of local governments with the federal government were all blamed on immigrants. This projective hysteria will bring about changes, most of them destructive, but the need for cheap labor to do the kind of work that American workers will not do, at least for minimum or below-minimum wages, will persist. The messages from politicians trying to match the mood of voters will be convoluted, to say the least.

We are particularly proud to present this case study as part of the Case Studies in Cultural Anthropology, and believe that it will prove a most useful and important publication for students everywhere who are trying to understand the perplexing end-decade of the 20th century—a time of displacement, threat, ambiguity, instability, and discontinuity. The situation of the undocumented workers makes one despair, yet their courage and endurance make one hope.

GEORGE AND LOUISE SPINDLER
Series Editors

Preface and Acknowledgments

My interest in Mexican migration to the United States is both personal and academic. When in 1980 I began research on Mexican migration into San Diego, I did not know a great deal about people who were commonly called illegal aliens. I had been back but a year from fieldwork in Ecuador and was still writing my dissertation on Otavalo Indians who had migrated into the town of Otavalo from the surrounding countryside to pursue their weaving businesses. I was familiar with the literature on migration, but I was most familiar with internal migration—that which occurs within a country. I was less familiar with international migration. I also lacked familiarity with the environs of San Diego. I had been living there for only a year, having come because my wife, Cathy Ota, decided to attend an area law school. Even during that year, I had spent most of my time holed up writing my dissertation.

But I could not help but become interested in immigration. San Diego is America's gateway to the Third World. Just 30 minutes from downtown San Diego is downtown Tijuana, Mexico. The two are separated by a political boundary—called the international border in English and *la linea* (the line) in Spanish—marked in some places by a fence with holes cut into it and in other places by nothing but the imagination. Communities on both sides share a common geographic space, and that closeness is the source of a never-ending series of problems. Rarely a day goes by in San Diego that such a story is not carried by the local television news programs, radio, or newspapers. One quickly becomes inundated with media coverage of border pollution, drug smuggling, capital flight, corruption, crime, and, occasionally, international cooperation. One of the most frequent and controversial stories is that of "illegal aliens."

It quickly became apparent to me that the media's picture of undocumented Mexicans was limited at best. Despite the frequency of their stories, they rarely reached beyond the most dramatic: the Border Patrol apprehending border crossers, raids on fields and factories, and crimes committed by illegal aliens.

I sensed that there was a great deal more to the story. Who were these people? I wondered about their lives, their motivations, and their aspirations for the future. I became convinced that the public and its policy makers needed a more complete picture of undocumented immigrants. What was missing was a sense of their everyday reality and experiences.

I believe anthropologists can offer a great service to whatever society they work in by easing the conflicts that arise as cultures mix, interact, and begin to share space, beliefs, and behaviors. Such situations lend themselves to tensions, misconceptions, and misunderstandings. The change that occurs as cultures intermingle is difficult and often painful. But culture is never static, and change is inevitable.

The American Southwest has a long history of contact among Indians, Mexicans, Anglos, Germans, Japanese, Chinese, Filipinos, and many other groups. Today's experiences and tensions between newcomers and natives are not new. I remember my great-aunt once telling me about the village in New Mexico where my family has lived since the early 1700s having a problem with immigrants. The immigrants, she said, were buying up the land, but did not speak the language, and did not understand the culture. I asked her where the immigrants were from, to which she replied, "*Pues* [Well], New York, New Jersey, and Boston." This reflection helped me to realize that we need to understand cultural change from many perspectives. Anthropology provides a method for challenging our assumptions about both ourselves and others in our world.

As I sat and wrote my dissertation, I began thinking about research on immigration to the United States. My opportunity arrived when the University of California in San Diego decided to start the Center for U.S.– Mexican Studies, bringing in as director Wayne Cornelius, a leading expert on Mexico and Mexican immigration. Despite my limited experience in the area, Wayne took a chance and hired me to conduct research on Mexican immigration into San Diego.

I was a bit naive when I began researching what turned out to be an immensely complicated subject. Perhaps it is naiveté that allows us to tackle such complex projects to begin with. I was not, however, so naive as to think of myself as completely objective. I knew I held subjective opinions and views, many of which I was not even aware. I had an underlying sense of community with Mexican immigrants; we shared, after all, a common ancestry. And yet I also knew that we were different. My family had dwelled in the southwestern United States for generations. My father's family has traced its genealogy in New Mexico back to the early 1600s. My mother's father was born in New Mexico in 1880. His own father migrated to the United States from Mexico to tend the sheep of other New Mexican ranchers; he was killed in 1885 by cattle herders.

So even though I share a common history with Mexican immigrants, I was considered a *pocho,* a derogatory term Mexicans use for a person of Mexican ancestry born in the United States. Moreover, my Spanish was pedestrian, which only confirmed my status as a pocho. As I set out to learn about life in the United States as experienced by Mexican immigrants, I knew that I needed to correct many of my own misconceptions and expectations, and that I would have to confront their perceptions of who I was as a pocho and as an anthropologist.

I would like to thank here the many individuals and organizations without whose help this book could not have been written. First and foremost, Paul Espinosa has contributed to this work in numerous ways. We have collaborated on two documentaries for the Public Broadcasting System—"In the Shadow of the Law" and "Uneasy Neighbors"—and shared many ideas and concerns about immigration and the lives of immigrants. Many of these ideas and concerns found their way into this book. Irma Castro, Yolanda Martinez, Roberto Martinez, Rafael Martinez, Marco Antonio Rodriguez, and many others (who will forgive me for omitting their names) provided me with insight and inspiration. Javier Gonzalez introduced me to valuable contacts. In addition, I thank the Chicano Federation and the Centro de Asuntos Migratorios for their support, and the Catholic Church for allowing this prodigal son access to parishioners on various occasions.

I am indebted to Wayne A. Cornelius and the Center for U.S.– Mexican Studies for our many years of fruitful association. I thank Ana Garcia for sharing with me some of the songs she has collected about the immigrant experience. I am grateful to Jorge Bustamante and El Colegio de la Frontera Norte for the two years I spent there as a research associate, and to Jorge Carrillo and Alberto Hernandez for many years of friendship. I also thank Estevan T. Flores and Marta Lopez-Garza for having the patience to work with me on our 1986 research project.

Along the way, I have received support from various funding agencies, including the Rockefeller Foundation, the National Science Foundation, the Committee for Public Policy Research on Contemporary Hispanic Issues, and the Corporation for Public Broadcasting.

Don Bartletti, a photographer with the *Los Angeles Times,* made a special contribution to this book by allowing me to use some of his captivating photographs of undocumented immigrants in San Diego. For this, I am truly grateful.

This book would not have been possible without the help of the many Mexican and Central American immigrants who shared their lives with me. I owe them all more than I can say. They gave me information in the altruistic hope that the lives of all undocumented immigrants would somehow be improved thereby. If this work contributes to a greater understanding of their lives, their trust will have been well served.

Finally, I thank George and Louise Spindler, the general editors of the Case Studies in Anthropology series, for urging me to write this case study, and my publishers at Harcourt Brace. I fully appreciate their constant support and suggestions while this book was being written.

Table of Contents

Introduction / Transition and Incorporation

Driving north on the San Diego freeway, I could occasionally see the ocean on my left as I passed through beach communities interspersed with farmland and nurseries. The sun hovered on the western horizon just above the orange haze of pollution that every San Diegan blames on Los Angeles. After I turned east near Oceanside, fields of fruit and vegetables became increasingly common sights. I soon passed the old Mission San Luis Rey, then turned right onto a road that led to a new condominium complex. The road came to a dead-end at a small hill that marked the boundary between the encroaching suburban growth and land still used for planting crops.

As I stood on top of the hill looking west, the fields glistened like an ocean at sunset. Farmers in this part of northern San Diego County plant crops, such as tomatoes and strawberries, that can be raised profitably on relatively small parcels of land. But such crops are also labor intensive. To protect the strawberries, workers must spread a sheet of plastic over each row and meticulously cut by hand a hole for each plant. The long rows of plastic reflecting the California sunset under a darkening sky made the gently rolling hills shimmer surrealistically.

Two men walked across the field, their silhouettes visible against the evening sky. They were making their way back to their camps nearby after a day's labor. In the ravines on the edge of the fields they tend, groups of two, four, six, sometimes eight men set up makeshift camps for cooking and socializing. Each sleeps alone, however, under the bushes. As I walked I could see the flicker of other fires. At peak season, as many as 300 men live along this particular ravine. In northern San Diego County there are many farms and nurseries, and many have their own retinue of workers living in the nearby canyons and hillsides.

For the first-time visitor, the darkness and unfamiliar landscape instills fear. Out here, anything could happen.[1] Though surrounded by housing developments, shopping centers, and freeways, one feels isolated, distant from and unnoticed by the larger society. Walking into a ravine full of strangers is disconcerting; not only can't you be sure of their reaction, but other dangers lurk about as well. People sometimes come to the fields to rob and beat the workers, if not worse. Walking in the fields at dusk is not without its moments of doubt—even for the most intrepid anthropologist.

---

[1] Indeed, on February 5, 1983, teenagers robbed and shot four farmworkers, killing two of them, in this same area (Weintraub, 1984).

How different visiting the farmworkers was from interviewing Jorge Díaz[2] in Pacific Beach. Jorge, a self-employed cementer and bricklayer, lives a comfortable, blue-collar life in that predominantly Anglo beach community. His apartment faces a busy street, where he parks a truck he uses for work and a late-model compact car he uses at other times. His apartment is furnished with a color television, a stereo, and pictures of his children. Although still less than fluent in English after 16 years in the United States, he can communicate with his English-speaking clients. Jorge is comfortable with his life

The men in the fields and Jorge Díaz represent the two ends of a continuum of experience found among immigrants living and working in the United States illegally. At one extreme are the temporary farmworkers, who, except for work, do not interact with the institutions and members of the larger society. At the other extreme are those individuals and families who have spent years, decades in some cases, in the United States and now feel a part of this society. In many ways, they have become integrated into U.S. society and culture. They follow a pattern set down by previous generations of immigrants, except that all these immigrants remain "illegal aliens," and thus face obstacles to full incorporation into the larger society.

My conclusions have not come easily. They are the result of almost a decade of work, during which I learned a lot about what it means to live without legal immigration documents. I also learned a lot about myself, about subjectivity and objectivity, and about conducting research in a diverse and dispersed population that would prefer to remain hidden.

ANTHROPOLOGY AND UNDOCUMENTED MIGRATION

My anthropological interest in immigration reflects work undertaken with increasing frequency by anthropologists in complex societies. In some respects, rural-to-urban migration led anthropologists to work in complex social settings. Anthropologists working among tribal and peasant groups in Africa and Latin America followed informants who migrated to urban areas for work (Hannerz, 1980).

The crossing of *political borders* adds many complications to the question of how migrants experience new situations. Some cross international borders without permission from the authorities of the receiving country. They are illegal border crossers who must live and work in their adoptive country clandestinely.

Working with undocumented immigrants poses unique problems and challenges for anthropologists and other social scientists. Often, as in this case, migrants leave Third World countries (those with underdeveloped or developing economies) for countries with highly developed, technology-based economies such as that of the United States. As a result of such movements, we are faced with a number of dilemmas and paradoxes. As I sat and talked with the men in the fields in northern San Diego County, such paradoxes became apparent.

---

[2]A pseudonym, as are the names of all interviewees mentioned here.

I was in one of the most affluent regions of the United States, an area known for its modernity: It has expensive tract housing, a major research university, and a growing high-tech industry. Yet here I sat talking with men who slept under bushes and cooked over an open fire. Many were Mixtec-speaking Indians from traditional communities in the Mexican state of Oaxaca. The boundaries between modern and traditional, between the First World and Third World were never more meaningless as under that darkening sky in the ravines of northern San Diego County.

How do we conceptualize this movement of peoples between such disparate realities?

Eric Wolf posed a similar question in *Europe and the People Without History*. He concluded that such realities are not disparate at all, but are part of the same reality; they are both part of a system created by European expansion and the advent of capitalism, and that system connects the economically and technologically advanced countries to those less developed. For anthropologists, this concept represents a move away from a view of societies as completely separate units to a view which stresses the interconnections between social groups. As Wolf points out:

> The concept of the autonomous, self-regulating and self-justifying society and culture has trapped anthropology inside the bounds of its own definitions. Within the halls of science, the compass of observation and thought has narrowed, while outside the inhabitants of the world are increasingly caught up in continent wide and global change. (1982, p. 18)

Perhaps nowhere is this interconnectedness as apparent as when studying international migration (Portes, 1978). Mexico and the United States share a 2,000-mile border. The American Southwest was once part of Mexico. U.S. economic interests and investments in Mexico helped build Mexico's railroads, connecting them to rail lines on the U.S. side (Cardoso, 1980). U.S. employers have used Mexican labor for most of this century, helping to establish patterns of migration from specific regions in Mexico. Indeed, the use of Mexican labor in the United States and the supply of this labor from Mexico means that for all practical purposes the two ostensibly separate political territories are linked into one international labor market (Bustamante, 1983).

Anthropologists working in complex societies have recently posed an additional challenge. As anthropologists, we must not lose sight of the people caught up in sweeping changes and global economic trends. As Marcus and Fischer have argued, abstract concepts found in contemporary theories

> must be translated by ethnographic inquiry into cultural terms and grounded in everyday life. One gains a thorough understanding of human subjects who exist buried as abstractions in the language of systems analysis. Without ethnography, one can only imagine what is happening to real actors caught up in complex macroprocesses. Ethnography is thus a sensitive register of change at the level of experience. (1986, p. 82)

A number of questions follow from this perspective and guide this work. How do the people who migrate perceive the penetration of the U.S. economy into their lives? How does the existence of job opportunities in the United States actually influence decisions to migrate? What does it mean to cross the United States–Mexico border? What can we learn from the experiences of the undocumented immigrants living and working in the United States?

MIGRANTS AND SETTLERS

Looking for answers to these questions led me to the fields, other workplaces, and homes of undocumented Mexicans. I wanted to see firsthand the types of jobs they have and ask them about their lives in the United States. I came to understand that there is a difference between a migrant and a settler. A *migrant* comes to the United States and then returns to his or her country of origin. A migrant's stay in the United States may be brief, lasting from a few days to many months or even a couple of years. A *settler* resides in the United States for years, perhaps even an entire lifetime. Yet the distinction is not always clear-cut, least of all to the settlers, who may cling to the dream of someday returning to their country of birth. Those longings, however, are offset by the passage of time in the United States, raising a family, and working.

That many undocumented migrants actually settle in the United States was a bit unexpected. The literature on the subject stresses the temporariness of their stay (Cornelius, 1978). Migration scholars refer to their subjects as "temporary migrants," "seasonal workers," and "target earners" who return home after earning a targeted sum of money (Piore, 1979; Porte & Bach, 1985). Many, however, do stay in the United States. I concluded that the important story to be told is that of the transition people undergo as they leave the migrant life and instead settle in the United States.

In his classic work *Rites of Passage,* Arnold van Gennep (1960) underscores the importance of the transitions individuals undergo as they pass from group to group and from one social status to another. A person's life is marked by such transitional moments as birth, coming of age, marriage, beginning an occupation, and death. These moments are typically accompanied with rites or ceremonies that enable the individual to pass from one defined position or status to another. For example, graduation from high school and college is marked by ceremonies that include the awarding of a diploma. Afterward, the individual is considered a "graduate," with the rights and responsibilities of that new status.

More often than not, crossing the border illegally is a monumental event in the lives of Mexican and other undocumented immigrants. A potential migrant usually has to gather some resources from family and friends, since for most getting to the border and finding someone to help them cross is an expensive undertaking. After the preparations have been completed and only the actual crossing remains, the moment of truth arrives; a successful crossing can only be hoped for, not guaranteed. For undocumented migrants, crossing the border is a territorial passage that marks the transition from one way of life to another. No matter how similar it may seem to the way of life left behind, or how many relatives and friends await the new arrival, life in the United States is different for the undocumented immigrant.

A territorial passage, like more conventional rites of passage, can be divided into three important phases: *separation* from the known social group or society, *transition* (the "liminal" phase), and *incorporation* into the new social group or society. These phases are not always of equal weight or importance in a particular territorial passage. As van Gennep notes:

> The length and intricacy of each stage through which foreigners and natives move toward each other vary with different peoples. The basic procedure is always the same, however, for either a company or an individual: they must stop, wait, go through a transitional period, enter, be incorporated. (1960, p. 28)

The chapters that follow examine separation, transition, and incorporation as experienced by undocumented immigrants. They are most concerned, however, with transition and incorporation. In most rites of passage, incorporation occurs when the participant acquires the appropriate knowledge, experiences, and behaviors, then successfully completes the proper rituals. Territorial passages, such as those undocumented immigrants experience, also have their rituals of incorporation, such as the appointment with the Immigration and Naturalization Service (INS) at which legal residency is conferred, or the naturalization ceremony for new citizens. Such rituals, however, mark only the culmination of efforts and experiences at the end of the passage. What about the experience itself? By examining practical, everyday experiences, modes of behavior, and knowledge acquired by undocumented immigrants during their territorial passage, we can begin to understand this transition and the problem of the undocumented immigrant's incorporation into the larger society.

Undocumented immigrants face many obstacles to their incorporation. In examining why this is so, Benedict Anderson's notion of "imagined communities" may prove useful. Members of modern nations cannot possibly know all their fellow members, and yet

> in the minds of each lives the image of their communion. . . . It is imagined as a community, because, regardless of the actual inequality and exploitation that may prevail in each, the nation is always conceived as a deep, horizontal comradeship. (1983, p. 15–16)

The notion of imagined communities raises important questions concerning undocumented immigrants. Does the larger society imagine undocumented immigrants to be part of the community? And to what extent do undocumented immigrants imagine themselves part of the larger community? To approach these questions, we must place the settlement of undocumented immigrants in a specific context—in this case, San Diego, California.

The case of undocumented immigrants in San Diego suggests that for some the transition phase begins with crossing the border, but never comes to a close; these people never accumulate enough links of incorporation—secure employment, family formation, the establishment of credit, capital accumulation, competency in English, and so forth—to allow them to become settlers and feel part of the new society. They remain "liminals," outsiders during their stay in the United States, often returning to their country of origin after a relatively brief time (Turner, 1974). However, even individuals who have accumulated a great number of such links may find full incorporation into the new society blocked because of their undocumented status and the larger society's view of them as "illegal aliens."

This observation gives added significance to the questions this book poses. Why do undocumented immigrants come to the United States? How do the experiences of undocumented migrants influence their decision to return home or settle in this country? Why do undocumented immigrants choose to settle in a country in which they have no legal status? What strategies do migrants and settlers employ to survive? How do they change, and how do they resist change? What are the major concerns in their lives?

ANSWERING THE QUESTIONS

To answer these questions, I draw upon observations, data, and interviews gathered over most of the 1980s. My experience suggested that long-term fieldwork with one family, one apartment complex, or one neighborhood would not capture the various lifestyles among undocumented immigrants. I decided that the best strategy would be to interview undocumented immigrants living in various places and to use multiple methodologies.

Most of the information on the lives of undocumented immigrants presented here was gathered in unstructured interviews, sometimes with the same people on more than one occasion. I also participated in a number of social events, during which I had countless informal conversations with undocumented immigrants. On numerous occasions, I participated in projects sponsored by community organizations to provide information to undocumented immigrants.

I also refer here to information from structured interviews from two surveys I conducted, one in 1981–82 and one in 1986. These provide additional weight to suggested behavior patterns. The surveys also provide information on the relationship of people living together. Use of multiple methodologies in this way gives us a fuller understanding of the undocumented immigrant's experience.

Even though I am concerned primarily with undocumented Mexicans, I contrast here the Mexican experience with those of undocumented immigrants from Central American countries such as El Salvador, Guatemala, Honduras, and Nicaragua. It is especially important to compare the reasons given by undocumented Central Americans for leaving their country with the reasons given by Mexicans.

FIELDWORK: FINDING THE UNFINDABLE

When I first set out to actually interview undocumented immigrants, I faced a mystery. Where were they?

Undocumented immigrants are dispersed throughout the county. Many also live among citizens and legal residents, from whom they rarely differ in any noticeable way. This is a setting different from that typically encountered by anthropologists—as in, for example, my own experiences in Otavalo, Ecuador. Otavalo Indians wear distinctive clothing that sets them apart from non-Indians; whether in the small town of Otavalo or the surrounding villages, I had merely to walk around the streets and pathways to meet people to interview. I could even sit in the home of the Indian family with whom I lived and wait for their friends and relatives to visit. San Diego, however, is no small community, but a typical California conglomeration of small communities and neighborhoods connected by roads, highways, and freeways.

In this context, finding undocumented immigrants is no easy task. One cannot simply select random telephone numbers or addresses from a phone book and expect to find them. And even if they could be found this way, why would they talk willingly to a stranger? How could they know that I was a legitimate researcher and that talking to me would not lead to their deportation? Their rational course of action, given their undocumented status, is to avoid contact with strangers as much as possible.

I decided that my best strategy was to begin by contacting individuals and organizations that provide legal and religious services to undocumented immigrants. A measure of trust exists between undocumented immigrants and such service providers, and I hoped to tap into that trust in our initial meetings. Once we met, it would be up to me to explain my purpose, develop rapport, and convince them that I had no connection to the INS. If they agreed to be interviewed, I would then ask them in turn to introduce me to a friend or relative. Finding interviewees in this way is known as "snowball sampling" (Cornelius, 1982; Biernacki & Warldorf, 1981).

And so, in early 1981, I set out to contact as many individuals and organizations providing services to undocumented immigrants as possible. To name all would take up too much space, but I should mention a few of the most important. One was the Chicano Federation, a service organization providing information on housing, social services, and legal advice to low-income Latinos and immigrants. I sought help from the Centro de Asuntos Migratorios (Center for Migration Issues), which provides legal services to undocumented immigrants, and the Migrant Education Program, which has groups of parent representatives throughout the county. I also turned to the Catholic Church, which is experiencing an upsurge in membership as a result of the new immigration. These organizations and others were sources of help, insight, and contacts.

After gaining entry into a group of possible interviewees, I then had to take the equally difficult second step: to present myself, discuss my aims, and convince people to cooperate. This meant talking to many persons and families, sometimes individually, but often to small groups, such as parent representatives to the Migrant Education Program and groups affiliated with the Catholic Church.

On one such occasion, I found myself standing at the pulpit of a Catholic church before some 400 people celebrating Mass in a predominately Spanish-speaking *barrio,* or neighborhood, near downtown San Diego. I was raised a Catholic, and even though I rarely attend church services now, I have always viewed the transept and apse of the church building, where stand the pulpit, altar, crucifix, and other religious objects, as sacred and revered places. Only the priest and chosen individuals were allowed in that sacred area. Standing up there, with everyone's eyes upon me, I was filled with confusing and contradictory feelings. I began with *"Buenas tardes"* ("Good afternoon"), to which the audience unexpectedly responded *"Buenas tardes"* in unison. I took a deep breath and began to explain who I was. Afterward, many people came up and gave me their names, addresses, and phone numbers.

Such cooperation from individuals and organizations was not without its responsibilities. The *quid pro quo* that I reached with them was to make a long-term commitment to the area. This meant making the data I would collect available to the organizations that had assisted me and also presenting my findings and their implications to interested nonacademic audiences.

Over the following years, I held up my end of the bargain, establishing my credentials in the San Diego community. This not only made my continued research infinitely easier but also served to bring to my attention other issues I would have overlooked had I not actively sought out the insight of community-based individuals and organizations.

Although I did not live with the informants, I found that I was emotionally drained after each interview session. The people I interviewed shared their lives and experiences openly. Each interview was stamped with its own nuances and individual importance. My experience was similar to that of Emily Martin, who noted:

> Doing a study based on interviews meant that I gave up the rich, multilayered texture of life that I would have experienced by living in a community or with a family. I tried to make up for that by participating in as many ongoing organizations as possible. . . . All of us doing interviews often felt swept away by them—either exhilarated or cast down—and the emotional effects lingered, as if we had had the most profound events of someone else's life shoehorned into our own. (1987, p. 9)

ROOTS OF MEXICAN IMMIGRATION IN THE 20TH CENTURY

My study of immigration into San Diego County must be placed within the broader historical patterns of Mexican migration to the United States. Mexicans migrating into the U.S. Southwest are moving into territory that was once part of Mexico. Many Mexican Americans (Americans of Mexican descent, also called Chicanos) can trace their roots to settlements in the U.S. Southwest as early as 1595. For these Mexican Americans, the history of immigration included the movement of U.S. citizens into Mexican territory, resulting in the eventual loss of that territory after the Mexican War, 1846-48. Immigration of Mexicans into what was now U.S. territory began shortly after 1848 but did not emerge as a major movement until the 20th century.

An understanding of contemporary Mexican immigration requires a brief history of its origins. Porfirio Diaz, president of Mexico from 1876 to 1911, laid the groundwork for both the Mexican Revolution and Mexican migration to the United States (Cardoso, 1980). One of Diaz's goals was to modernize Mexico. To accomplish this he invited foreign investment from Europe and the United States and separated the Mexican *campesino* (peasant) from the land, thus creating a mobile labor force for capitalist development. By the time his presidency came to an end with the revolution, 5 million rural Mexicans had lost their rights to land. In villages and towns across the Mexican countryside, upwards of 98% of the farmers had no land to farm. During this time, the railroads were built, with U.S. financing, connecting the interior of Mexico with U.S. and European markets. The railroads also provided the rural labor force with a cheap means of transportation to Mexico's growing urban-industrial centers and to the northern border.

The growing demand for labor in the American Southwest was attractive to Mexicans. In the early part of the 20th century, New Mexico, Arizona, Colorado, and Oklahoma needed workers for their booming coal and copper mines. In California, the deserts of the Central and Imperial valleys were being transformed into rich, labor-hungry, agricultural lands. A growing population and economy meant large-scale construction in expanding cities throughout the Southwest, but especially Los Angeles, San Diego, San Francisco, and Denver (Romo, 1983).

In its search for a labor force to meet these new labor demands in the Southwest, the United States turned to international sources. Chinese immigrants were brought to work in the agricultural fields and mines and on the railroads. Their immigration was virtually stopped with the Chinese Exclusion Act of 1882, a response to the "Yellow Peril" campaigns against the Chinese. The Japanese followed, but they, too, were characterized as a competitive threat due to their success in farming, fishing, and other economic endeavors. The "gentlemen's agreement" with Japan in 1907 closed the door on their immigration (Takaki, 1989).

In the early 1900s, Mexicans became a preferred alternative labor force in the Southwest for a number of reasons. Mexican culture was not so different from American culture, relative to Asian cultures. U.S. employers already had experience with Mexicans through their investments in Mexico. And Mexicans had a long history in the area; their presence was not new or exotic. In addition, Anglo Americans commonly characterized Mexicans as indolent, passive, noncompetitive, inferior "half-breeds" who lacked ambition and who were satisfied with their lot in life, or at least believed there was little they could do to alter their future (they were, in other words, fatalists; De Leon, 1983). They were portrayed as people who would not become economic competitors with their employers. And finally, Mexicans were viewed as the quintessential temporary migrants who would return like "homing pigeons" to Mexico rather than stay permanently in the United States. With such characteristics, Americans viewed Mexicans as providing ample labor at little cost.

So pervasive were these perceived characterizations of Mexicans that in 1911 the Dillingham Commission, which was established to study the immigration issue, argued that Mexican immigration should be promoted as the best solution to the Southwest's labor needs (Portes & Bach, 1985). It even went so far as to exempt Mexicans from the head tax for immigrants that was established under the immigration laws of 1903 and 1907. With the higher wages offered in the United States compared to Mexico, and with active recruitment campaigns by American employers, Mexicans with few opportunities in Mexico became attracted to jobs in *El Norte* (The North, literally; the United States, figuratively).

By the 1920s, a pattern of immigration had been established, and the stage was set for the first large immigration of Mexicans to the United States (Cardoso, 1980). The postrevolutionary years in Mexico were chaotic and violent, especially in the countryside. Across the border, the United States needed labor. The American economy was growing, but perhaps more important for Mexicans, the United States shut the door to low-skilled labor from Europe. The immigration laws of 1921 and 1924 severely restricted the immigration of southern and eastern Europeans. Once again,

Mexicans became a suitable alternative for America's labor-hungry agricultural fields and factories. American businesses often sent recruiters to Mexico in search of laborers for work in the Midwest, including Chicago, where the communities they established continue today.

Immigration from Mexico and the rest of the world came to a virtual stop during the Great Depression of the 1930s. In fact, many Mexicans returned to Mexico, some willingly, others unwillingly. Anti-immigrant, especially anti-Mexican, sentiments flourished during the early 1930s. President Herbert Hoover even blamed the Depression on the presence of Mexican immigrants, providing another example of scapegoating immigrants during difficult economic times (Hoffman, 1974). As a consequence, the U.S. Immigration and Naturalization Service (INS) routinely rounded up Mexicans and repatriated them to Mexico, forcing them to take their American-born children, who were U.S. citizens, with them. Close to 500,000 Mexicans were repatriated during the Depression.

Although Mexicans were eschewed during the 1930s, the 1940s witnessed a renewed recruitment of Mexican labor. World War II ushered many American men and some women out of the labor force and into military service. Many other women went to work in factories, but a labor shortage still existed. The United States turned to Mexico for unskilled and semiskilled laborers who would work in the United States on a contract basis for a few months. Beginning in 1942, this program became popularly known as the "Bracero Program," *bracero* meaning "arms" in Spanish. Although the Bracero Program was to last only during the war years, its advantages as a ready source of cheap labor, especially in agriculture, proved irresistible. The program continued until 1964.

During the course of the 22-year Bracero Program, hundreds of thousands of Mexicans were recruited to work in the United States (Craig, 1971). Mexican workers came from many states, but principally from the highly populated central states of Jalisco, Michoacán, Zacatecas, Querétaro, Guanajuato, and Puebla. While in the United States, bracero workers learned about opportunities in the American labor market and they established contacts with American employers. When the Bracero Program ended in 1964, the demand for the labor these workers provided did not vanish. Employers still needed the workers in their fields and on their ranches, only the workers could no longer immigrate to work legally as braceros. Not surprisingly, the number of illegal immigrant workers rose dramatically after the termination of the Bracero Program. The system of employer-employee contacts, migration routes, and social networks continued to operate, only clandestinely. The same Mexican states that supplied workers for the Bracero Program are the principal source of most Mexican immigration today.

Since the 1960s, use of Mexican labor has diversified, especially in the Southwest. Once working primarily in agriculture, undocumented Mexicans are now found in many urban and suburban jobs, performing work that typically pays low wages and offers few benefits and that therefore is not generally attractive to U.S. citizens.

Although many, if not most, undocumented immigrants come to the United States for relatively brief periods and then return home, some do settle and add to the existing population. Because undocumented immigrants are a clandestine population, making accurate estimates of their numbers is difficult. Some reasonable assessments are, however, available. About 200,000 undocumented immigrants settle in the United States each year rather than staying for a short time and then returning to their home country (Woodrow & Passel, 1990, p. 57). This estimate of undocumented settlement has changed little over time, which suggests that the monumental 1986 immigration law, which was designed to stem the flow of undocumented immigrants, had little effect on the number who settle in the United States each year. These estimates also suggest that the number who settle is much less than the millions of illegal aliens often said to come and, by implication, stay in the country.

Undocumented immigrants come from many countries, such as China, Ireland, and Colombia. Mexicans and Central Americans, however, make up a large proportion of the undocumented population. For example, Mexicans made up about 70% of the undocumented population in 1988, and Central Americans accounted for another 25% (Woodrow & Passel, 1990). Undocumented Mexicans and Central Americans

A young migrant worker sits at his campsite after a day's work.   Don Bartletti

tend to be relatively young; most are 18 to 34 years of age (Borjas & Tienda, 1993, p.717). Historically, most undocumented immigrants were males, but the proportion of females has increased so that most studies of community-based undocumented immigrants and the newly legalized immigrants find that females account for more than 40% of the population (Borjas & Tienda, 1993; Chavez et al., 1990; Montes Mozo & Garcia Vasquez, 1988). Undocumented Mexicans and Central Americans on average have 6 to 7 years of education (Chavez, 1994; CASAS, 1989).

More than 80% of undocumented immigrants live in five states: California, New York, Texas, Illinois, and Florida (Passel & Woodrow, 1984). California attracts the largest proportion of undocumented immigrants of all nationalities. For example, Cornelius (1988) found that in 1987, California had approximately half (1.74 million) of the nation's undocumented immigrants. Not surprisingly, most undocumented immigrants from Mexico also choose California as their state of residence. California alone absorbs at least half of the total flow of undocumented Mexican immigrants (Cornelius, 1988, p. 4). Of the approximately 3 million people legalized under the 1986 immigration law, most (55%) lived in California (CASAS, 1989).

The stories I heard from undocumented immigrants in San Diego illustrate these historical patterns. I listened to what they had to say about their personal dramas, fears, joys, and dreams. I learned that history is about people who take action, make decisions, and follow often difficult roads, not knowing where they will finally end.

OVERVIEW OF CHAPTERS

The book is organized in a manner that loosely follows the three phases of a territorial passage: separation, transition, and incorporation. However, each of these is not given equal space or attention. My objective is to explore the transition through which undocumented immigrants go—from temporary migrants to settlers in the United States. As a consequence, I spend more time on the transition and incorporation phases of their experiences.

Chapter 1 provides an overview of the setting. The San Diego area, a conglomeration of cities and smaller communities, begins at the U.S.–Mexico border and extends north some 55 miles, where the immigration checkpoints at San Clemente and Temecula symbolically define its northern limits. Despite a long history of Mexican immigration, San Diegans are at best ambivalent about undocumented immigrants, and at worst openly hostile.

Chapter 2 examines separation—why undocumented immigrants choose to migrate to the United States, leaving family, friends, and community. Mexican men and women migrate because of economic necessity and a desire for economic mobility. Their conception of the marketplace for their labor is not restricted to a local area inside Mexico, but extends to the U.S. side of the border. Social links to the United States have developed over generations as part of family strategies for finding alternative sources of income. In contrast, migration from Central America is relatively recent, and many of the reasons migrants give for leaving home relate to the political strife in their countries.

Chapter 3 explores what it means to cross the border. I argue that crossing the border marks the beginning of the transition phase, when migrants move from one way of life to another. The border over which illegal crossers must navigate is described, and personal experiences of the crossing are recounted to explore the various strategies migrants use to gain entry to the United States.

Chapters 4, 5, and 6 focus on the experiences of recent arrivals, especially those living in encampments of makeshift housing. Chapter 4 describes the living condition of farmworkers in northern San Diego County. Lacking affordable housing, many live in canyons and ravines, sleeping under bushes or in makeshift housing. They work, and thus contribute to the U.S. economy, but have few experiences that might incorporate them into the new society. Many return to their homeland after a period spent as outsiders in U.S. society.

Chapter 5 examines the case of Green Valley, where undocumented migrants and recently legalized immigrants built a community of makeshift housing in the middle of a relatively affluent suburban area near the Pacific Coast. I examine the views of the surrounding community concerning migrant workers and their camps and then life in the camp itself. Unlike other makeshift campsites in northern San Diego County, Green Valley was home to many women and children and was serviced by two restaurants.

Chapter 6 continues the Green Valley saga. The men of the campsite typically sought work by standing on a busy nearby boulevard, hoping for an employer to stop and offer them a job. Women in the camp sought work as housecleaners or in one of the many service jobs in the area. The larger community's frustration with the continued presence of the Green Valley camp eventually led the county health department to condemn the site and forcibly remove its inhabitants. But Green Valley is a drama without a proper ending, since the problems associated with migrant workers continue in northern San Diego County.

Chapters 7, 8, and 9 focus on the experiences of undocumented immigrants who settle in San Diego. As chapter 7 shows, those who stay for an extended time in San Diego begin to form families, whether by bringing family members from back home or marrying someone they meet locally. Over time, their families grow, as do their social networks of other relatives and friends from back home and new acquaintances in the area.

Chapter 8 examines the work experiences of undocumented immigrants. Undocumented immigrants seek steady work, and those who find such jobs often find them an important inducement for staying longer than originally planned.

Chapter 9 examines the fears and experiences of undocumented immigrants trying to survive without lawful permission. No matter how long they have lived in the United States, they still face the constant threat of apprehension and deportation.

Chapter 10 examines the incorporation of undocumented settlers into the larger society. Undocumented immigrants become incorporated in various ways: economically, socially, culturally, and personally. As a result, many desire to continue living in San Diego and consider themselves part of the local community. However, full incorporation into society is hampered by the larger society's view of them as outsiders.

The epilogue examines events that have occurred since the original publication of *Shadowed Lives*. During the 1990s, public discourse and public policies reflected a major rethinking about the place of immigrants, both documented and undocumented, in American society. In 1994, the voters of California passed Proposition 187, which sought to deny undocumented immigrants health care, education, and other social services. In 1996, the U.S. Congress passed welfare and immigration reform laws, both of which targeted immigrants, cutting them off from most social services. In San Diego, the INS's Operation Gatekeeper has meant a new fence along the U.S.-Mexico border and more Border Patrol officers. In the meantime, migrant workers in San Diego continue to live in makeshift campsites. One of the largest of the camps was in McGonigle Canyon, along a creek bed between Rancho Peñasquitos and Del Mar. The residents of the camp called it Rancho de los Diablos (Village of the Devils). The circumstances around its eventual destruction are examined.

1 / The Setting

"It's another beautiful day in Paradise" is a common refrain of radio deejays and television newscasters when referring to San Diego. San Diegans are proud of their mild climate, miles of beaches, and nearby mountains and deserts. Added to this has been a prosperous local economy based on a mixture of tourism, the aerospace industry, computer-related businesses, and agriculture.

San Diego's population is diverse, and includes Blacks, Asians, and Mexican Americans, as well as immigrants from a number of other countries. According to the 1980 Census (U.S. Bureau of the Census 1984, pp. 6–1206), minorities (Asians, Latinos, and Blacks) make up more than a quarter of San Diego County's population. Latinos—or individuals of Spanish origin as designated by the Census Bureau—are the largest group, accounting for 14.8% of the population. Among Latinos, persons of Mexican origin are in turn the largest single group; of the 14.8% Latino population, they account for 12 of those percentage points. San Diego's mild climate and thriving economy attract both U.S. citizens from other states and immigrants from throughout the world. Foreign-born individuals, mostly from Mexico, Asia, Europe, and Canada, accounted for 12.7% of San Diego's population in 1980. Included among these are about 50,000 undocumented immigrants, of whom about 34,000 (68%) are from Mexico (Passel, 1985, p. 18). The rest of the undocumented population includes increasing numbers of people from El Salvador, Nicaragua, and Guatemala.

I use the term *undocumented immigrants* when speaking of individuals who have crossed the border clandestinely, without permission from the INS, and who reside in the United States. Undocumented immigrants themselves use terms such as *pollos* (chickens), *indocumentados* (undocumenteds), *ilegales* (illegals), and *majados* (wetbacks), most of which echo English words. I believe "undocumented immigrant" is the most nearly neutral of these terms, referring simply to immigrants without documents from the INS. The other terms have other connotations. Describing oneself, and others, as a pollo symbolically posits one's defenselessness and vulnerability. The metaphor becomes symmetrical when one considers that the name for the person who guides undocumented migrants across the border is *coyote.* Coyotes, of course, are the natural antagonists of chickens, on whom they prey.

The term *illegal alien,* though popular, is imprecise. The legality of undocumented immigrants' presence in the United States is best determined by an immigration judge, and is therefore not something on which I wish to make, or even imply, a judgment. Moreover, some immigrants find the word *alien* offensive. One immigrant woman at a public hearing I attended said, "Aliens are from outer space!" The term *wetback* is also inaccurate and, to some, pejorative. It was popularized in Texas, where illegal border crossers typically wade across the Rio Grande, arriving wet. But most of the undocumented migrants in San Diego cross over the hills, arriving dusty and tired. Such terms are not merely descriptive; they speak to underlying perceptions of who is an outsider to society, who is a member of the community, and ultimately, who is an American. (Although I recognize that everyone living on the American continents can lay claim to being American, I use the term here to mean a member of U.S. society, which corresponds to its meaning as a folk term in American English.)

San Diego County begins at the U.S.–Mexico border and ends some 55 miles later, north of the city of Oceanside. Within San Diego County, it is possible to distinguish three broad regions: northern, central, and southern. The central region, where downtown San Diego lies, is the administrative, political, and economic hub of the county. It also boasts the first Spanish mission in California as well as the oldest non-Indian residential area, a Spanish settlement. (The site is now a tourist center called "Old Town.")

The southern region extends to the U.S.–Mexico border. Some farming is still carried out in this region, particularly near the border. Many of this region's farm-

workers have acquired legal residence in the United States but live in Mexico, crossing the border daily to work on nearby farms. In addition to farming, the southern area has also recently begun to capitalize on its proximity to Mexico by developing manufacturing plants that have, or will have, twin plants, called *maquiladoras,* on the Mexican side of the border.

The northern region extends to the Camp Pendleton Marine Base and the Orange County border. Once known for its rural qualities and extensive farm land, this region is undergoing rapid population growth and housing construction. It also has experienced growth in the number of computer-related industries. Many people moving into this region have been attracted by the new high-tech information and service industries as well as by the University of California at La Jolla. Despite these trends, agricultural production, including avocado farms, nurseries, and flower farms, remains important to the northern region's economy.

The three regions display noticeable differences in ethnic population. Closer to the U.S.–Mexico border one finds a higher density of Mexican immigrants. Mexican Americans are found throughout the county, but in larger numbers and greater concentration in the central and southern areas. The northern region is composed predominantly of people of non-Mexican origin.

In the southern and central regions, ethnic and racial diversity is more pronounced. Not only are there more Blacks, Asians (particularly Filipino Americans and Southeast Asians), and Latinos, but there is also an observable diversity in income within these groups. Among Mexican Americans and Mexican immigrants, one finds representatives of the affluent and middle class, as well as blue collar and poor.

In the northern region such diversity is more limited, found only in isolated pockets, for example, in Solana Beach and Encinitas. Otherwise, the northern region, particularly along the coast, can be broadly characterized as having two social and economic groups: the affluent Anglos and the Mexican immigrants who service this population (as maids, gardeners, restaurant workers, and so on) or work on farms and nurseries. It is an area of sharp human contrasts:

> Northern San Diego County is today a land unlike any other along the U.S.– Mexico border. . . . A place where squalid, plywood-and-cardboard shacks sit in the shadow of $1-million mansions, where the BMW and Volvo set rubs elbows at the supermarket with the dusty migrants fresh from the fields, where the haves routinely run head-on into the have-nots. (Bailey & Reza, 1988, Sec. 1, p. 36)

As this description suggests, the northern region is polarized in terms of ethnicity, work, and income. Such contrasts influence the nature of the relations between the Anglo residents and undocumented immigrants in the area.

The context must also be set from another perspective. The moment undocumented migrants illegally cross the U.S.–Mexico border they enter a liminal space, one "betwixt and between" categories in a number of senses (Turner, 1974; van Gennep, 1960). This liminal space begins at the very border itself, as we shall see in chapter 3.

Migrants find themselves in an ambiguous space when they leave their natal country and enter a territory such as San Diego—or similar areas of the U.S. Southwest—where they encounter friends, relatives, and a prevalence of the

Spanish language. To Mexicans, San Diego is both foreign and familiar at the same time. Finally, San Diego itself is betwixt and between borders of sorts. Bounded to the south by the international border with Mexico, San Diego is also bounded to the north by immigration checkpoints at San Clemente (in the west) and Temecula (in the east). These checkpoints are extensions of the international border, meant to capture any undocumented immigrants who have made it safely into San Diego but are trying to reach economic opportunities or relatives somewhere else in the United States. For many undocumented residents of San Diego, the northern immigration checkpoints symbolize all of the constraints on their lives. Undocumented immigrants frequently told me that because of their illegal status they were not free to enjoy life, often citing as an example the fact that they were unable to take their children to Disneyland because of the immigration checkpoint at San Clemente.

UNDOCUMENTED IMMIGRANTS AND THE LARGER SOCIETY

Despite a long history of experience with immigrants (Alvarez, 1987), San Diegans follow a cyclical pattern of concern about immigration that is also found in the rest of the country. These concerns about immigrants are not new; they are as old as America itself (Higham, 1985). Consider the following comment Benjamin Franklin made in 1751:

> Why should the Palatine boors be suffered to swarm into our settlements, and, by herding together, establish their language and manners, to the exclusion of ours? Why should Pennsylvania, founded by the English, become a colony of aliens, who will shortly be so numerous as to Germanize us, instead of our Anglifying them . . . ? (Steinberg, 1981, p. 11)

About 140 years after Franklin's lament, anti-immigrant hysteria reached a new high, only this time the immigrants were from Ireland, Italy, and Eastern Europe. An editorial in *The New York Times* on May 15, 1880, was one of many such articles sounding the alarm:

> There is a limit to our powers of assimilation and when it is exceeded the country suffers from something very like indigestion. We are willing to receive immigrants just as fast as we can make them over into good American citizens. . . . [But] we are not in need of any more aliens at present. Foreigners who come here and herd together like sheep remain foreigners all their lives. We know how stubbornly conservative of his dirt and his ignorance is the average immigrant who settles in New York, particularly if he is of a clannish race like the Italians. Born in squalor, raised in filth and misery and kept at work almost from infancy, these wretched beings change their abode, but not their habits in coming to New York. . . . A bad Irish-American boy is about as unwholesome a product as was ever reared in any body politic. (Simon, 1985, p. 186)

Fears that immigrants will have lasting and harmful effects on the economy, society, and culture of the United States wax and wane. Such fears seem to be at their highest intensity during and shortly after periods of economic downturns (Cornelius, 1980; Craig, 1971). The 1920s, the 1930s, and the 1950s witnessed periods of anti-immigrant feelings in which public policies were implemented to restrict the entry of, and in some cases deport, immigrants (Reimers, 1985). More recently, the public's concern over immigration heightened as the country experienced economic "stagflation" during the late 1970s and another brief economic downturn in the early 1980s. The early 1980s also witnessed increased Congressional efforts to pass legislation stemming the flow of undocumented immigrants, efforts that would finally prove successful in 1986 with passage of the Immigration Reform and Control Act (IRCA).

In addition to economic cycles, the last 20 years have witnessed a dramatic increase in the number of people immigrating to the United States (Reimers, 1985). During the 1980s, more than 600,000 people legally immigrated to the United States each year. Although immigrants once came primarily from Europe, Asians and Latin Americans now account for the lion's share. This shift occurred after the Immigration Act of 1965.

Before 1965, immigration was governed by quotas based upon national origin, with Europeans receiving the largest share of the available quotas. The 1965 immigration law abolished that system and established a more egalitarian system, giving each country an equal number of slots for possible immigrants. The law also established a preference system based upon the ideal of reuniting families, so that, for example, U.S. citizens and legal immigrants could petition to bring family members from other countries (Reimers, 1985). As a consequence of these changes in the law, the "Golden Door" that previously had been open primarily to Europeans was now thrown open to Asians and Latin Americans, who in 1980 constituted about 80% of legal immigrants coming to the United States.

The changing complexion of legal immigrants, from white Europeans to people of color from Asia and Latin America, drew attention to the influx of foreigners to our shores. But two other immigration movements piqued that interest: the arrival of political refugees and of undocumented workers. Political conflicts abroad have motivated additional migration to the United States. Over the last few decades, large numbers of Cubans, Vietnamese, Salvadorans, Guatemalans, Nicaraguans, Russians, and others have come seeking political asylum.

In contrast to political migrants are the undocumented workers. Estimates of the number of undocumented immigrants now living in the United States range from 2 million to 12 million, with roughly 3 million generally considered a reasonable figure. In addition, researchers for the U.S. Census Bureau estimate that between 100,000 and 300,000 undocumented immigrants stay in the United States each year, adding to the existing population (Passel & Woodrow, 1984). Although Mexicans account for about 55% of this total, undocumented immigrants also come from Central and South America, Asia, and Europe (Passel & Woodrow, 1984). Boston, for instance, may be home to as many as 100,000 undocumented Irish immigrants (Fulwood, 1990).

Increased levels of legal immigration, the influx of refugees, and untold numbers of undocumented workers have all contributed to the public's interest in the impact of this new immigration on the country. Some statements sound similar to those of Benjamin Franklin and *The New York Times* in earlier centuries:

At today's massive levels, immigration has major negative consequences—economic, social, and demographic—that overwhelm its advantages. . . . To solve the immigration crisis, we Americans have to face our limitations. We have to face the necessity of passing laws to restrict immigration and the necessity of enforcing those laws. If we fail to do so, we shall leave a legacy of strife, violence, and joblessness to our children. (Lamm & Imhoff, 1985, p. 3)

Concern over immigration during the late 1970s and early 1980s culminated in the 1986 immigration law, IRCA, which consists of provisions designed to limit undocumented migration, including an amnesty program to legalize some undocumented immigrants already in the country and penalties for employers who hire undocumented workers. [1]

LOCAL REACTIONS TO "ILLEGAL ALIENS"

Residents and government officials of San Diego County have expressed their own concern over the presence of undocumented immigrants. Representatives of the San Diego Police Department have broadly characterized undocumented immigrants as criminals:

These new criminals are undocumented aliens from Mexico, some of whom live here but many of whom sleep in their native land and cross daily into the United States to commit their crimes. At the end of their workday, they go back into Mexico with a few dollars to show for their efforts. (Quoted in Gorman, 1986)

A member of the County Board of Supervisors has blamed undocumented immigrants for the county's budgetary problems, and at one point proposed suing the federal government for $23 million she claimed the county spent on jail costs, health care, and court costs for undocumented immigrants (Reza, 1986a). Such public denunciations fan the public's anger toward undocumented immigrants.

Official solutions have also been directed to the emotions of local citizens, as a flurry of suggestions to the media in 1986 indicates. The controversy began with San Diego County's sheriff calling for Marines to be stationed every 15 or 20 feet, day and night, along the border (Meyer, 1986). Then-Senator Pete Wilson, who had once been mayor of San Diego, said he would support this proposal if the border situation deteriorated and immigration reform did not help (Gandelman, 1986). A local member of the House of Representatives then suggested that the National Guard be stationed at the border, which would be a politically palatable alternative to calling in the Marines (McDonnell, 1986). The sheriff's rationale for the original proposal that set off this round of public debate is illuminating:

Illegal aliens are gradually affecting the quality of life as we know it. For example, now we have to admit illegal aliens into our colleges, which means my grandchildren may not be granted entry because of an illegal alien and they'll probably require her to be bilingual. (Quoted in Meyer, 1986)

[1]There were an estimated 3 million applicants nationally for legalization under the 1986 immigration law. Of these, 1.8 million applicants have been in this country since before 1982 and 1.2 million are special agricultural workers, or SAWs (CASAS, 1989, p. 1).

Some San Diegans have also taken to expressing their concern with undocumented migration by staging "Light Up the Border" rallies. At these rallies, occurring about once a month in 1989 and 1990, scores of San Diegans line up their cars and shine their headlights at the border to symbolically state their opposition to illegal immigration. They also display slogans such as "Order on Our Border" and "Support the Border Patrol" (Miller & McDonnell, 1990). Overlapping these events, a group of San Diegan teenagers took to dressing up in camouflage outfits and "hunting" undocumented border-crossers, sometimes wounding them with BB guns (Chavira, 1990).

The northern part of the county has been the site of particularly strong emotions concerning the presence of undocumented immigrants. This area has undergone rapid growth from open land and farms to suburban development. With such changes has come mounting tension between the established residents and the migrant workers, who live in makeshift campsites and stand on busy streets waiting for offers to work.[2] These tensions erupt periodically, as when it was feared that migrant workers were about to precipitate a malaria epidemic or when they were accused of extorting lunch money from schoolchildren (Dawsey, 1988; San Diego Union, 1986a, b).[3] For example, angry parents in the community of Rancho Peñasquitos demanded that a local Catholic church stop taking food and other items to migrants living near a school bus stop, arguing that such efforts attracted migrants to the neighborhood (Bailey & Reza, 1988). In 1986, a candidate for the County Board of Supervisors conveyed these themes using images of war, disease, and disaster:

> Nowhere else in San Diego County do you find the huge gangs of illegal aliens that line our streets, shake down our schoolchildren, spread diseases like malaria, and roam our neighborhoods looking for work or homes to rob. We are under siege in North County, and we have been deserted by those whose job it is to protect us from this flood of illegal aliens. (Quoted in Weintraub, 1986)

These and other fears sometimes lead to acts of violence. For example, there have been cases in which unidentified men have driven by in trucks and used sticks to club fieldhands walking along the street; a Mexican fieldworker waiting for a bus was shot in the back, paralyzing him from the waist down; and a Mixtec Indian from Oaxaca was tied up, beaten, and left with his head covered by a paper bag bearing the message *"no mas aqui"* ("no more here"; Freedman, 1990). Such tensions and behaviors reflect a widespread xenophobia in the area.

I am sometimes asked to address these fears at public meetings. On one such occasion in 1985, I spoke to members of the adjacent North County communities of Encinitas and Carlsbad who were upset about undocumented workers in their area. I

---

[2]Tensions also arise between Latinos generally and the Anglo community. For example, in the beach community of Leucadia, a Mexican American psychologist found that local residents blamed all Latinos for what they saw as increasing problems in the high school caused by gangs and undocumented immigrants. As he said, "My child was referred to as a 'dirty Mexican.' That was her fourth-grade experience. I see a subculture developing here. North County is for affluent people now. Nobody can afford to live here if they are not rich or professionals" (Stevens, 1979).

[3]Although some undocumented immigrants do commit crimes, their involvement in crime is often exaggerated, which adds to local concerns (D. Wolf, 1987).

walked into the auditorium and found about 250 angry residents. I made my presentation on the economic and political causes of undocumented migration and then listened as one person after another rose to speak about how they felt threatened by the "aliens," whose campfires they could see flickering in the canyons and hills beyond their houses.

They blamed undocumented workers for creating tensions in their community because they "are unkempt and unsanitary," "urinate and worse in public," "are a health risk, with who knows what diseases," "loiter on the streets and harass women who pass by," and "are contributing to the rising crime rate in the area." No one in the audience stood up to present the counterview: that these immigrants do work most Americans will no longer do, bring with them the work ethic, and contribute through their labor to the general productivity and welfare of the country.

One member of the audience left a lasting impression. She was an elderly-looking woman who stood up and said,

> Every night I can see the campfires those men make. I know what they are doing out there. I know they are just waiting for the right time to rob us, or worse. I just want you to know that every night I go to bed with a pistol under my pillow to protect myself from them.

Undocumented immigrants are not generally regarded as members of the community; they are society's "Others," who are, as Michel Foucault (1970, p. xxiv) notes, "for a given culture, at once interior and foreign, therefore to be excluded (so as to exorcise their interior danger)." As a consequence, the larger society often endows the identity, character, and behavior of the illegal alien with mythic qualities. And like most myths, these help justify and give meaning to the social and economic order. The larger society's beliefs and attitudes concerning undocumented immigrants may be seen as an expression of what Marxist theorist Antonio Gramsci called hegemony:

> the permeation throughout civil society . . . of an entire system of values, attitudes, beliefs, morality, etc. that is in one way or another supportive of the established order and the class interests that dominate it. . . . [T]o the extent that this prevailing consciousness is internalized by the broad masses, it becomes part of "common sense." (Greer, 1982, quoted in Martin, 1987, p. 23)

This view of undocumented immigrants stresses their transience, and thus their ostensible lack of commitment to the community's well-being. As *illegal aliens* they are not legitimate members of the community. The "illegal" component of this term underscores that they exist outside the legal system that governs society. *Alien* is synonymous with *outsider, foreigner,* and *stranger.* In short, the undocumented immigrant's image consists of a conglomeration of negative values and missing qualities. (Even the term *undocumented* stresses the *lack* of documentation.)

The dominant values, beliefs, and attitudes that define "illegal aliens" must be taken into account when one considers the immigrants' incorporation into society. Although undocumented immigrants may settle in San Diego, their incorporation into the larger society does not depend on them alone. A society that is unwilling to view undocumented settlers as part of the existing society limits their incorporation. Undocumented immigrants are, for example, the targets of government policies that attempt to limit their participation in tax-supported programs such as health care, education, and housing (Chavez, 1986, 1988). The state also attempts to limit their ability to work. INS agents raid workplaces where the presence of undocumented immigrants is suspected, and Congress passes laws that make it illegal to hire undocumented workers (Chavez, Flores, & Lopez-Garza, 1990; U.S. House of Representatives, 1986). Even away from the workplace, undocumented immigrants constantly fear apprehension and deportation (Chavez & Flores, 1988; Chavez, Flores, & Lopez-Garza, 1989). Governmental representatives make it very clear that undocumented immigrants are unwelcome, actively seeking to restrict their economic opportunities and discourage their continued presence in the country.

At the same time, undocumented workers are part of the economy. Employers view undocumented laborers as dependable and hard-working, and some industries—such as hotels, restaurants, and domestic services—have come to rely on their labor (Cornelius, 1988). And even though the 1986 immigration law was designed to stop the hiring of undocumented workers, employers in small businesses and service-oriented businesses (such as restaurants and landscapers) have found ways to circumvent the law. To avoid employer sanctions for hiring undocumented workers, employers must require potential workers to show identification establishing that they are legal residents of the United States. Employers who believe they need immigrant labor have found that a flourishing industry in forged social security cards and immigration documents has resulted in plenty of workers with "identification." Such employers are thankful that the 1986 law has been relatively ineffective. As the personnel manager at a luxury hotel told me, if the new law had worked there would have been

> severe damage. A lot of properties would have a terrible situation. A majority of your staffing would suffer tremendously. Your food service industry would shut down, your hospitality [hotels] industry would suffer tremendously. Your pricing [would] go up. You'd see in this industry alone a lot of rooms closed. You'd see a lot of permanently closed properties. [But] no one has really suffered an impact other than creating additional paperwork flow. [4]

Obviously, the larger society harbors complex and contradictory attitudes about undocumented immigrants. In *Orientalism* (1978), Edward Said suggests that such attitudes can form part of society's perception of the "Other." For example, Said, a Palestinian-born professor of literature, believes that European views of the Middle East are contradictory. He argues that to understand such complex views, we must realize that the relationship between the two areas is not a purely imaginative one, but one that is based on material foundations, especially the history of what he calls French, British, and American "imperialism" (Jackson, 1989, p. 150). Similarly, the generally negative, but contradictory, views of undocumented immigrants have a material foundation, and they serve a purpose: They obscure the

---

[4]In 1987 I conducted 20 interviews with employers in firms of various sizes in San Diego and Orange Counties as part of a research project, undertaken by the Center for U.S.– Mexican Studies, on the effects of the employer-sanctions provisions of the 1986 immigration law.

undocumented immigrants' contributions to the economic well-being of the communities in which they settle.

Consequently, undocumented immigrants exist as marginal persons, as outsiders. Why, then, do undocumented immigrants settle in an environment with such obvious obstacles to their full incorporation? Do they themselves ever feel a part of the community?

2 / Separation

Beatriz and Enrique Valenzuela live southeast of downtown San Diego. Their two-bedroom house is on a street lined with other modest, single-family homes in an older, relatively low-income neighborhood. A block away runs a major avenue, along which the walls of some buildings are covered with graffiti. As we sat in their living room sipping on sodas, they talked about their lives as undocumented immigrants. They were very open about their experiences. It had been more than 15 years since each had left Mexico for San Diego, having made the journey separately before meeting, and marrying, here. As we talked, Beatriz slowly began to cry. "I was afraid because I had never left home before," she said. "So when I was on my way here, I was very afraid. All the way from Manzanillo to Tijuana I cried—the whole way."

For Beatriz and others I talked with, leaving home was an important event. They separated themselves from family, friends, and community in Mexico to live in the United States as undocumented immigrants. The fundamental reason was work. A laborer can earn seven to ten times as much working on the U.S. side of the border as on the Mexican side. But there is more to the story than this. Personal histories of undocumented immigrants reveal a complex array of motives for migration. They provide insight into why Mexicans view migration to the United States as something within the realm of their possibilities.

The idea of migrating to work in the United States is not something that just happens. It is socially and culturally constructed. The idea grows out of a history of behavior and social interaction between individuals and families in both Mexico and the United States. It is infused with many layers of meaning, or significance, for the people involved.

Mexicans become aware of the possibility of working in the United States through a number of sources. Employers sometimes lure workers to the United States. Migration is often a part of family history. Friends and relatives who have been to the United States return and tell stories about what it is like there. Migration to the United States is also a part of local folklore. For example, it has been a theme in popular Mexican songs throughout this century (Herrera-Sobek, 1979). From *corridos* (ballads) sung at informal social gatherings or in *cantinas* (drinking establishments) to modern rock and roll heard on the radio, songs tell of migrating, the dangers encountered, the successes, the failures, and the reasons for leaving Mexico. These songs are popular expressions of an experience millions of Mexicans have had, either through their own migration or that of a relative or friend. By listening to such songs, one gets a sense how pervasive such migration is in Mexican culture, history, and society. Later, I will present some of these songs to show how deeply embedded the migration experience is in the lives of undocumented immigrants.

Undocumented immigrants express many reasons for leaving home and migrating to the United States. I have grouped these reasons into a number of categories that have helped me to understand the experience. The categories are not always mutually exclusive. Also, the stage individuals have reached in life influences their reasons for leaving home. Young, unmarried individuals, for example, give different reasons than married individuals. Spouses and children left behind have their own reasons for joining the original migrant in the United States (chapter 7). Women who married, had children, and then suddenly became single mothers through death, divorce, or abandonment, express yet another set of motives.

MIGRATION AS A PART OF FAMILY HISTORY

As we sat and talked in his living room, Enrique Valenzuela told his story of coming to the United States. He was raised on a *rancho*—a very small agricultural community, usually consisting of only a few families, in the state of Puebla (see map). His family's land depended upon rainfall to grow corn and beans. "If it rains, there is work for six months. If it doesn't rain, there is no work." During periods of little or no work, his father migrated elsewhere, including the United States, to earn money.

His father worked in the United States under the contract labor program known as the "Bracero Program." The term *bracero* is derived from *brazos,* or "arms," and refers to laborers, especially agricultural workers. In 1942, the U.S. government instituted the Bracero Program as a short-term solution to the agricultural labor shortage created by the influx of American men into the armed services during World

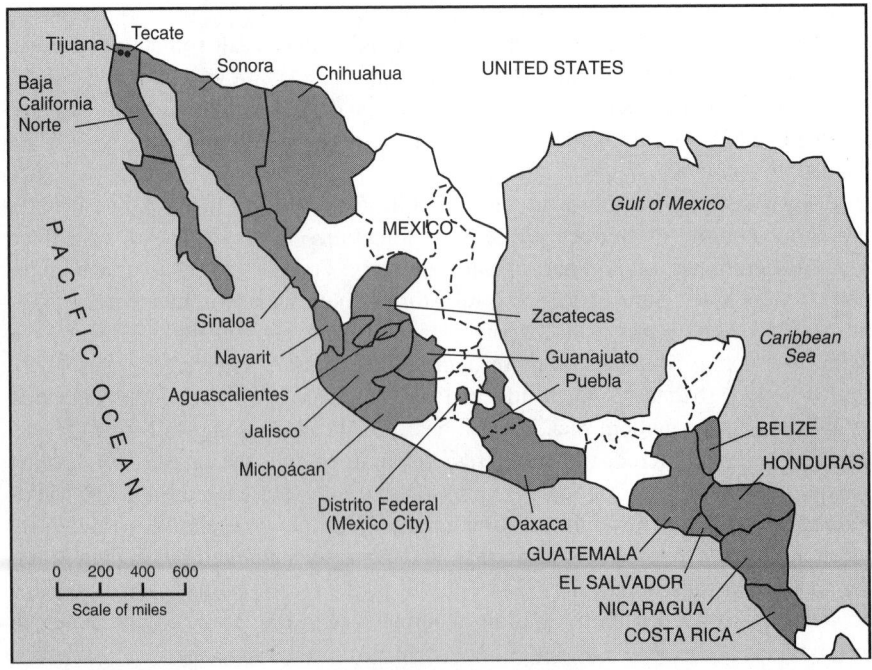

War II. The program allowed American employers to hire, under contract, Mexican laborers for specific periods of time, usually a few months. Although it was originally a short-term program, the benefits of bracero labor resulted in the program's extension well beyond the war years. It was finally phased out in 1964. Over this 22-year period, hundreds of thousands of Mexicans were hired to work temporarily in the United States (Craig, 1971).

Enrique's father worked as a Bracero for 12 years. "Sometimes he'd get a contract for three months, six months, and then he would return to the rancho, to Mexico. And then the next year he would return [to the United States] again. He did that until the Bracero Program ended." During this time, Enrique worked on the rancho. He was the oldest child and as such, he said, "[from the time] I was very young, I had to work to help feed my brothers and sisters and mother."

In 1963, when he was 16, Enrique decided to leave the rancho because "there was no work there. We were very hungry. We earned enough to barely get by. But I wanted to do better, to get out of poverty, to do something with my life." And so Enrique migrated to Mexico City, where he found a job in the market selling tomatoes and chiles for 50 pesos (about U.S. $4) a week. After two months, he found a better job in a small factory, making car accessories such as antennas and mirrors. When he left that job, in 1970, he was earning about 275 pesos a week (about U.S. $22).

After working in Mexico City for the same employer for nearly seven years, Enrique felt he needed a change. "I only earned enough to eat with and pay rent." He remembered his father talking about work in the United States. "My father would say that when it was good, you could get ahead. And that's how later I thought that someday I would come to this country." After the Bracero Program ended in 1964, Enrique's father continued to migrate to the United States as an undocumented worker, relying on contacts made with employers during his years as a bracero. His father always tried, however, both in person and in his letters to Enrique, to discourage Enrique's interest in migrating to the United States, "My father had told me that it was very hard and that he suffered a lot. 'When you first come to this country you suffer,' he would tell me. He tried not to have me come here."

In 1970, his father was working on a ranch in northern San Diego County. Enrique decided to take advantage of the situation and convinced his father to help him migrate. Before leaving, Enrique had to inform his employer, who tried to dissuade him from pursuing his plans:

> I told my boss that I was going to come and try my luck here. He didn't like that. He told me Mexicans were not wanted here [in the United States] and that I would be treated very poorly. He said that with him I would have work for a lifetime, that it would not work out for me here and that I would never progress. So I told him that I wanted to try my luck because I had been with him for seven years and could not do anything more. So he got mad at me.

Despite his employer's objections and warnings, Enrique migrated to San Diego. He was 23 years old. His experience reflects a number of themes found in the migration experiences of undocumented Mexicans. The need for labor in the United States and the resulting Bracero Program created the opportunity for Enrique's father's migrations, which in turn laid the foundation for Enrique's own migration. His father's experiences provided Enrique with a psychological and social bridge between himself and the United States.

Migration to the United States is not always a one-step movement. Some undocumented immigrants, such as Enrique, move first to urban areas in Mexico. After this, they then migrate to the United States. Quite often, those who migrate to the United States, like Enrique, may have a job in Mexico, but desire greater economic mobility than is possible given existing circumstances. It is this desire for future economic and social improvement through hard work that motivates many undocumented immigrants to leave their jobs and seek a better life in the United States.

The story of Andrea Portrero provides another perspective of an even deeper historical relationship to the United States. Andrea was 52 years old in 1986. The matriarch of a large, three-generation, extended family in the San Diego area, she has twelve children and ten grandchildren, seven born in the United States. On the day we spoke, a Sunday, many of these children were at home and intensely interested in the interview.

Andrea's links to the United States extend back two generations to her mother's parents. Her mother had been born in Los Angeles in 1918. At the time, Andrea's grandparents were working for a railroad company making boxcars there. In 1922, the family returned to Mexico, to visit family in Val Paraiso, Zacatecas. While there, her grandfather was killed. As a result, Andrea's mother decided to stay in Zacatecas with her children. Later, a maternal aunt and uncle of Andrea moved to the United States, eventually becoming legal immigrants. Andrea's mother remarried in Zacatecas and did not return to the United States until recently, after her second husband died, to visit Andrea.

In 1969, Andrea, her husband, and their children had left Val Paraiso and moved to Tecate, in the Mexican state of Baja California. They left Val Paraiso, she said, because of the following:

> Back where we're from it was a very poor community. There was no work there. Subsistence is mostly from corn and cattle, for those who have it. We just planted corn. My father-in-law owned a small piece of land. But bad business and things like that ended it all. So, when we saw that we could not support ourselves, well, we said we have to start looking elsewhere.

In Tecate, Andrea washed and ironed clothes. Her husband worked in construction. The two oldest daughters, then 13 and 14, began working as domestic maids. Later, a friend of Andrea's husband was able to find these two daughters work in an electronic company, one of the American-owned *maquiladoras,* or factories, that assemble goods for sale in the United States. About a year later, Andrea's husband started working in the same maquiladora.

Maquiladoras are assembly plants set up by American and other foreign companies in cities and towns along the U.S.–Mexico border. By setting up maquiladoras, foreign companies are able to take advantage of the assembly-plant program established by the Mexican government in 1965. The maquiladora program makes it possible for foreigners to invest in factories that assemble goods in Mexico but sell them outside of its borders. American, Japanese, and European companies can pay Mexican workers the prevailing minimum wage (as low as 50 cents an hour) to assemble computers, televisions, clothing, or anything else from existing parts, then ship those products back to the United States, paying only a small tax on the value added to the product by its having been assembled. Because of their potential for increasing profits, maquiladoras have sprung up in many towns and cities along the U.S.– Mexico border, such as Juárez, Tijuana, and Tecate.

Two years after arriving in Tecate, Andrea and her family found they were having trouble earning enough money to provide for their large family, even with four members working. Andrea's maternal aunt who had settled in Fresno offered to help Andrea find work. Andrea discussed with her husband the possibility of leaving the family to work in the United States:

> "Well," he said, "Maybe I should go to the United States." I told him, "Look, you shouldn't quit your job. If you like, I'll go. I can work a few days and then come back." He said, "Well, if you want to go with your aunt and see what kind of luck you have, well go then." So that's why I went to my aunt's.

Andrea took the three youngest children with her. She found work in Fresno caring for an elderly woman. Her aunt watched Andrea's children while she worked. Andrea lasted only three months on this first migration. "I told my aunt, 'I can't stay here because I have [the rest of] my children down there [in Tecate] and I better go.' So I came back."

Andrea migrated to the United States to help support her family. Her grandparents' migration to the United States early in the 20th century created the link that eased Andrea's own migration. Her family connection in the United States meant that she, not her husband, was best suited to migrate and find work, which she soon did again. Andrea's story underscores the long historical relationship Mexicans have with the United States. Five generations of Andrea's family, spanning most of the 20th century, have lived and worked in the United States.

TARGET EARNERS

One common theme in the reasons undocumented immigrants give for leaving home is the need to earn money for a specific, or targeted, purpose. These "target earners" typically desire to earn a certain sum and then return home after a short period—anywhere from a few months to a couple of years. This is quite common among young, unmarried men and women, who said they left to help their parents. Comments such as the following, by two women, were typical: "My family needed money for planting and food," and "I came to work and send my parents money." Men occasionally said they came for similar reasons; one man, for example, said of his first trip to the United States: "My family was very poor and I came only for three or four months and then returned to help my father." Such reasons suggest the importance of family in the decision to migrate. Sending a member to the United States, or even a nearby urban area in Mexico, is often part of an overall family strategy to find as many sources of income as possible, to ensure the family's economic survival. Family members working away from home are, in essence, "agents" of the family, sending back, or bringing back with them, needed resources.

The goals of target earners may be quite explicit. For example, one fellow came to get a grubstake, or capital to finance a business venture—"to start a clothing business, making and selling clothes." Others came to earn money to continue their education in Mexico; one young man said, "I was unable to continue studying and so I came to work a while to save money so that I could continue my studies." For another fellow, "I wanted to get married and I needed money to build a house." Another man came to earn money "to build a house in Guadalajara and I am almost finished." As these examples suggest, migrating to work in the United States is an accepted way of obtaining an economic start in life. It offers one of the few opportunities for young people to get capital if their family is poor.

DISSATISFACTION WITH LOCAL ECONOMIC OPPORTUNITIES

Many undocumented immigrants say they came to the United States to work because they were dissatisfied with their opportunities in the local Mexican economy. This was the most common reason given by both Mexican men and women. In the words of three women, "I came to look for a way to live better because there were few jobs in my country," "My job was no good," and "I came because of the scarcity of jobs in my country."

Men generally agreed. One said, "I came because of the devaluation." In 1982, the Mexican economy experienced a downturn, known as *la Crisis,* setting off a series of devaluations of the peso. Hemmed in by the devalued peso and the obligation to pay off its large foreign debt, the Mexican government could invest little capital in the creation of jobs, a situation which has continued into the 1990s. The economic crisis exacerbated the factors already pushing Mexicans to the United States. As one woman commented, "Mexico was in bad shape economically." Mexicans felt hard pressed to make ends meet. One fellow who preferred to take his chances as an undocumented immigrant explained that in Mexico "it was difficult to survive. Salaries in relation to the cost of living weren't fair."

This sense of economic despair was the theme of a song popular on Mexican radio stations after the economic crisis began. "El Otro Mexico" ("The Other Mexico") defends Mexicans who left to work in the United States.[1] It also criticizes wealthy Mexicans who take their money out of Mexico, a phenomenon known in English as *capital flight* and in Spanish *sacadolares* (referring to those who "take dollars out" of the country).

No me critiquen porque vivo al otro lado. No soy un desarriagado. Vine por necesidad.	Don't criticize me because I live on the other side. I have not lost my roots. I came out of necessity.
Ya muchos años que me vine de mojado, mis costumbres no han cambiado ni mi nacionalidad.	Now it's been many years since I came as a wetback, my customs have not changed nor have I changed my nationality.

---

[1]"El Otro Mexico," composed by Enrique Franco. Recorded by Los Tigres del Norte. Quoted by permission of Tigres del Norte Ediciones Musicales.

Soy como tantos otros, muchos, mexicanos que la vida nos ganamos trabajando bajo el sol, reconocidos por buenos trabajadores, que hasta los mismos patrones nos hablan en español.	I am like so many other Mexicans who make a living working beneath the sun. Renowned for being such good workers that even employers speak to us in Spanish.
¿Cuándo han sabido que un doctor, un ingeniero, que se han cruzado de braceros porque quieran progresar? O que un cacique deje tierras y ganado por cruzar el Rio Bravo? Eso nunca lo verán.	When have you heard that a doctor or an engineer has crossed the border as a bracero because they want to better their lives? Or a landowner leave land and herds to cross the Rio Bravo [Rio Grande]? That you will never see.
El otro México que aquí hemos construido es el peso de lo que ha sido territorio nacional. Es el esfuerzo de todos nuestros hermanos y latinoamericanos que han sabido progresar.	The other Mexico that we have constructed here, that is our burden, was once national territory. It's the courage of all our brothers and Latin Americans that has improved our lives.
Mientras los ricos se van para el extranjero para esconder a su dinero y por Europa pasear. Los campesinos que vinimos de mojados casi todo se lo enviamos a los que quedan allá.	Meanwhile the rich ones go abroad to hide their money and to travel through Europe. Farmworkers like ourselves who came as wetbacks send almost all of our money to those who stayed behind.

I point out here that the overwhelming majority of Mexicans do *not* migrate to the United States, even during periods of economic crisis. Most Mexicans stay in Mexico and develop strategies for dealing with hard times, rather than undertake a migration that would mean leaving family, friends, and country for long periods of time.

Mexicans typically learn about the possibility of migration from a family member or friend who now lives in the United States or who has returned and provides them with the information necessary to make the journey and find work. Others may have acquired personal experience with *el otro lado* ("the other side") from living in a border community such as Tijuana. Without such knowledge or social contacts, it is very difficult for a person to imagine migrating to the United States. With such knowledge, however, sudden unemployment at home raises the possibility of migration to the United States. One woman who lived in Tijuana and had visited San Diego a few times said, "The hospital I worked at in Tijuana closed down and so I was out of work. I decided I would either return to Mexico City or move to San Diego. So I moved to San Diego to look for work."

The theme of migrating to the United States because of dissatisfaction with limited economic opportunities in Mexico is an old one. It did not begin with *la Crisis* in 1982. Popular songs, especially the corridos from early in this century, speak of leaving Mexico for similar reasons, especially the economic devastation caused by years of fighting the revolution of 1910–15. For example, "Defensa de los Norteños" ("In Defense of the Northerners") criticizes other songs that depicted undocumented migrants and their experience negatively.[2] Through such songs, Mexicans carried out a national debate on the merits of migration to the United States:

[2]"Defensa de los Norteños" was published in *The Mexican Corrido as a Source for Interpretative Study of Modern Mexico (1870–1950),* by M. E. Simmons, 1957, Bloomington: Indiana University Press (pp. 444–445).

Lo que dicen de nosotros casi todo es reali-
dad; más salimos del terreno por pura
necesidad.

What they say about us is almost all true;
but we leave our land through sheer necessity.

Pero la culpa la tienen esos ingratos pa-
trones que no les dan a su gente ni para
comprar calzones.

The fault lies with those ingrate bosses who
do not give the people enough to buy paja-
mas.

El rico en buen automóvil, buen caballo,
buena silla, y los pabrecitos peones pelona
la rabadilla.

The rich have a good automobile, a good
horse, a good saddle, and the poor peons
ride bareback.

Yo no digo que en el Norte se va uno a estar
may sentado, ni aún cuando porta chaqueta
lo hacen a uno diputado.

I do not say that up north one goes to sit and
relax, and even if one wears a jacket one
does not become a congressman.

Allí se va a trabajar macizo a lo americano,
pero alcanza uno a ganar más que cualquier
paisano.

One goes to work there, hard, American-
style. But one is able to earn more than any
of our countrymen.

Aquí se trabaja un año sin comprarse una
camisa; el pobre siempre sufriendo, y los
ricos risa y risa.

One works here a year without buying a
shirt; the poor people always suffering; and
the rich laugh and laugh.

Ansia tenemos de volver a nuestra patria
idolatrada, pero qué le hemos de hacer si
está la patria arruinada.

We are eager to return to our beloved country. But what can we do if the homeland is
ruined?

Que no vengan de facetos les digo a mis
compañeros. Amigos, yo no presumo,
porque soy de los rancheros.

I entreat my fellow workers not to return all
a-bragging. Friends, I am not a show-off because I am a farmworker.

Similar themes were emphasized by Margarito, a man in his mid-thirties, whom I met in 1988 in a squatters' settlement known as Green Valley (see chapter 5). To Margarito, the underlying economic problem pushing him and others to migrate was that the wealth of Mexico does not trickle down to the peasant. He said about his native state, and of Mexico in general, "Oaxaca has a lot of minerals, vegetation. There is silver, gold, trees, mountains. Mexico has a lot, plus oil, a lot of natural resources, fish. But the wealth stays with very few. It never goes to the farmers."

Undocumented immigrants often believe they faced limited economic opportunity in Mexico because they lacked the necessary social connections or education. The oldest children in the family often felt obligated to begin work while young to contribute to the family's resources, so that younger siblings might seek schooling.

Jorge Díaz's experiences reflect these circumstances. Jorge is relatively tall and thin, yet strikes one as a person of subdued strength. He is a man of few words, but appears sure of what he says. His few words betray no shyness or lack of confidence. Jorge says what he thinks with an economy of expression, like a Mexican Gary Cooper. Jorge is from Mascota, a small rural community in the state of Jalisco. He first came to the United States in 1970, when he was 28 years old. Before that, he worked in construction. "I have two brothers and a sister. All three of them have good jobs. I am the oldest. I didn't receive any training, and schooling only up to junior high. But from the time I was very young I dedicated myself to construction."

Jorge's siblings all moved to Guadalajara. Jorge, however, believed he had little chance for a better economic future in Mexico because of the type of work he performed. "In Mexico, if you don't work for yourself you really can't live because another person, the person you work for, will take it all from you. You just can't make it." Jorge began to think about crossing to the United States. Friends who had worked there told him about the opportunities that existed for construction workers. It became a real possibility when his sister's employer sent her to San Diego to learn English.

> It was a difficult decision because I had to leave my family. But I had decided I had to change my life because I realized that life in Mexico was too difficult. There is much poverty. The jobs were very difficult to obtain. If you had family members that were involved in politics, then you would have a good job. If not, and if you are not well educated, then you do not have a good job.

So, Jorge went to the United States to try his luck. He worked for a while as a gardener, then returned to his parent's home. But Jorge decided to return to the United States in 1972. "I liked it [the United States], and I stayed. I have made my life here. I am married and I have children and I work, like the rest of the world."

THE IMMIGRANT'S DREAM

Another major theme in the reasons given for leaving Mexico is what I call "the immigrant's dream," which is similar to "the American dream." Undocumented immigrants view the United States as the land of opportunity, where the streets are paved with gold, and where hard work and sacrifice can earn them upward mobility, at least for their children if not for themselves.

Such ideas pervaded the discussions and interviews I had with undocumented immigrants. They believe the United States offers them the opportunity to *progresar* (make progress) and *mejorar economicamente* (better themselves economically). They hope to *superarse* (surpass their current situation or circumstances), for both themselves and their families. They believe jobs in the United States offer a chance to *subir* (rise). As one fellow put it, "I always wanted to be a mechanic and here I had better opportunities to rise (to that position)." Thus, many immigrants symbolically equate the idea of journeying north *geographically* with rising *economically and socially.*

Before they came, undocumented immigrants believed that the United States held out chances for a *mejor vida* (better life). One man struck a common chord when he said, "I came to earn dollars; I had the belief that one could live better here." Many of these perceptions result from stories told by returning migrants. One man said, "They speak so beautifully of the United States that I decided to come." Another said, "I had some friends who came and it went well for them. I wanted to progress like them." Or as a woman said, "I heard that when you change your salary into pesos you get a lot of money."

Before Angelina Ortega and her husband left Mexico, leaving her children with her sisters in Santiago, Guanajuato, she already had a clear perception of what she would encounter. Her sister had migrated a few years earlier and written her. She was convinced a better life was possible.

> She would always write and tell me it was very pretty and that you could live here better. And that people here don't have to be very skilled to live better. And it's true. When you work along with your husband, it brings you many things. You can have everything. Whatever you want you can give yourself.

There is little in such affirmative declarations that might be construed as a fatalistic attitude or a resigned acceptance of one's lot in life. On the contrary, undocumented immigrants express an optimism and hope for the future that must be seen as part of their immigrant ethic. They come ready to accept sacrifices in return for a better tomorrow.

FEMALE IMMIGRANTS

Women's reasons for migration are similar to men's. For some women, however, economic motives are complicated by a relationship with a man, as was the case of Isela Díaz, Jorge's wife. Isela is a wiry, energetic woman, as talkative as Jorge is quiet. She met Jorge in November of 1975. Both were from the same hometown—Mascota, Jalisco—and had left to seek opportunities elsewhere. On one occasion, they happened to meet while in Mascota visiting their respective families at the same time. They soon became involved in a relationship.

At the time she met Jorge, Isela was living in Tijuana. An ambitious woman, she had felt stifled in Mascota, where there were few jobs and little opportunity for continued education. As Isela said,

> Mascota is a small town that to me is very beautiful. I like it very much. But the problem is that there are no possibilities to study, not for adults. . . . In Mascota, there are hardly any jobs for women. You can only be a teacher or a nurse and a few others. But very few. The majority of jobs are for men.

She migrated to Tijuana because of the economic development it was experiencing. Factories there, especially the maquiladoras, hire many women. She found that "There are more opportunities for women who seek jobs. For example, in the factory, positions are the same for men and women. Women can learn a position which men also perform." She viewed Tijuana as providing the opportunity to work and support her continued education.

When she married Jorge, a few months after meeting him, he was eager to return to San Diego to live and work. Isela was hesitant. She had been to the United States on two other occasions. When she was 15, she spent a year with relatives in San Fernando, California, where she exchanged housework and childcare for room and board. Three years later, she returned for another year. She liked the United States, but was determined to finish her studies and become a nurse.

> At first, he wanted to come and I didn't want to come until I had finished my nursing studies. But I had married and so I had to come with him to live here, with the dream

that I would continue my studies and complete them. But it was impossible because I became pregnant with our son and I was unable to do anything. Later, after our daughter was one year old, I began to work. Before that time, he didn't want me to work.

Isela reluctantly came to the United States at her husband's request, even though she thought the timing bad. But she was unwilling to live in a transnational family, coexisting in two countries. As a consequence, she deferred her own objectives to carry out what she considered her responsibilities as Jorge's wife.

Other women migrate to the United States to escape or avoid a relationship. One woman said, "I left because I got divorced and I wanted to escape from my husband." Another "ran away" from a married boyfriend. Other women, either widowed or else divorced or abandoned by their husbands (both formal and common law), suddenly found themselves struggling as single mothers, a situation with low social status.

Some undocumented single mothers believed the United States offered an escape from society's harsh judgment of them as "abandoned women" and mothers with children out of wedlock. The United States, they believed, also provided more job opportunities for women than could be found in Mexico. María Delgado made this point very clearly. María is in her mid-thirties and lives with her two teenaged children in a house on a busy boulevard southeast of downtown San Diego. As we sat in her small, well-kept living room, I noticed pictures of another daughter, who, I found out, had recently married. María first came to the United States in 1977. "I came to look for work. What I earned was no longer enough."

Before coming to the United States, María lived in Ensenada, on the coast of Baja California. Her father worked as a fisherman and María made handicrafts for the tourist trade.

> I had a macramé business when macramé became popular in 1975 and 1976. It was a very good business. But later everyone else wanted to do it and would sell it for less. It was no longer a good business for me and I needed money. I had my children and they were little.

María had a friend who suggested going to the United States to work. The only problem was what to do with her children. Her friend suggested that she leave the children with María's mother, find work as a maid or housecleaner, get settled, and bring the children later. "That's how I did it," María said. "Once I was working and I could pay rent, I brought my children [about two years later]."

Similarly, Alicia Herrera left her hometown of Chiautla de Tapia, in the state of Puebla, in 1977 when a friend who was working in San Diego as a maid "sent word to my mother that they needed somebody because her employer was going on vacation and that I should come. So, it was an opportunity." Struggling to support herself and her family, Alicia left her children with her parents. She made the decision to leave quickly because

> I was left by myself. My husband left me and there was an opportunity for me to come. I decided to come here because I wanted to try living here, know what it is like here. I saw that it was easy for me, although I had to struggle because it was hard to understand people. But I've struggled for my children more than anything else.

The same kind of pressures felt by Alicia when she left Mexico are still present for single mothers. I met Isabel in January 1989. She had been in the United States one month and was living in makeshift housing built of plywood, cardboard, and plastic on a hillside in Carlsbad (see chapters 5 and 6). She had left a daughter, age 6, and a son, age 3, in Oaxaca.

> I came here because there is no work over there. Oaxaca has no factories, no large busi-
> nesses to employ people. When you do find work it's very difficult. You work from
> nine in the morning to nine at night for little pay and it's hard to find another job. I was
> told that there were good wages here and that there was plenty of work for women.
> Right now I do housekeeping, but sometimes I do that and sometimes I don't. It's not
> stable [work].

Isabel came with a girlfriend and was pleasantly surprised to find other Oaxa-cans living in the campsite. Their presence comforts her, and they alert her to any job possibilities that may come up. She knows she cannot return without having earned enough money to make her trip worthwhile.

> I don't have any money to go back right now. I came here to work and send money to
> my children. There's no use in my having asked [relatives] for a loan to come here and
> return with nothing and still have that debt.

FAMILY CONFLICTS

I previously noted that many young people migrate to help their parents economi-cally. This portrayal emphasizes the importance of the family in the decision to mi-grate. However, family life is not always a model of unity and cohesion. Conflict between family members can also be a powerful influence to migrate. One man said, "I left because of family problems. I couldn't tolerate living in the same place where many things happened." Another said, "I left to see what it was like. My fa-ther always sent me away. He didn't want me." Some men left after a divorce, echo-ing this man's sentiments: "I didn't have any obligations, and I wanted to try new worlds." For another, his wife left him and so "I came to look for [her]."

People who had migrated because of family conflicts often expressed a deep personal anguish to me. As we sat in her living room, Beatriz Valenzuela's eyes moistened as she spoke of her mother and of the conflicts between her and her brothers.

Beatriz was in her mid-forties and had the tired look of someone who regularly worked long days. She showed a sly sense of humor when she spoke. She was born and raised in Manzanillo, Colima, where her family owned a large bakery. Because of the family business, Beatriz was able to study through high school. But in 1964, when Beatriz was 20 years old, her father died, setting off a period of bitter conflict between her and her two older brothers, who believed they alone were entitled to their father's inheritance. Beatriz believed that her brothers, especially the oldest one, were taking advantage of her since she was the youngest child. She believed that she, too, deserved some of the inheritance. This led to a period of intense con-flict, which eventually caused her to leave for the United States.

We were feuding, especially with my oldest brother. I didn't fight with my sisters because they were already married. But it was with the two boys that I fought every day. My oldest brother kicked me out of the house. He would kick me out just like that, saying "Leave my house," because the house was left in his name. We lived in a very large house.

During this time, Beatriz had friends whose married sisters lived in the United States but often returned to Manzanillo. "They would tell me about the United States and invite me to go back with them." Beatriz declined their invitations until finally the pressure of feuding with her brothers became too much to bear.

I tolerated them [her brothers] for five years, but only for my mother, only for her. I would tell her that I wanted to go to another place or come here [the United States], and she would start to cry. When I couldn't stand it anymore, that's when I asked her for permission to come here.

Beatriz did not migrate to the United States for economic reasons. Family conflict drove her out of her home. "If it hadn't been for the problems with my brothers I wouldn't have to come here because I worked in our own business." She received advice and encouragement from her friends, who arranged for a place in the United States for Beatriz to stay and told her their relatives would assist her in finding work. She accepted their help but "they didn't know about my family problems because I didn't talk about that with anyone." Beatriz's memory of her trip from Manzanillo to Tijuana recalls the loneliness and fear felt by someone who had never left home before. "I was afraid and I would think of my mother. So the whole way I cried." When I heard her story, it had been about 17 years since Beatriz had last seen her mother.

ADVENTURE AND CURIOSITY

Undocumented immigrants also migrate to join family members already in the United States, a theme I take up in chapter 7. But here I continue with some of the broader reasons undocumented immigrants migrate, among the most common of which are simply "for adventure" and to satisfy curiosity about what life is actually like in the United States. One woman said, "I came because I wanted to know San Diego." A man said, "I wanted some adventure." Another woman said, "I came on vacation and I stayed." And for yet another woman, "I came to acquaint myself with the United States and then study English." Some, however, found the adventure more difficult than expected, like this fellow: "I came for adventure to the richest country, where we live like dogs."

Migration to the United States for adventure is the theme of many a Mexican song. "El Lavaplatos" ("The Dishwasher"), written in the 1920s, is a humorous corrido that tells the story of a fellow who went to Hollywood to seek his fame and fortune as a movie star.[3] His adventure did not go as planned:

Soñaba en mi juventud ser una estrella de cine. Y un día de tantos me vine a visitar Hollywood.

I dreamed in my youth of being a movie star. And one of those days I came to visit Hollywood.

Un día muy desesperado por tanta revolucion, me pasé para este lado sin pagar la inmigración.

One day very desperate because of so much revolution, I came over to this side [of the border] without paying the immigration.

Qué vacilada, qué vacilada, me pasé sin pagar nada.

What a fast one, what a fast one, I crossed without paying anything.

Al llegar a la estación, me tropecé con un cuate que me hizo la invitacion de trabar en "el traque."

On arriving at the station, I ran into a friend, who gave me an invitation to work on "the track."

Yo "el traque" me suponía, que sería algún almacén. Y era componer la vía por donde camina el tren.

I supposed "the track" would be some kind of store. And it was to repair the road where the train ran.

Ay, qué mi cuate, ay, qué mi cuate, como me llevó pa'l traque.

Oh, my friend, oh, my friend, how he took me to the track.

Cuando me enfadé del traque me volvió a invitar aquel a la pizca del tomate y a desahijar betabel.

When I became angry with the track, he invited me again, to pick tomatoes and gather beets.

Mi cuate, que no era mage, él siguió dándole guerra y al completar su pasaje, se devolvió pa' su tierra.

My friend, who was no fool, continued giving them a bad time. And on completing [enough] for his fare, he returned to his land.

Y yo hice cualquier bicoca y me fui pa' Sacramento, cuando no tenía ni zoca, tuve que entrarle al cemento.

And I earned but a trifle and I left for Sacramento, when I had nothing I had to work with cement.

Ay, qué tormento, ay qué tormento, es el mentado cemento.

Oh, what torment, oh, what torment, is that famous cement.

Echale piedra y arena a la máquina batidora, cincuenta centavos la hora hasta que el pito no suena.

Toss some gravel and sand in the cement mixer, fifty cents an hour until the whistle blows.

En la carrucha mentada se rajaron más de cuatro y yo pos' como aguantaba, mejor me fui a lavar los platos.

Four or more of us strained at that famous pulley and I, how could I stand it, I was better off washing dishes.

Qué arrepentido, qué arrepentido estoy de haberme venido.

How repentant, how repentant I am for having come.

Es el trabajo decente que lo hacen muchos chicanos, aunque con l'agua caliente, se hinchan un poco las manos.

It is decent work done by many Chicanos, although with the hot water, the hands swell a little.

Pa' no hacérselas cansadas, me enfadé de tanto plato, y me alcancé la puntada de trabajar en el teatro.

To make it short, I got tired of so many dishes, and the thought came to me of working in the theater.

Ay qué, bonito, ay qué bonito, circo, maroma, y teatrito.

Oh, how pretty, oh, how pretty, circus somersaults and little shows.

Adiós sueños de mi vida, adiós estrellas del   Goodbye dreams of my life, goodbye movie
cine, vuelvo a mi patria querida, más pobre   stars, I am going back to my beloved home-
de lo que vine   land, much poorer than when I came.

CENTRAL AMERICAN IMMIGRANTS

Undocumented immigrants from El Salvador, Nicaragua, Guatemala, and Honduras whom I have interviewed migrated to San Diego for some of the same reasons as Mexicans. Few, however, had the historical connections to the United States that their Mexican counterparts did. Many, however, left for reasons similar to those of Mexicans.

For example, dissatisfaction with local economic opportunities was a common theme among Central Americans. A man from Honduras said, "I came because of the economic situation in my country and I wanted to give my children a better education, a better way of living." A Salvadoran man echoed this sentiment: "The country's economy was getting worse, few jobs, and I had to look for a better future."

Some came because of the immigrant's dream of the unlimited opportunities to be had in the United States. A Salvadoran man said, "I came because they say such beautiful things about the United States, and I thought I could come, stay a while and bring my wife when I am doing well." A woman from El Salvador said, "I thought it was a better life [in the United States], I could get ahead [*superarse*] and earn some money." A Honduran man said, "I wanted some adventure and I thought I'd make a lot of money, but at least here one can live tranquilly."

The desire to assist parents economically was also an evident theme. A woman from El Salvador said, "I wanted to come to the United States to work, in this way to help my parents."

Single mothers leave to support their families. One Salvadoran woman said, "I lost my job and I had to leave my country because I had no other way to provide for my two children." Another said, "There are no guarantees in life, and less for a woman." And yet another from El Salvador said, "I came for my young children, what I earned was not enough, that's why I decided to come."

As important as these motives were, they were overshadowed by the frequent references to the danger interviewees felt in their homelands because of political conflicts, a reason rarely given by Mexicans. Salvadorans, Guatemalans, and Nicaraguans frequently mentioned their fear of guerrilla activity and the dangers presented by the state's attempts to repress it. I suspect that the economic motives some interviewees gave for leaving may have actually reflected the devastation to local economies caused by the political turmoil these countries have experienced.

Table 2.1, which shows the proportion of Central Americans who gave political reasons for migrating to the United States in a survey I conducted in 1986, demonstrates how important political motives were in their decision to migrate. My question was open-ended, which means they could respond in any way they desired. A person could cite more than one reason, but if at least one of the reasons for leaving was related to political conflict and turmoil then the person is listed here as having a political motive for migrating.

TABLE 2.1.   UNDOCUMENTED CENTRAL AMERICANS AND THEIR
             REASONS FOR MIGRATING

Interviewees' Nationality	Total Number of Interviewees	Percent (%) with Political Motives
El Salvador	92	65.2
Honduras	24	20.8
Nicaragua	15	60.0
Guatemala	11	54.5
Total	142	56.3

A majority of the Salvadorans, Guatemalans, and Nicaraguans cited a reason for coming to the United States that included a reference to the political turmoil their country was experiencing. Their motives offer a striking contrast to those found among undocumented Mexicans.

To begin with, many undocumented Central Americans left their homelands because of a general fear that their lives were in danger. They were concerned about being caught in a political, and a very real, crossfire. Said one Salvadoran woman, "There is much danger because of the rebels and the army." A Salvadoran man added, "Because of the conflicts in El Salvador, there's no respect for the life of others." A Salvadoran woman explained the reason for her hasty departure in this way: "The relationship between the government and the people is impossible, and I had to leave the country, to escape the danger." A woman who left Nicaragua was exasperated with the situation there: "I was escaping the problems of my country." A man from Guatemala had a similar complaint: "The political situation is bad in my country, and before they took everything I had, I emigrated."

Others specifically linked the disruption of the economy to the political turmoil their country was experiencing. A man from El Salvador said, "Why did I come to the United States? That's a simple question. I wasn't able to work because the guerrillas started fighting." Another Salvadoran man said, "I was out of work and soon the guerrillas began looking for me to get me to go with them. Because of this danger, my family and I had to abandon our country." Salvadoran women cited similar reasons for leaving, as in this woman's comment: "In my country there is much poverty, and I was shot in the foot; that's why I decided to come." A man from Guatemala had a similar reason: "I came because of the political situation in my country and the poverty in which I lived."

Some of the people I interviewed also expressed a great deal of anxiety over their children's safety. As a Salvadoran woman noted, "I wanted to protect my children from the situation in my country." A Salvadoran man also expressed such fears: "I was alone, without a wife, and the situation was very difficult. I had to leave the country because of the guerrillas. They don't respect ages. My young children are afraid." A Nicaraguan woman I interviewed worked in San Diego as a live-in maid. She had left her 17-year-old son in Tijuana, where she supported him with her earnings. She had left her husband and younger children in Nicaragua because the Sandinistas "were drafting boys my son's age to fight the *contras.*"

Young people also expressed these fears. As a 19-year-old man from El Salvador said, "I left because of the situation in my country; one cannot live peacefully when one is young." Another said he left, "Because in my country, and more so in the city where I lived, the military persecutes young people like me."

Another major theme was the threat individuals felt because they had served either in their country's armed forces or with an antigovernment group. They believed they were targeted by the other side because of such activities. A Salvadoran man's comment was typical: "I was in the army because that was the law. When I left the army, the guerrillas began to look for me at my house. I left to feel safe."

Some had served in the army and believed the rebels were pressuring them to also serve with them as a way of making up for having been in the army. This Salvadoran's comment was similar to others: "I got out of the army and then people that I knew belonged with the guerrillas invited me to go with them. It was a dangerous situation." Some wish to avoid the army altogether, as this Salvadoran man did: "I didn't want to go into the army to fight against my own people." Some interviewees merely wished to avoid taking sides altogether, and found emigration their only escape from being forced to join one of the two camps.

Association with a faction or government can place people in politically sensitive situations. For example, I met Isabel and her husband in summer 1986 through a friend of mine, Yolanda Martínez, who was working at the Chicano Federation (a social service agency). They walked in unemployed and desperate for help. Isabel, a Nicaraguan, said her association with the deposed Somoza government had led to problems with the new Sandinista rulers, ultimately resulting in their migration. They left their children to come to the United States because, as she said, "I was the secretary for four police chiefs, and they [representatives of the new government] arrested me for 15 days." The new government wanted her to attend revolutionary meetings at night in Managua, about two hours from her home. She was unwilling to attend the meetings, believing the "request" amounted to harassment. About a year after Isabel and her husband left, her four children arrived with her brother, his wife, and their three children. Her brother decided to join Isabel because her letters had led him to believe there were greater economic opportunities in San Diego than Nicaragua. He and his family had little chance of obtaining political asylum, however, and would therefore have to live as undocumented immigrants. Isabel's case points to the interplay between migrations that are politically motivated (Isabel's) and economically motivated (her brother's).

Cecilia's experiences also exemplified the relationship between economic and political circumstances that influence migration. Cecilia left Usulutan, El Salvador, at the end of 1974, leaving behind her common-law husband and their five children, "because we were very poor there." She joined her brother in San Diego and found work as a restaurant cook. A year and a half later, her husband joined her after his sister was killed by unknown assailants, leaving him with her own two children to raise as well. "He had to come to earn enough to support the family."

One nation's conflicts sometimes cause repercussions in a neighboring country. Some Hondurans who left for economic reasons considered the spillover of regional conflict to be one reason their own economy was in trouble. One Honduran said, "I came to try my luck in the United States because my country is very poor, and [because of] the situation that it finds itself in with the Nicaraguan refugees."

Let me end this section with the case of María Favala, who gave her distress over the daily dangers in El Salvador as the reason she and her husband left. I met María in December 1988. She was living in makeshift housing in a campsite known as Green Valley (see chapters 5 and 6). María was pregnant, 22 years old, and had left three children—ages 5, 3, and 2—with her mother-in-law when she and her husband migrated from El Salvador. Seven years earlier, some men had burst into María's family's home. "They killed my father. They killed him at home in front of us." María also spoke of the other atrocities she has witnessed: "They come to take a man out of his home and the next day you'll find him dead on the road, with no head. They'll [plant] . . . a stick with the head on top in the middle of the road, and they'll leave the body thrown over to the side."

María and her husband had been in the United States, at this campsite, for 6 months. They joined her husband's father, who had been there 3 years and had also fled El Salvador out of fear. On learning that his son had been arrested and held briefly, the father had feared for his son's life, and sent word for him and María to join him in San Diego. Maria herself believed, because of her husband's arrest, that they were in danger from pro-government vigilante squads operating clandestinely in the country. "They were looking for my husband. They would leave us notes saying that if they didn't find him then they'd get his wife. So he was afraid. He said, 'If I leave, something will happen to you here.' So, that's why we came over here."

FINAL THOUGHTS

Violence, or the threat of it, has led many Central Americans to leave home. Separation under these circumstances, and the recentness of the onset of migration from their countries, constitute major differences between these undocumented immigrants and those from Mexico.

What is striking about Mexican immigrants, in contrast, is not merely that they migrate primarily for work; it is how history, social relationships, and economic structures have converged to expand many Mexicans' conception of where they may legitimately work. They do not consider themselves restricted to jobs in their local economy. Their possible labor market includes places in the United States where they (or a relative or friend) have worked before. The political border between Mexico and the United States does not limit this expanded concept.

The possibility of migration has been created by the demand for labor in the United States. For most of this century, U.S. employers have sought Mexican workers, often actively recruiting them, as in the Bracero Program. This need for labor has pulled many Mexicans north to jobs they know are waiting for them. Mexicans have also felt the push at home of economic necessity and limited opportunity. These two processes, the pushes and the pulls leading Mexicans to migrate to the United States, did not occur independently. The historical and social links between Mexico and the United States examined here are evidence of the overlap in economic structures that have bound the two countries together during this century.

Mexican workers and U.S. employers are part of one international labor market. That they are separated by a political border has not hindered this labor market from functioning.

Once undocumented Mexicans, and those from other countries as well, decide to leave their families, friends, and communities, they have initiated the first phase in their territorial passage, that of separation. When they leave, they embark from the world they know and begin a journey to a new and different society. In the following chapter, we explore the second phase in this passage, transition, which is marked by crossing the border into the United States.

3 / Crossing Borders

Critics of border enforcement policies often claim that the line separating Mexico from the United States is useless because so many people cross it illegally. Others claim that the border is a political fiction, that in the minds of those who cross it is merely an inconvenience, a temporary bother en route to fulfilling dreams and economic responsibilities. As true as such observations may be, we cannot take for granted the powerful role the border plays in the lives of undocumented immigrants. The border is both a symbolic and a physical separation. It is a divide that must be crossed, a barrier that must be surmounted, a moment that must be transcended.

In the previous chapter we discussed the stage of separation in a territorial passage, when people decide to leave home and migrate to the United States. This chapter concerns the actual crossing of the border. Preparations for the crossing include consulting a border specialist (called a *coyote,* or guide), paying for his or her services, planning for the crossing, and the nervous wait before embarking on the journey. Then the migrants must begin the crossing, which marks the stage of transition that migrants must endure. It is the moment that Victor Turner (1974, pp. 231–232) describes as "betwixt and between," when an individual is no longer in the old world but has not yet moved into, or been accepted into, the new world. This liminal period is typically a time of ambiguity, apprehensiveness, and fear. The participant does not know what the outcome of the migratory experience will be, nor the trials and obstacles he or she will have to endure.

THE BORDER ZONE

There are many ways to cross the border illegally. Some carry greater risks than others. To understand this, one must know some of the border's geography. Nature and politics have created a border that is not uniform, but rather has tiny niches that present specific opportunities and obstacles to the intrepid migrant. Border crossers follow the path of least resistance. If the Border Patrol increases surveillance, and thus detentions, in one area, the border crossers shift to another, less guarded, area.

The border begins at the Pacific Ocean, at Imperial Beach on the U.S. side of the border and at Playas on the Mexican side. A chain-link fence follows the hillside down to the beach and then stops. Families often meet at the beach near the fence, with family members casually wandering across from the U.S. side to the Mexican, and vice versa. There is no fence in the water. A Border Patrol officer often sits on a bluff overlooking the beach in an attempt to discourage illegal crossings.

Heading east from the beach, the coastal hills turn into low mountains and then drop down into a plain through which flows the Tijuana River canal. The border

Border Patrol officers and people waiting to cross the border face each other along the Tijuana River canal. The city of Tijuana is in the background. The United States begins to the right of the street. Don Bartletti

Migrants crossing into the United States. Don Bartletti

continues east along the canal. On the Tijuana side, houses and streets come right up to the border. On the U.S. side lies a buffer zone of farm acreage and undeveloped land. Just inside the border on the Mexican side, a road passes alongside the border and the canal. Adjacent to the canal runs a chain-link fence, but holes have been cut in it at convenient locations. On almost any afternoon you may see individuals and small groups standing on the edge of the canal, where they wait for the darkness of night to shield their attempts to cross the border.

On a number of occasions I have toured the border with the Border Patrol. Their view is that the coyotes station themselves in hotel rooms across from the canal. From these command stations, the coyotes observe the position of the Border Patrol vehicles sitting a few yards away on the opposite side of the canal and direct the migrants (called *pollos,* or chickens). The Border Patrol is convinced that the coyotes deliberately direct some migrants to their officers, thus sacrificing them, but in so doing occupying the officers so that larger groups of migrants may cross unhindered. The coyotes are also said to give preferential treatment to the "sacrificed" migrants on their next attempt to cross the border—usually the next night. Once a migrant makes it past the canal area, the communities of Imperial Beach and San Ysidro are but a short distance away. In its continuous attempt to discourage border crossers, the Border Patrol's latest tactic has been to place large floodlights along this part of the border to reduce the advantage migrants gain with darkness.

Further east, the border runs into downtown Tijuana and the formal border-crossing station. Known as the San Ysidro Port of Entry, it is the world's busiest border crossing. Every year, millions of people cross the border legally through the San Ysidro checkpoint. According to the INS and the U.S. Customs Service, 38,300,000 people crossed into the United States during 1984. This breaks down to approximately 3,200,000 northward crossers per month, or 107,000 per day. Most of these crossings are in vehicles. Of these people crossing into the United States, some 46% are U.S. citizens. The remaining 53% are legal immigrants (many of whom live in Mexico but work in the United States), foreign tourists, and individuals with border-crossing cards. Such cards, known locally as "shopping cards" or "local passports," allow the holder to visit the United States for 72 hours and travel up to 25 miles from the border.

The border continues east, with Tijuana residences jutting right up to the edge of the border. At this point, still within a few hundred yards of the official port of entry, the U.S. city of San Ysidro also comes right up against the border. The border fence continues east from the port of entry, but here, too, holes have been cut at convenient places. The fence offers little resistance to passage. Some local teenagers on the Mexican side claim they sometimes go to the nearby McDonalds for hamburgers and then return home. For illegal border crossers, the streets of San Ysidro are but a quick jaunt away, but this is an area that receives heavy surveillance by the Border Patrol.

The terrain from this point east is hilly, with plateaus separated by canyons and ravines. Few buildings stand on the U.S. side of the border. A maze of dirt roads—created by continuously patrolling Border Patrol vehicles—has left the hillsides visibly scarred. At night, these hills come alive as migrants and the Border Patrol try to outwit one another. On most nights, the Border Patrol sets up a surveillance point on a particularly high hilltop not too far east of the official port of entry. Looking south, one gets a spectacular view of the lights of Tijuana at night. The officers use an infrared night scope to scan in any other direction. At certain times, little green fluorescent images in the broad shape of human bodies flicker across the screen. If the images are moving north, the officer radios other officers of the direction of the movement. More often, the images are merely gathering in a group, waiting for the proper moment to cross, a decision usually made by the coyote.

On the nights I rode along with the Border Patrol in this area, it always amazed me how close we could come to the groups of men and women standing on the hillsides. As the Border Patrol vehicles approach, the people merely back up a few yards, knowing that they need only run the short distance back into Mexico for safety. Border Patrol officers know this as well, so they typically wait until the crossers have moved a significant distance from the border before attempting to apprehend them.

The terrain continues like this eastward until coming to one of the most important areas on the border: Cañon Zapata, or the Soccer Field, as it is called on the Mexican and U.S. sides, respectively. About 15 miles east of the Pacific Ocean, Cañon Zapata is a broad plateau on which migrants often play soccer while waiting for night to fall. The Soccer Field extends north from the border and is actually in the United States. The only clue to the existence of the border, however, is that the houses on the Mexican side come to an abrupt stop. No fence or demarcation of any kind separates the two countries.

A number of canyons and ravines extend from the Soccer Field, like twisted fingers pointing the way into the United States. Migrants must find their way through these canyons and ravines during the dark of night, a journey that can take many hours. The paths are fraught with obstacles, including sensor devices placed by the Border Patrol. As migrants pass over these sensors, officers are alerted to their location and merely have to station themselves at the top of the canyons, where the migrants must eventually emerge. Dangers also lurk within the dark

Migrants wait for night at the Soccer Field.   Don Bartletti

canyons. Migrants sometimes encounter bandits waiting to rob them, with rape and murder also all too frequent (Redfern, 1979; Frank, 1979).

Although the Soccer Field is on the U. S. side of the border, it has long served as a staging ground for thousands of people waiting for their chance to enter the United States. It was, in essence, the *unofficial* port of entry into the United States throughout the time of my fieldwork. Since 1989, however, the number of migrants crossing at the Soccer Field has decreased. Instead, many now try to cross at the canal area in Tijuana. Explanations that I have heard for this shift are that the Border Patrol has increased surveillance at the Soccer Field, and that even though the risk of getting apprehended is greater in the canal area, the distance to the United States is shorter, thus reducing the risk of being robbed, raped, or killed. But this shift toward the canal area may be only temporary.[1] If floodlighting makes it too difficult to cross at the canal area, the flow of migrants through the Soccer Field, or some other nearby area, will more than likely increase once again.

Beyond the Soccer Field is the Otay Mesa, a flat plateau just past the Tijuana Airport. Driving on the Mexican side of the border toward Otay Mesa, one is struck by the absence of a border fence in some areas. At Otay Mesa itself, the development of an industrial park has resulted in buildings coming right up to the border, where they meet similar Mexican developments. Otay Mesa is also the site of the Otay Mesa Border Station. This new port of entry opened in January 1985, and about four or five thousand vehicles now pass through it daily to the United States.

East of this area, it becomes more difficult to cross the border illegally. Crossers must cover a greater distance to get to a settled area. They face a greater chance of getting lost, given the lack of roads and lights. The mountains also jut up, presenting a geographic obstacle. With these natural barriers to the east, and the ocean to the west, most illegal border crossings must occur within a span of about 20 miles.

The experiences of undocumented immigrants who navigate the border are the focus of the rest of this chapter. Both the decision to cross the border and the crossing experience itself are unique to each individual and family going through them. Yet there are similarities in the experiences. How and where one crosses depends on many things, including previous personal experience crossing the border (or a coyote's experience and preferences), and the amount of risk one is willing to take. These factors influence the strategies migrants follow for getting themselves and family members across the border.

The most dangerous risks are encountered by those who cross the border on foot over the hills. As we shall observe below, single men and women are often willing to take such risks. Families with small children also sometimes cross through the canyons and over the hills. Many people I have interviewed, however, tried to find less risky ways, even though the alternatives may be more costly.

---

[1]This information was provided by Jorge Bustamante, President of El Colegio de la Frontera Norte (COLEF), in Tijuana, Mexico. He and his team of researchers have been monitoring the flow of migrants through the Soccer Field for a number of years. Every day they take three photographs of the Soccer Field, count the people, and record the information on a computer.

THE SOCCER FIELD EXPERIENCE

Many undocumented immigrants in southern California crossed at the Soccer Field, or had a very similar experience crossing over the hills. Consequently, the Soccer Field is a convenient place at which to begin examining the crossing experience.

During the day at the Soccer Field, people wait around, talking in small groups. More and more people wander into the area as the day progresses, with the peak numbers arriving shortly before dusk. Most of those waiting are men, but women and children are also scattered throughout the various groups. Some local entrepreneurs have set up tables and makeshift wooden stalls from which they sell items the migrants may need. Near the entrance to the Soccer Field, one family sells sweaters, jackets, and tennis shoes. Farther into the field is a stall where a woman prepares and sells food. A few men brace their spirits at a stall where liquor is sold. A woman with children in tow passes from group to group selling bottles of soda from a bucket.

The Soccer Field (like other places along the border) is a place of geographic liminality. Although legally inside the United States, it is an ambiguous place betwixt and between the United States and Mexico. It is in the United States but the migrants use it as a staging area, a place to gather and wait for the right moment to try to migrate north. Even though they stand on sovereign U. S. territory, the people at the Soccer Field are not treated as if they have officially entered the United States. The Border Patrol watches what goes on in the Soccer Field, but makes little attempt to assert control over it. People seem to understand implicitly that the Soccer Field is neutral ground. As such, it is reminiscent of a time when politically independent communities were separated by a zone of uncontested terrain over which no one had control. The Soccer Field, metaphorically speaking, stands between the domestic and the foreign from the perspective of people on both sides of the border. For the migrants who congregate there on any given day, it is the threshold to a new society and a different life.

Because of this ambiguous context, unusual things sometimes happen at the Soccer Field—things that might seem out of place, given the seriousness of the Border Patrol's efforts to catch illegal border crossers and the migrants' fear of being apprehended. But such events become understandable once the area's liminal status is understood.

For example, the cat-and-mouse game played by the Border Patrol and the migrants is sometimes suspended. On more than one occasion I have seen a Border Patrol vehicle slowly drive up to the area and stop. Although the migrants backed up slightly, it was clear that the officer did not intend to try to detain someone. On some occasions, the Border Patrol officer strikes up a conversation with the people standing and waiting. One time, I heard an officer say, "Good luck. I'll be seeing you."[2]

Another occasion shows how the seriousness of the crossing can break down, if only momentarily, and give way to a truly bizarre event. One night I took my class on a ride along with the Border Patrol. At about 11 P.M., our van came upon a group

---

[2]This event is chronicled in the documentary "In the Shadow of the Law," on which I was associate producer and coauthor.

of 35 to 45 migrants already a good distance into the United States and far from the Soccer Field, yet still not safely past the Border Patrol. The officer driving the van flicked his lights on and off a few times. The border crossers apparently could see that the lone vehicle was flicking its lights as a signal of some kind. We approached the group slowly. The vehicle stopped, and out jumped my students to talk to the migrants. The group saw that we were not Border Patrol officers and came to the vehicle. The officer just sat in the van as scores of migrants and my students talked, took photographs, and wished one another well. The migrants showed little fear, realizing that for the moment traditional rules were suspended.

Another altogether unusual event occurred on April 19, 1987, which was that year's Good Friday. Suddenly in the Soccer Field there appeared a procession dramatizing the Passion of Jesus Christ. Among the participants was a priest who worked with a social service organization providing assistance to migrants in Tijuana. A man dressed as Jesus Christ carried a cross, guarded by others dressed as Roman soldiers. After the various events leading up to Christ's crucifixion were enacted, a Mass was celebrated for all the migrants about to leave for the United States. As I stood on a hilltop watching the crowd of people around the priest and the Christ figure, the sky darkened, and people began to stream toward the eastern edge of the Soccer Field, from which they would depart to the United States.[3]

At other times, the Border Patrol has given out Christmas presents at the Soccer Field. Politicians, including San Diego mayor Maureen O'Connor, and INS officials have visited the Soccer Field to "assess the situation" or to have their photograph taken with the Soccer Field as a backdrop to some political message. At times, it is hard to remember that the Soccer Field is on the front line in the battle to "keep our borders secure," as some rhetoric has it.

Talking to people as they wait for sunset at the Soccer Field can hold its surprises. People not only have interesting stories and motives for being there, but they sometimes surprise you with unexpected requests. On one occasion, I interviewed a man and a woman from Oaxaca who were on their way to the agricultural fields of northern California. With them were two of their children, who appeared to be in their early teen years. The woman explained why she was bringing her children on this trip:

> So they can work and help out. I have seven children and I know that my salary alone is not enough to support the children. That's why you separate yourself from your residence and abandon your town, to make your way.

The man and woman had previously worked in the United States a few years before this trip. Even though they had crossed through the Soccer Field on four occasions, she said she was still afraid. However,

> even if you are afraid, you see how you have to face all kinds of things in life . . . we always get work. The hard part is this right here. The getting across is difficult for us . . . If we make it today or tomorrow it doesn't matter.

At the time I talked with her, the 1986 immigration law had already passed. She knew that the law was an attempt to stop undocumented workers from finding employment in the United States. She unexpectedly asked:

---

[3]This event is also portrayed in the documentary "In the Shadow of the Law."

Do me a favor. Tell [then-President] Reagan to let all the illegals work in peace in California. We all come out of necessity, because of economic reasons, to be able to support our children. That's why we come to suffer in the United States. That's the only favor I ask of you. That's all.

The Soccer Field is an ambiguous place, and this woman had already separated herself from her native community and entered the liminal stage of transition. It is precisely during such moments that a person achieves such high levels of self-awareness (Turner, 1974, p. 255).

MEMORIES OF CROSSING THE BORDER

Crossing illegally anywhere along the border leaves indelible memories in the minds of those who experience it. For many undocumented immigrants, the experience is not something that happens once and then is done with. They must cross again if they return home to visit family or if they are apprehended and sent back. They may find they have to cross yet again to bring other family members into the United States.

Héctor Gómez has crossed many times, and for all these reasons. He left his home in Aguascalientes to find work in the San Diego area in January 1972. He decided to try his luck in Escondido, where his cousin had a job lined up for him. But his trip was ill-fated from early on. When he arrived in Tijuana, he found that he did not have enough money to pay for crossing the border and the ride to Escondido. As he said,

I arrived in Tijuana. I found a coyote and I told him I wanted to go to [Escondido]. He said, "Do you have money?" I said, "No. They will pay [when I get there]." We called the telephone number from Tijuana, but couldn't get through. So he said, "Well, let's go and we will take care of it there."

After crossing over the hills near the Soccer Field, Héctor and the coyote went to Escondido and searched for the address. But

We just couldn't find it. We searched all the streets. The streets were sometimes hidden. Finally, we asked at a place and they told us "That street continues on the other side." The street ended in one place and then continued later. We finally had found it, but the house was deserted. There was no one there. Then I felt discouraged. So he said, "Well, then, I'll take you back to Tijuana again." I agreed because here I did not know anyone. So we returned to Tijuana and he left me there.

Back in Tijuana, Héctor tried to find work. Not finding any, he returned to his home in Aguascalientes. There he found out that his cousin had moved to San Marcos, where he lived and worked on an avocado farm. Héctor returned to San Diego with the new address and found his cousin. "Then, I felt encouraged," he said.

Héctor plays guitar, and, with some of his friends, often performs at parties, baptisms, and church events. Many of the popular songs he sings tell of the border-crossing experience. Listening to Héctor sing, I knew the songs told of his own experiences. For example, one song, "Los Alambrados" ("The Wire Fence Jumpers") tells of crossing the border into northern San Diego County.[4]

Ahora si muchachos a ganar muchos dolares. (hablado)

Now boys, to earn lots of dollars. (spoken)

De México habían salido, hasta Tijuana llegaron. Por no traer sus papeles, de alambrados se pasaron. Se cruzaron por el cerro, Su rumbo habían agarrado.

They left Mexico and arrived in Tijuana. Since they didn't bring any papers, they crossed as "wire fence jumpers." They crossed over the hills, that was the direction they took.

Iban rodeando veredas como lo habían aportado. Era de noche por eso, la vigilancia burlaron. Y por allí en Chula Vista, dos tipos los esperaron.

They turned and twisted on the paths as they had been directed. It was night, and for that reason, they eluded the surveillance. And there in Chula Vista, two guys waited for them.

Un helicóptero andaba queriendolos encontrar, pero entre los matorales nada pudieron mirar. Lo que hay que hacer en la vida para dólares ganar.

A helicopter searched attempting to locate them, but with all the bushes they couldn't see anything. The things one must do to earn some dollars.

Hasta Encinitas llegaron casi ya de madrugada. De los que los recogieron no se volvió a saber nada. Allí pasaron dos noches y sin poder hacer nada.

They arrived in Encenitas almost at daybreak. Of the two who picked them up, they never heard again. There they spent two nights, not able to do a thing.

Más tarde se decidieron a dar la vida o la muerte, pero la fé que tenian los llevó con mucha suerte. Ahora andan en Chicago con dólares se divierten.

Later they decided to face life or death, but their faith brought them luck. Today they are in Chicago enjoying themselves with dollars.

For years, Héctor migrated back and forth between work on the farm and his family in Aguascalientes before they eventually joined him in 1977. During these crossings Héctor was apprehended and sent back to Mexico at least 15 times. On many of his return trips, Héctor paid a coyote. "I did pay a lot of money for several of my returns. The first time I came I paid $150. Later I paid $125, $100, in that range."

Sometimes Héctor would cross without a coyote. He believed he had enough experience to go it alone and he would save the money he would have paid otherwise. However, on one such occasion it turned out just as costly anyway.

One time I already could cross by myself. I came in taxi from San Diego. The taxi driver asked, "Do you have money?" I said "Yes." He said, "I'll charge you 23 dollars to Escondido." I told him I had the money. I had a hundred-dollar bill in my shoe. He said, "OK, let's go." We arrived at my boss's house and he said, "OK, here's the address you gave me." I handed him the hundred-dollar bill. I said, "Where's my change?" He took out about 8 dollars and some change. It wasn't even 9 dollars. He said he didn't have any more change. I told him, "But you still owe me a lot." He said, "I don't have anymore." I was afraid to shout or get tough with him. . . . I was safer if I let him keep the money. So that's what I did.

[4]"Los Alambrados," words and music by Marco Antonio Solis. Interpreted by Los Bukis. Fona Visa, Inc.

Héctor's persistence, despite his initial failure to find his cousin and the adversity he faced on his many trips, attests to the depth of his determination to cross the border and work in the United States, much like the theme of another popular song that Héctor sings. "Los Mandados" ("The Commands") tells of the experiences of a man who has migrated many times to the United States.[5] It expresses his bravado and determination to cross the border, as well as his knowledge of the border region. The song says, in part:

Por Mexicali yo entré y San Luis Río Colorado, todas las lineas crucé de contrabando y mojado, pero jamás me rajé, iba y venía al otro lado.	I entered through Mexicali and San Luis Rio Colorado, I crossed all the borders as contraband or wetback, but I never gave up, I came and went to the other side.
Conozco todas las líneas, caminos, ríos y canales desde Tijuana a Reynosa, de Matamoros a Juárez, de Piedras Negras a El Paso y de Agua Prieta a Nogales.	I know all the borders, streets, rivers and canals from Tijuana to Reynosa, from Matamoros to Juarez, from Piedras Negras to El Paso and from Agua Prieta to Nogales.
La migra a mí me agarró tres cientas veces digamos, pero jamás me domó, a mí hizo los mandados. Los golpes que a mí me dio, se los cobré a sus paisanos.	The *migra* [INS] got me, let's say, three hundred times, but they never tamed me, they jumped at my command. The beatings they gave me I charged to their countrymen.

Despite the bravado many undocumented migrants express when talking about crossing the border, the experience can be unnerving the first time. One does not know exactly what may happen. Should the crossing be successful, getting past the immediate border is only the first step. As Héctor's case illustrates, contact still must be made with a relative or friend in the United States. Sometimes that contact, however, does not turn out as anticipated. For the first-time crosser, there is much to learn. When Enrique Valenzuela left Mexico City and arrived in Tijuana in 1970, he

> thought it would be easy to cross. I thought that I would arrive, let's say, tonight and tomorrow I would cross. But that wasn't the case. I was there for eight days before I was able to get word to my father so that I could cross into this country. I had run out of money because I was paying 100 pesos a day to stay in a hotel, that was four dollars [U.S.]. That was a lot of money for me. I didn't have a lot of money. So I ran out of money and my father sent me 20 dollars. He got someone, a coyote, to cross me. He was going to charge me $125. But I didn't have any money. So my father paid it.

Enrique's father, who was working on a farm in northern San Diego County at the time, arranged for the coyote through friends he had made in Tijuana. But Enrique was apprehensive. He had heard of the dangers of crossing the border over the hills and the attempts of some coyotes to rob migrants such as himself. Moreover, he found unnerving his lack of familiarity with the area, the landscape, and the route he was to take. As he said,

---

[5]"Los Mandados," by Jorge Lema. © 1978 Peer International Corporation. International copyright secured. All rights reserved. Used by permission.

I felt afraid because I didn't know this person. I had arrived in Tijuana without knowing anyone. The coyote got to the hotel, asked for me by name, and introduced himself. He said that he was here to pick me up and take me to the other side. He had a plan about when we would cross. He said we would cross at 11 P.M. near one of the neighborhoods. I didn't know my way around Tijuana then. Now I know that it is the Colonia Libertad [neighborhood near the Soccer Field]. So he crossed me, but I was very afraid because I didn't even know where we were supposed to end up. We walked through the mountains and I couldn't see the United States. We walked a lot and got to a place where it was more inhabited. From there he got someone, or someone was waiting for him, I don't know, but we got into a car and he took me all the way to the farm. He took me to my father. But there was no work there for me, only for him.

Having finally crossed the border and found his father, Enrique was faced with a dilemma. He could not stay with his father. He also had a brother-in-law working in Encinitas, but he, too, lived where he worked and could not offer Enrique work or a place to live. Enrique heard from other workers he met that La Jolla had a lot of restaurants that needed dishwashers.

So I went to La Jolla without knowing anyone, just like that, as they say, threw myself into it. Some other Mexicans, although I didn't know them, gave me the opportunity to live with them and pay rent in a motel in La Jolla.

Although the meeting with his father did not turn out as Enrique expected, he was flexible and determined to find work. He was determined not to return to Mexico without having earned some money, as happens to the protagonist of one song heard often on Spanish-language radio in the San Diego–Tijuana area, "El Bracero Fracasado" ("The Failed Bracero").[6]

Cuando yo salí del rancho, no llevaban ni calzones, pero sí llegué a Tijuana de puritos aventones.	When I left my village I didn't even have a pair of underwear, but I arrived in Tijuana by hitching rides.
Como no tenía dinero me paraba en las esquinas para ver a quién gorreaba los pesruezas de gallina.	As I didn't have money, I would stand on street corners to see who I could get to buy me chicken necks [to eat].
Yo quería cruzar la linea a la unión americana. Yo quería ganar dinero porque eso era mi tirada.	I wanted to cross the line to the United States. I wanted to earn money, that was my goal.
Como no tenía papeles, mucho menos pasaporte, me aventé cruzar el cerro yo solito y sin coyote.	As I didn't have any papers, much less a passport, I ventured out across the hills by myself and without a coyote.
Después, verá cómo me fué. Llegué a Santa Ana con las patas bien peladas, los guaraches que llevaba se acabaron de volada.	Later, you should see how it went for me. I arrived in Santa Ana with my feet skinned, my shoes wore out right away.

---

[6]"El Bracero Fracasado," composed by Ernesto Pesqueda. Performed by Las Jiguerillas ("15 Auténticos Éxitos"). Produced by CBS/Columbia Internacional, S.A. © 1983.

El sombrero y la camisa, los perdí en la carrera, que me dieron unos güeros que ya mero me alcanzaban.	My hat and my shirt I lost in a chase that some white men gave me, they almost caught me.
Me salí a la carretera, muerto de hambre y desvelado. Me subí en un tren carguero que venía de Colorado.	I left the highway, almost dead with hunger and sleepy. I jumped a freight train coming out of Colorado.
Y con rumbo a San Francisco, donde me fuí colgado pero con la mala suerte que en Salinas me agarraron.	Heading for San Francisco, I hung on but with my bad luck they caught me in Salinas.
Después, verás como me fué. Llegó la migra, de las manos me amarraron, me decían no sé qué cosas, en inglés me regañaron.	Afterwards, you should have seen how it went for me. The *migra* [INS] arrived, tied my hands, they said I know not what things, they told me off in English.
Me dijeron los gabachos, "Te regresas a tu rancho." Pero yo sentí muy gacho regresar a mi terreno de bracero fracasado sin dinero y sin hilacho.	The white men told me, "You return to your village." But I felt badly about returning to my native land as a failed bracero, penniless and the worse for wear.

CROSSING THE HILLS WITH FAMILY

It is one thing to cross the hills as a single person. It is another to cross with small children. The risks involved in such a crossing loom large in the memories of those who have done so.

When Federico Romero and his wife Patricia remember crossing the border they become angry. We sat in their small, one-bedroom apartment in one of San Diego's blue-collar neighborhoods. It was about two weeks before Christmas, 1986, and the joyous rooms were in marked contrast to their drab, rundown exterior. A Christmas tree glowing with colored lights and silver tinsel filled about a third of the small living room. Christmas wreaths, Christmas cards, and pictures of Christ decorated the walls. A multitude of dolls and stuffed animals sat on the back of the sofa, adding to the Christmas spirit.

We sat at the dining table, which was also in the living room, engaging in what would appear to be small talk to a layman but what to an anthropologist is the beginning of the interview. It is the time to set the interviewees at ease. Talk is general and is as much about me as them. They must get a sense of my identity as a person and my objectives as a social scientist. I reassured Federico and Patricia that my motives were genuine, and that I was not out to cause them harm in any way; they needed to know that I would protect their anonymity. When Federico offered to open a new bottle of tequila to toast the Christmas spirit, I laughed and readily agreed.

As we sat sipping on tequila and *sangrita,* a red, nonalcoholic drink often served in Mexico with tequila, Federico talked enthusiastically about his life. He loved to talk and did so quite well. Both he and Patricia had an urbane air about them, and the light complexion common to many people from Mexico City. As we talked, it was clear that Patricia had to battle her husband for speaking time, which meant she often listened to his avid rendering of events. But when she wanted to clarify a point, or make her perspective known, she jumped into the conversation, as she did when the topic came to why she came to San Diego. She explained that after Federico had been in the United States for about 10 months she felt she could no longer continue in Mexico without him. It was her decision to join him.

> We [she and their child] came because I told him that I could no longer remain over there [Mexico City] without him. He didn't want us to come, but I told him that I didn't think it was right for us to be separated. I told him, "I'm sorry but I'm coming, like it or not."

Federico was opposed to Patricia's joining him in the United States because he still intended to return home after earning some money.

> I never asked her to come. I just wanted to earn one thousand dollars and return to Mexico. In Mexico, that would be plenty of money with which to begin again. It was possible then. But now, not even ten thousand dollars is enough in Mexico.

Having decided to migrate, Patricia and their ten-month-old son took a bus to Tijuana, Mexico, where Federico met them. The evening they planned to cross, a friend of Federico met with them in Tijuana and introduced them to a coyote he had brought along. The friend then said that it would be safer if he took all their luggage, money, and other valuables across, since he was able to cross legally, and then he would meet them on the other side and take them to downtown San Diego.

As Patricia noted, "He worked in the same place as my husband worked. It was logical to think that he would help us. It wasn't just adults [who would be crossing], but a baby was coming along."

Shortly after darkness fell upon the hills, the Romero family began their trek across the border, leaving from the Soccer Field. It was a dark, cool night in June 1980. About halfway across the desolate hills, their guide refused to go farther. According to Federico, "He claimed that we hadn't paid him. But I had paid my friend, the bad friend."

Because they refused to give him more money, the coyote abandoned Federico, his wife, and infant son. As Patricia lamented, "He left us on this [the U.S.] side, in the wilderness there, in the badness there."

It was the middle of the night and they had only the faintest idea of which way to go. There were no roads or signposts that the Romeros could rely on to suggest which way to go. Adding to their plight, Patricia was unprepared for the unexpected coldness of a June night in open brush land. It was something completely alien to her experiences in Mexico City. As Patricia remembered,

> I didn't know anything. I was wearing light clothing. Only a thin sweater with the baby in my arms. It was a very bitter experience, an experience you don't tell anybody. For me it was difficult. I wasn't used to this. In my life never did I imagine that I would experience something like that. You imagine many things when you're about to come [to the United States], but not something as unpleasant as that. I only had a bottle for the baby in hand. But he didn't wake up, even while I ran. He fell asleep in Tijuana and woke up here [in San Diego].

For about four hours the Romeros walked, ran, and walked some more, finally finding themselves huddled together in a hotel parking lot. As they caught their breath, a flashlight appeared. "Then the night watchman appeared," Federico said. "He was a black man who told us we couldn't stay there. I said, 'Well, give me a moment, this is my family.' He flashed the light and saw the baby in my wife's arms. He said, 'OK, but you can't stay for long.'"

Finally, at about three in the morning, the Romeros found themselves in the backyard of another house. The baby started to cry, waking the people in the house. The house belonged to a Chicano family who felt sorry for Federico and his family. They invited the Romeros into the house and warmed the baby's milk. Later that morning, Federico gave them his ring for taking them to Federico's small studio apartment in downtown San Diego, where, as Federico said, "there are a lot of winos." The clothing, money, and other goods the Romeros gave the so-called friend were never seen again.

Thinking back on the experience in the warmth of their small apartment some 6 years later, Patricia grimaced at the memory. Crossing the border illegally was something she would never like to do again. She has not returned to Mexico since coming to the United States, and says she will do so only when she can cross back legally, or if she returns to Mexico to stay. Federico returned about 3 years later to help their teenaged son and daughter cross the border, once again over the hills.

AVOIDING THE HILLS

Crossing over the hills and through the canyons presents risks that some individuals and families attempt to avoid. Various strategies attempt to blend illegal border crossers in with the thousands of people who daily cross legally at the official port of entry. Many apply for a temporary visiting permit, or shopping card, and use it as a pass across the border, staying beyond the time limitations. Beatriz, Enrique Valenzuela's wife, entered with such a card. As she remembered,

> I applied for a permit to cross. I went to Guadalajara and . . . they gave me a permit. So I came with a friend of mine. We got to Tijuana and . . . a sister of hers picked us up. My friend also had a permit. So there in San Ysidro they stamped our permits and we crossed. I came here on August 2, 1969.

Beatriz has returned to Mexico only once, for a few days in Tijuana in 1972 to have her first child. She has not been back since. As we sat on her sofa talking, Beatriz cried as she spoke of her longing to see her mother.

> During all these years I wanted to go but I am afraid of crossing the border and won't risk it. You know how they say that they assault people, murder women. I'm scared of crossing and that's why I don't go to Mexico. That's my problem.

Like Beatriz, many undocumented immigrants fear recrossing the border. This puts pressure on them to stay in the United States until they are sure they want, or are forced, to return home. This seems especially true for women, who very often immigrate on their first and only trip to the United States.[7]

Perhaps realizing the desire to avoid the dangers associated with crossing the border, coyotes also offer relatively safe passage by providing shopping cards that have been lost or stolen. Or, they make arrangements for women and children to pass through with other persons, particularly Americans, who make unlikely suspects for transporting illegal border crossers.

Beatriz found herself in need of such services in 1972, when she was ready to return to the United States after having her baby in a Tijuana hotel.

> I was in Tijuana and because I couldn't stay there my friend found someone to cross us. She sent a very young American guy. One of those guys who doesn't work, but wants money. He came after me and brought us. I didn't have any problems. They just asked him where we were headed. He said San Diego and they let us through without problems. That was the only time I left here [San Diego], but it was out of necessity.

Parents are particularly apt to choose these relatively safe methods for crossing the border. Although such arrangements are expensive, they are often willing to pay the price to reunite their families, especially if they have not seen their children for a number of years. Alicia Herrera came to San Diego in November 1977 and arranged for her five children to join her in December 1980. Her children arrived, by bus, in Tijuana. Then,

> I went to see a woman who told me that she knows a man who knows somebody. She said, "Don't worry." I gave her my phone number and then the woman who brought them [her children] called me and told me it would be $600, but that in an hour and a half I would have my children.

The cost of the crossing was high in relation to Alicia's resources. She is a single mother. Her husband abandoned her in Mexico, and the need to support her children was a principal motive for migrating to San Diego, where she cleans houses for a living. She was willing to pay such a comparatively large amount so that her children could cross in a car and not undergo the risks of the canyons. In the end, Alicia's optimism and dreams for a better future balanced out the relatively high cost of bringing her children.

> They didn't have to run [through the canyons] and it's preferable that way. I paid too much money, but everybody struggles for something. The important thing is that they brought me my children and that is worth more than anything to me. I wanted to see them more than anything. I wanted to see them very badly. They came very young and now they're grown. This pleases me but sometimes it is difficult for me because I'm the only one who works for everything. But in the end I have to come out ahead.

Undocumented immigrants who came relatively young sometimes cross back into Mexico posing as American citizens. When questioned, they provide appropriate answers based upon their experiences. For example, Eva Portrero, who was 27

---

[7]I present more detailed information on migration patterns in my articles (Chavez, Flores, & Lopez-Garza, 1990, and Chavez, 1988).

when I first interviewed her in 1987, attended a year of high school in San Diego. She used to cross frequently into Tijuana using a shopping card, but lost the card a number of years ago. She then tried crossing without it, saying she was an American citizen. When asked where she grew up, she cited a specific neighborhood and high school in San Diego. But such subterfuge creates quite a bit of anxiety, because of which

> I stopped going [to Tijuana] for a long time. Then you find yourself in situations where you'll be out with friends and let yourself be carried away with the idea of going to Tijuana. You feel like you want to say "Let's go." But then you start to doubt [the idea] because of your status.

Although some undocumented immigrants such as Eva learn enough of local San Diego culture to substantially increase their chances of passing through the official border freely, they are often unwilling to take such risks. Should the border guard become suspicious and ask for identification, it could lead to apprehension and deportation, jeopardizing the equity they have built up at work over the years and any other wealth they have managed to acquire. In short, recrossing the border imperils the life they have created in the United States. As we shall see below, this vulnerability is a major theme in the lives of undocumented immigrants.

CENTRAL AMERICANS: MANY BORDERS TO CROSS

Undocumented immigrants from El Salvador, Guatemala, Nicaragua, and other Central American countries cross several borders. At the very least, they have to cross into Mexico and then make their way to the U.S. border. With more borders come increased risks. Often desperate to flee dangerous situations, undocumented Central Americans find themselves vulnerable to exploitation.

I met María Favala at the Green Valley camp in Carlsbad (see chapter 5). She is an outgoing 22-year-old with three young children in El Salvador. Concerning her trip north, María said,

> The trip was treacherous because we had to cross so many borders. We had enough money because [my husband's] father had sent him some, plus what we had. But the Mexican police came out as soon as we came off the train and asked if we had any money. They took it all away. They stripped us naked, both men and women, to find out where we carried the money. Some hid it well, but they still found it. They pointed their guns at us and we were very afraid. They took all our money. They left us penniless, not even enough to buy food.

With thousands of miles to go, María and her husband were disheartened but determined. They scrounged for food and received help from other travelers like themselves. Since they could not pay for tickets, they had to hop freight trains: "The train rushed by and we had to run after it. But we would fall. I arrived here injured all over." It took a series of such rides to reach the U.S. border. "When the train would stop we'd have to walk at night, despite the rain, wind, and cold."

After a month of arduous travel, María and her husband arrived in Tijuana. They found a coyote who helped them cross the hills and canyons, and then took them all the way to San Diego's Green Valley camp, where they joined her father-in-law. Even though the camp offers nothing more than makeshift shelters, María was relieved to arrive after her tiring and dangerous ordeal.

Despite the bravado and joking that some (especially successful migrants) express about the experience, crossing the border is not a frivolous undertaking. The journey poses risks, the least of which is apprehension by the Border Patrol. Border crossers face the ever-present possibility of being robbed, raped, or killed by a border bandit. They may meet up with an abusive Border Patrol agent. Or they may be injured or even killed in an accident. And yet hundreds of thousands, perhaps even millions, take that risk in order to seek work or find relative safety in the United States.

RISKS OF SEPARATION

When one family member leaves for the United States, family left behind experience some justifiable anxiety about the potential dangers of the journey. The worst-case scenario is that the person is hurt or killed, with the family back home never receiving notification.

This is not an idle fear. Undocumented border crossers often carry no identification so that if apprehended they can use a false name, avoiding a record of their arrest. But this also makes it difficult to identify the person in the event of an accident.

Crossing the border is filled with dangers. Bandits of both countries rob, rape, and even kill unsuspecting migrants crossing the border over the hills and through the canyons (Frank, 1979). Death can also be more random. On May 18, 1990, a 12-year-old Mexican boy, on his way to his parent's apartment in Orange County, was gunned down as he and family members walked along a border hillside. A 23-year-old U.S. citizen who lives in the area was charged with the murder. According to witnesses, the alleged killer, who was standing on the balcony of a friend's apartment, said, "Let's shoot some aliens," and fired a hunting rifle toward a hillside where many undocumented border crossers were gathered. This same person was also charged with assaulting undocumented immigrants for "beer money" earlier on the day of the murder (McDonnell, 1990a). Violence committed against undocumented border crossers appears on the increase. In 1982, two killings and 60 robberies were reported. During the first eight months of 1990, nine killings and 228 robberies were reported (Miller & McDonnell, 1990).

Death can also occur from a crossing gone awry from bad planning. In July 1980, a party of 26 Salvadorans paid $1200 to a coyote to cross into the United States. Their guide then left them in the Arizona desert. With an inadequate water supply and inappropriate dress (the women wore high-heeled shoes and jewelry), 13 perished in the desert (Maggio, 1980). Indeed, so many ill-equipped border crossers die in the Arizona desert during the hot summer months that the Yuma County Department refers to it as the "season of death" (Curry, 1986).

In addition to natural hazards, clandestine border crossers occasionally find themselves in danger as a result of Border Patrol actions. They have been accidentally run over by Border Patrol vehicles. On April 18, 1985, a Border Patrol officer shot and wounded Humberto Carrillo, a 12-year-old boy standing on the Mexican side of the border. The officer said the boy was about to throw a rock at him over the chain-link fence (La Ganga, 1985). According to one observer, 11 more minors have been beaten or shot, four fatally, by Border Patrol agents between the time of the Carrillo case and December 1990.[8] Between January and the end of November 1990, at least five undocumented border crossers were wounded by immigration authorities, including a 15-year-old boy who made his living selling gum and newspapers at the border (McDonnell, 1990). The youth was standing with one foot in Mexico and one foot in the United States when he was shot for allegedly holding a rock to throw (Miller & McDonnell, 1990).

Accidents also occur when immigration agents attempt to capture undocumented immigrants. In one incident, a Border Patrol agent fired his revolver into a van loaded with undocumented immigrants, hitting one 16-year-old Mexican boy twice in the head (McDonnell, 1990). Although the Border Patrol says such incidents are few in relation to the huge number of people detained by agents, the Mexican government has expressed concern that these incidents raise questions about the use of force in situations where a threat to the officers is questionable (Miller & McDonnell, 1990).

Border Patrol and INS officers sometimes chase undocumented workers into waterways, where they drown. In one case, three undocumented workers were walking across a railroad trestle bridge in an agricultural area near Santa Paula, California, when INS agents arrived. Two of the men allowed themselves to be taken, but one jumped into the Santa Paula Creek, then flowing at about 25 miles an hour, and was apparently afraid to take the hand of an agent who tried to pull him out of the water *(Los Angeles Times,* 1982). According to one source, 15 farmworkers drowned between 1974 and 1986 during INS raids in agricultural areas (Rural California Report, 1990, p. 4).

On February 15, 1988, in Madera, California, INS agents conducted a raid on a group of farmworkers, most of whom were Mixtecan Indians from Oaxaca. Most of the workers ran. But one 17-year-old was caught by a relatively large agent who threw him down on the asphalt, causing head injuries from which he died a few days later (Rural California Report, 1990, p. 4). The fear and physical contact experienced during raids creates the potential for life-threatening events.

Once across the border, newcomers unaccustomed to life in the United States sometimes take unnecessary risks. In their zeal to get into the United States, some undocumented migrants jog across Interstate Highways 805 and 5, which run north from the border. I have witnessed this on a number of nights. I also have seen lying on the roadside the bodies of unfortunate ones who misjudged the speed at which cars travel on a freeway. In four years, 1985–88, 57 undocumented immigrants were killed crossing Interstate Highways 805 and 5 near the Mexican border. This death rate seems to be on the increase; between 1987 and August of 1990, 83 people were killed. Between January and August 11, 1990, 16 were killed *(Los Angeles Times,* 1990).

Similar deaths have occurred on Interstate 5 near the San Clemente checkpoint. Undocumented migrants sometimes try to evade detection at the checkpoint

---

[8]Roberto Martinez of the American Friends Service Committee's U.S./Mexico Border Program, located in San Diego, has compiled these cases.

by hiking through the hills to the east or circling around to the west, which means crossing the freeway. This maneuver is particularly dangerous for the young and aged. For example, on August 8, 1990, an 8-year-old Mexican boy, the last in line behind his mother, brothers, and sisters, was killed shortly after midnight while crossing the freeway just north of the San Clemente checkpoint (McDonnell, 1990). A teenaged Latino male was also killed that day, and an older couple had been killed the week before while on their way to visit their son in Los Angeles. On September 27, 1990, an 80-year-old immigrant from Mexico was killed when his son, who was driving, became nervous and told him to cross the freeway, that he would pick him up on the other side. Ironically, the immigration checkpoint was not operating at the time (Reyes, 1990). Between 1987 and August 11, 1990, 33 migrants were killed near the San Clemente checkpoint (*Los Angeles Times,* 1990). These tragic events led the California Transit Authority to post signs near the checkpoint stating, "CAUTION—WATCH FOR PEOPLE CROSSING ROAD." Another sign simply has the word "CAUTION" above a picture, in silhouette, of a man, woman, and child running.

Migrants also take other unfortunate risks. They sometimes hop trains only to have the boxcar door inadvertently locked from the outside. Railroad personnel find their suffocated, dehydrated, or starved bodies at the train's destination. Life-threatening accidents also occur on the job, in automobiles, or in a number of other ways. For example, farmworkers are exposed to pesticides, which sometimes reach fatal exposure levels.[9]

Undocumented immigrants crossing the freeway. Don Bartletti

[9]*Los Angeles Times*; A:22, March 5, 1990. José Campos Martínez died on January 20, 1990, while spraying the pesticide parathion on an almond orchard in Lost Hills, California. According to the article, he apparently had somehow swallowed some of the pesticide.

In addition, undocumented immigrants are the victims of random crimes committed by individuals with an irrational hatred or fear of them. For example, in November 1988, two teenagers in the community of Escondido, motivated by their dislike for Mexicans, used an AK-47 assault rifle to gun down two Mexican workers walking along a field of avocado trees (Miller & McDonnell, 1990). Ironically, the two workers were actually legal immigrants.

As these examples suggest, leaving home to migrate north initiates a profound and serious separation. Those left behind realize that sending a loved one off to the United States is an event whose outcome is in the hands of fate, and that some will pay an awful price for the privilege of earning minimum wage in a foreign country. Songs often speak of the risks inherent in the migration experience. For example, "Vendites los Gueyes" ("You Sold the Oxen"),[10] tells of a migrant worker who dies while in the United States.

Mi negro del alma te juites pa'l norte dejates las siembras por una ilusión. Vendites los gueyes para el pasaporte. Maldita miseria la de esta región.

Dark one of my soul, you went to the north, you left the sown fields for an illusion. You sold the oxen for a passport. Evil misery of this region.

Con un burro flaco hicimos labranza, hicimos la escarda con azadón. Miramos al cielo con una esperanza, las nubes se fueron como maldición.

With a skinny burro we did the farming, we did the weeding with a hoe. We looked up to the sky with hope, the clouds disappeared like a curse.

Mis hijos lloraban, dejándome sorda. Me fui pa' la hacienda, yo quise robar. Les truje nopales y un cacho de goma, y yo ya, sin fuerzas, me puse a rezar.

My children cried, leaving me deaf. I went to the hacienda, willing to steal. I brought them cactus and a wad of gum, and I now, without strength, began to pray.

Los gringos mandaron la plata a montones, con unos papeles que había que firmar. Mi prieto había muerto en las fundiciones. No quise la plata y me puse a llorar.

The gringos sent piles of money with some paper I had to sign. My dark one had died in the foundries. I didn't want the money and I began to cry.

Family members left behind by migrants live with the knowledge of such risks and potential dangers. They are part of an underlying tension created by separation. Geographic separation also strains relations between family members, especially spouses, but also between migrating parents and the children left behind. These fears, tensions, and emotional stresses contribute to the pressure families feel to join members residing in the United States.

BORDERS AND LIMINALITY

Crossing the border is both a physical and symbolic experience that marks the beginning of the transition phase in the undocumented immigrant's territorial passage.

[10]"Vendites los Gueyes." Composed by Fernando Campo. Performed by Las Hermanas Padilla y El Mariachi Vargas de Tecalitlan (Album: "Con Sabor a Provincia"). Produced by Antilla.

Undocumented immigrants sleeping on a hill above the freeway. Don Bartletti

However, completion of the next phase, incorporation into the new society, is not guaranteed nor does it occur immediately after safely reaching a destination in the United States. Rather, incorporation occurs in stages. It is a process marked by a series of experiences, such as finding a job, forming a family, learning the local culture, establishing contacts with family and friends in the area, learning English, and moving from undocumented status to legal residence.

As we see in the following chapter, the transition phase is an extended one for many undocumented migrants. They have few experiences to incorporate them into U.S. society. Consequently, they remain liminals, or outsiders, who may find work but remain isolated from the larger society.

4 / Life on the Farm

Many undocumented migrants are drawn to northern San Diego County by the demand for labor in the strawberry, tomato, and avocado fields, as well as in large nurseries and flower farms. Scattered throughout this area, workers live in temporary camps near the fields that they tend. From Encinitas, Carlsbad, Oceanside, and Del Mar on the coast to the inland communities of San Marcos, Bonsall, Escondido, Rancho Peñasquitos, and Fallbrook, workers set up makeshift sleeping shelters of plastic, cardboard, tar paper, discarded wood, and anything else that is handy. These encampments can be found on hillsides covered by dense brush, and in canyons with pleasant-sounding names like McGonigle Canyon and Deer Canyon. Even though they are just moments away from middle- and upper-middle-class neighborhoods and communities, they stand in stark contrast to the growing affluence of north San Diego County. These camps resemble the living conditions I have seen in Third World countries (McDonnell, 1987).

Finding these encampments is not easy. Their shelters are placed as inconspicuously as possible. The ones on private property sometimes have guards, or at least a wary foreman posted, to discourage strangers from trespassing. I visited encampments in a canyon near the old Mission San Luis Rey on many occasions during

Worker and his makeshift shelter surrounded by suburbia.   Don Bartletti

1981 and 1982.[1] I got to know a few of the hundreds of men living there, many of whom were Indians from Oaxaca. I found conditions in the campsites similar to those found in other canyons in the area at the time, including Deer Canyon, which the *Los Angeles Times* called "The Canyon of the Damned" (Montemayor, 1980).

To arrive at the campsite, I headed east from the coast past the Mission San Luis Rey and then turned from the main highway onto a street newly built for a recently finished condominium complex. Parking the car where the road dead-ends, I made my way up a hill to find myself looking over a field with rows of strawberries gently curving with the contour of the land. Each row was covered with plastic to protect the delicate plants. The field gave way to the greenery of bushes and trees marking the edge of an extensive canyon that worked its way east past other fields and into the foothills. From this perspective, it was difficult to tell that as many as 300 to 500 men lived down in the canyon. Their campsites were down in that natural cover, hidden from sight as much as possible.

LIFE IN THE CAMPS

During the week I tried to arrive at the campsites at about 4:30 in the afternoon, when the workday would be winding down. Some workers were still in the fields. Others were making their way back to their campsites. Whenever possible, I struck up a conversation with the first man I encountered who was not working and then accompanied him into the canyons.

The makeshift campsites the workers set up are mostly empty during the day as the men work in the fields. However, I usually found some workers idle at the campsites. They complained that the foremen would tell them there was not enough work, but that they should stick around until the following day, when work might be available. For men who have migrated hundreds of miles to work, a continual on-again, off-again work schedule is frustrating. Then again, these idle workers serve as a reminder to the working men that they are easily replaced should they get sick or fail to work hard enough.

The men work as many hours as they can, with 10-hour or longer days not unusual. They also work as many days as possible, but usually not Sundays. They earn minimum wage, but are able to increase their earnings during the harvest by working piece-rate, that is, by the basketful. There have, however, been unfortunate cases of farmworkers complaining of being paid less than minimum wage, beaten up and shot at by hired thugs, and even forced to work without pay (Taylor & Montemayor, 1980; L. Wolf, 1989).

The campsites slowly come alive in the late afternoon. Standing on the edge of the canyons, one can see the flicker of fires through the brush and low trees. In the distance, on a ridge above the canyon, sits the *fayuquero,* a person selling food from a truck. Men slowly make their way to the truck, returning with tortillas, bread, sandwiches, sodas, beer, and other items.

[1]When I first visited the canyons in 1981, I was assisted by two excellent researchers, Richard Mines, who has written extensively on farmworkers in California, and Alberto Hernández, who at the time was a research assistant on the project I was involved in and who is presently a researcher at the Colegio de la Frontera Norte, in Tijuana, Mexico.

On Sundays, the campsites take on a community-like appearance. Men bathe, and wash their clothes, hanging them on trees and bushes, or on lines strung between the trees. Some men play soccer and basketball, using a hoop someone has rigged up. Others sit on old wooden crates or tree stumps as they relax, talk, and drink beer. Sometimes the men talk about fights from the night before. With little else to do, nowhere to go, and few outsiders to talk to, the men often drink beer to pass the time on Saturday nights and Sundays. Loneliness and boredom plague them during nonworking hours.

As we sat and talked one Sunday afternoon, one young man jumped up and pointed down into the ravine. "There she goes," he said, hitting another fellow on the arm. "Now's your chance." We all stood up and looked as the men laughed. Down below, a woman walked through the canyon with a number of men following her. As sometimes happens on Sundays, a group of prostitutes from Tijuana had arrived at the camp.

On one occasion, Alberto Hernández (a Mexican researcher assisting me) and I approached a campsite of men whom I had met before. I recognized Faustino, Ignacio, and young Miguel, all of whom had migrated originally from an Indian community in Oaxaca. Faustino motioned for us to sit down. Before long, they offered us a cola and beer, and we were talking about work, where they were from, and life in the canyon. One of the men warmed tortillas on a rusty lid taken from a discarded 55-gallon container found lying near the fields. They also used a makeshift grill to cook strips of meat. A meal of tacos was prepared and then eaten quickly. Faustino, about 36 years old, seemed respected by the men sitting around the campsite, who ranged in age from about 16 to 27.

Workers socializing after work.   Don Bartletti

Canyon campsite.   Don Bartletti

A worker and his shack, or canton.   Don Bartletti

Farmworkers refer to their campsites as their *canton,* which means the place where they live, conveying a sense of hominess, belonging, and even permanence to a living situation that seems far from permanent. The living conditions in these canyons and ravines are at the most basic level. The encampments have no running water or toilets. Water is brought in from the spigots and hoses that irrigate the fields. Lacking toilets, the workers use the immediate area to relieve themselves. Mounds of trash, especially soda and beer cans, pile up.

Looking around the campsites, it is clear that they are places used mostly for cooking, eating, and socializing by small groups of people. Some, such as Faustino's, had a makeshift table upon which food and a meager collection of plates, utensils, and other paraphernalia were piled. Leftover food also lay scattered on the table, drawing numerous flies.

In a few of the campsites scattered throughout the canyon I noticed that some men had constructed shelters for sleeping out of old pieces of wood and plastic. But many others, such as Faustino's, had no apparent place to sleep. I asked Faustino where he slept. He took me to a less conspicuous place just outside the campsite. He had cleared a space under some thick bushes just large enough for sleeping. He was lucky, he said, because he found some pieces of plastic to line the space with. The local press refers to these sleeping quarters as "spider holes," a term perhaps meant to suggest the metaphorical distance between men forced to sleep in "nature" while the rest of San Diego's residents sleep in houses and apartments, the products of "culture."

The main advantage of sleeping in a hole in the ground was the likelihood of remaining unseen by agents of the INS and Border Patrol, who frequently raided this and many other canyons in the northern part of the county. Although the encampments, nestled among trees and bushes, are difficult to spot from a distance, they are easily found once you are in the canyons themselves. The well-worn paths between encampments are a liability for men wishing to avoid the INS and Border Patrol, who often raid the camps at sunrise. On the other hand, a hole in the ground, discreetly hidden by bushes, has a greater chance of going undetected, leaving its occupants free to work yet another day.

The disadvantages of makeshift shelters are many. Men sleeping in the bushes are plagued by fleas, rats, and snakes. Moreover, the makeshift shelters offer little comfort during a storm. As he showed me his sleeping hole, Faustino made it clear that during heavy rains this place became useless to sleep in. And during severe storms, water flowed through the canyon, washing away huts built too close to the canyon floor.

Cold nights also pose a danger to men trying to keep warm. On May 15, 1981, a camp near some strawberry fields in Oceanside caught fire, killing one worker and severely burning three others. All four were from San Martín, a tiny Indian village in the remote northwestern mountains of Oaxaca. Their underground shelter was made of cardboard and plastic. It is believed that heated rocks used to warm the shelter on cold nights ignited the plastic and then the entire hut burned up around the four occupants. Adding to the tragedy was the 20 minutes it took to reach a telephone to report the fire and another 45 minutes for an ambulance to be dispatched (Walbert, 1981). Fire in the migrant camps is always a danger during the summer, when heat leaves the brush cover tinderbox dry. On one hot August day, an alleged arsonist apparently tried to get rid of a migrant camp by starting a fire that burned 650 acres east of Del Mar (Bowman, 1979).

A lack of provisions for hygiene poses an obvious health threat for farmworkers living in hundreds of camps found in the area. A county health worker, after a

Sleeping place dug into the ground and under bushes, called a "spider hole." Don Bartletti

tour of farmworker camps in October 1980, emphasized that even though workers handled the food being harvested, it was unlikely that disease would be transmitted from the workers to the consumers through the agricultural product; rather "When we have feces on the ground, when you have flies all over the place, the main danger is transmission [of disease] among [the farmworkers] themselves" (Montemayor, 1980).

Not surprisingly, farmworkers complain of recurring headaches, stomachaches, and diarrhea. Such symptoms may be attributable to more than the lack of storage facilities, running water, and toilets. While talking to Miguel, who was 16 years old, I noticed that he and the others stored their water for drinking and washing dishes in white plastic buckets. Upon closer inspection, I saw that they were discarded pesticide containers with a label that warned (in English) against using the container for anything that led to human consumption. When I attempted to explain the danger such a practice posed to their health, the workers merely shrugged it off, saying, "What else are we going to do?" Men who tend avocado trees in nearby fields have been known to drink water from the irrigation system, which also supplies fertilizers and zinc solutions for the maturing trees (Taylor & Montemayor, 1980).[2]

Seeing the conditions in which the farmworkers in the canyons and ravines live, it is not surprising that most return home after a short period—around 10 months. It is a hard life. One man I met, however, said that he had been living in this canyon for 3 years without a break.

Not all farmworkers in San Diego live under such trying conditions. In the southern part of the county farmworkers are generally legal immigrants, and many belong to a farmworker's union. Many of these farmworkers are "commuters"—they live in Mexico and commute daily to work on farms in San Diego. Not only is Mexico close but so is the Border Patrol, which may be why farmers closer to the border often rely primarily on workers who are legal immigrants.

Even in the northern section of the county, conditions vary for farmworkers, some of whom are also legal residents of the United States. On some farms, the owners provide an old trailer or mobile home where three to five workers can live. Although lacking many modern conveniences, such housing at least provides shelter from the elements. The larger farms and nurseries often do not provide such facilities, except perhaps for the foreman and his family. Lest I give the impression that all agricultural workers in the area live on farm property or in nearby canyons, many live with their families in apartments and houses. Or they crowd six or more single people into an apartment. Even though life under these crowded conditions has its difficulties and annoyances, the workers living in apartments have at least managed to move beyond the rudimentary life of the workers in makeshift shelters.

Back in the canyon, I found it interesting how the farmworkers managed to get from a small village in rural Mexico to a specific ranch in the United States while knowing so little about the environment in between. Some needed only the vaguest of directions, just a general description of the area and perhaps the name of a farm. The general consensus among the farmworkers, however, is that the surest way to make the trip is with someone who has already made at least one migration. This is not too difficult. The 17 Oaxacans interviewed in this one canyon had migrated an average of 4.4 times each, which means that all seem to know somebody who worked on the farm before, usually a relative or friend from the same village.

---

[2]A farmworker in El Mirage, Arizona, made a similar comment about a tank that drained into irrigation water: "The tank had a skull and crossbones on it. I used the water to drink, to bathe in, to wash dishes, to cook with, and to wash clothes" (Curry, 1980).

I found that the men around any particular campsite fire are frequently related in some way. Brothers, cousins, fathers, and sons tend to share a campsite. Miguel, for example, was here with his uncle, who had made the trip before. Of the 17 Oaxacans, 12 (70.6 percent) also had a relative working in San Diego. But there are other forms of relationship besides kinship. Men from the same village will find each other even if they had not migrated together. The Oaxacans I visited with most often in this particular canyon were all from the Indian village of San Geronimo del Progreso. However, the region and even the particular state a migrant comes from can also serve as the all-important link between people in a different country. Their mutual experience as migrants in a foreign land provides them with a sense of comradeship and communion. They become *paisanos* (countrymen) away from home. Extending comradeship in this way is common among all the immigrants I have met.

The farmworkers I encountered generally came from various states in Mexico, with Jalisco, Michoacán, and Oaxaca the most common homestates. People from Jalisco and Michoacán have been migrating to the United States for generations. Migration from Oaxaca is more recent (Kearney, 1986). Workers typically share many of the same characteristics. They are single or, if married, have left their families in Mexico. They have little education and few sophisticated work skills.

The Oaxacans I met in the canyon near the Mission San Luis Rey migrated from communities that are ethnically Indian. They tend to be shorter and darker than most other Mexican immigrants. They often speak an Indian language of the Mixtecan language group, and have learned Spanish as a second language. When I interviewed Miguel, it was clear that he did not understand some of the questions posed to him in Spanish. He, like many other young Oaxacan-Mixtecan migrants, had been away from his village but a short time and his knowledge of Spanish was still rudimentary.

The workers do not leave the confines of the farm and canyon very often. Except for an occasional walk to a convenience store, they are reluctant to leave their camps. When they do leave to go to a store, for example, they often must walk through residential areas. This raises the suspicions of local residents, who may complain to local politicians. In April 1983, a San Diego city councilman asked the Border Patrol to conduct sweeps in northeastern San Diego, especially near Rancho Peñasquitos and Rancho Bernardo. He took this action after residents of Rancho Peñasquitos complained of their fear of the undocumented workers who use their streets to reach a local convenience store. The councilman said, "There are no restrictions that keep them from entering neighboring communities, primarily for the purpose of obtaining liquor. When the situation reaches a point where San Diego residents are threatened and robbed, action must be taken to enforce existing laws" (Rangel, 1983).

The farmworkers in the canyons know little about the world outside the farm and its surrounding canyons, and what they do know adds to their reluctance to venture out. They talk about how the INS and police indiscriminately stop farmworkers and ask them for immigration papers. And they talk about workers being robbed, beaten, shot at, and even killed by local people. In one case in 1986, three teenagers in Encinitas dressed up in camouflage uniforms and attacked a group of farmworkers, firing at them with a .22 caliber rifle, .22 caliber handgun, and a pellet gun,

Agricultural workers arrested by the Border Patrol. Don Bartletti

wounding one person (Reza, 1986b). Other incidents occurred in 1984, when local off-duty Marines undertook nighttime "beaner raids" ("beaner" is a derogatory term for Mexican) on farmworkers near Fallbrook. The Marines beat, robbed, and even set a farmworker on fire (Smollar, 1984). The year before I began my research, three men from Carlsbad were arrested for fatally shooting a 17-year-old undocumented worker and for robbing 20 other Mexican farmhands *(Los Angeles Times,* 1980).

Since I initially went into the fields in the early 1980s, such incidents against migrant farmworkers have continued to occur in northern San Diego County. In the fall of 1989, workers living in a campsite in the hills near Poway complained of being "terrorized" by white youths shooting at them with pellet guns and rifles loaded with paint cartridges, which sent some workers to the hospital (Barfield, 1989). Youths in that area have also parked near migrant camps and yelled threats and obscenities at the farmworkers. On at least one occasion, several teens with baseball bats and knives drove a four-wheel-drive pickup truck through a camp late at night, frightening the camp dwellers and damaging their makeshift shelters (Barfield, 1989). On November 9, 1989, two Mexican fieldhands, ages 22 and 19, were shot to death by two local teenagers as they walked along an isolated stretch of Black Mountain Road, just east of Del Mar and near a number of nurseries and migrant camps (Serrano, 1989).

Stories of such incidents are told as the men sit around talking. One Sunday afternoon Faustino related what happened to him in a labor camp in Ventura County. One morning, he said, they were just waking up when a group of *cholos* (Mexican American gang members) burst through the door of the building. They had rifles and guns and demanded their money. The farmworkers gave their money to them, but the robbers shot at them anyway, killing one worker. Faustino became quite animated as he showed how he jumped out of a window to escape the flying bullets. Stories such as these, like most folklore, carry a message, and in this case they help instill a sense of caution and fear among the farmworkers.

RELATIONS BACK HOME

Farmworkers living in the canyons save as much of their money to take back home as possible. This is not as easy as it sounds. Food must be bought daily since there is no refrigeration or adequate storage. Clothes also wear out from daily use. Since they often buy these items from the fayuqueros, they often pay premium prices—often twice the retail price (Walbert, 1981). The farmworkers I talked with believed they were lucky if they were able to save one out of every three dollars they earned. If they could not find relatively steady work this proportion dwindled down to nothing.

The Oaxacans provide us with an example of the strong link the farmworkers maintain to their families back in Mexico. Many of the Mixtecan farmworkers working in San Diego are part of a migration stream out of Oaxaca that includes not just single men but whole families. Drought, soil erosion, and land pressure have forced Mixtecan Indians—as many as 90,000—into a migrant-labor circuit inside Mexico that leads to the citrus fields of Sinaloa and the tomato fields of Baja California Norte (Nagengast, Kearney, & Stavenhagen, 1989). Because they are Indian, the Oaxacan migrant workers often endure lower wages and worse living conditions than other farmworkers in Mexico and are forced to work without protection from pesticides (Kearney, 1986; Beckland & Taylor, 1980).

One result of this migration has been the growth of a community of Oaxacans in Tijuana, primarily in the neighborhood known as Colonia Obrera *(colonia* is the Spanish word for "neighborhood," and *obrera* the word for "worker"). Faustino's wife and two children live in Colonia Obrera, as do the families of other Oaxacans working in San Diego. The men usually return to their families after a few months working in the fields—typically in the fall, after harvest. They sometimes return sooner if apprehended by the INS or Border Patrol, in which case they enjoy a brief visit with their family, perhaps get a haircut, and go to a restaurant before returning to the fields in northern San Diego County.

When they return to their families they take with them whatever money they have been able to save. They also send money to their families through other Oaxacans who are returning. Out of 17 Oaxacans, 15 had sent money back home to relatives. The other two had not yet earned enough to send back. Men with families in Oaxaca also send money home, usually every two weeks, by telegraphic money order, a practice common among Mexicans in the United States.

A number of years after I first interviewed Ignacio, we met again on a visit I made to Colonia Obrera with Alberto Hernández. He asked me to return and visit his home and meet his family in Colonia Obrera on the upcoming Day of the Dead, November 2. As we sat eating chicken *mole,* Oaxacan style, Ignacio told us how he was going to quit farmwork for a while to work in construction in Tijuana. He said that life on the farms was just too harsh.

He showed me around the house he had built using money he had earned from farmwork. The house is on the side of a canyon, as are all the houses in this neighborhood. To the casual visitor from the United States, Colonia Obrera looks like a shantytown. The houses appear thrown together, built of plywood and a hodge-podge of building materials. And, indeed, the neighborhood has developed in a haphazard manner, as migrants have claimed unused land and begun to build shelters. Since it was on the fringes of city property, the neighborhood did not develop according to any building codes or central planning. It has neither paved streets nor piped-in water. Some of the houses have electricity, but most appear to be without it.

Ignacio's house was set on a concrete foundation rather than on the dirt, thanks to the money he earned in the United States. The walls were made of plywood. He had a small television, a radio, and a few other items purchased in the United States. Other than that, the house had a rural appearance, with chickens running in the dirt yard and most of the day's activities taking place outside. His wife spoke only Mixtec, and his children were bilingual (Spanish and Mixtec).

Ignacio's brother and his family lived next door. The inside of his house was dark because there were no windows. In the front room, a table was adorned with pictures of Catholic saints in honor of the holiday. Chicken mole, tortillas, fruits, and soda were also set on the table for the souls of family members who had died. This display was set up just as it would have been in their native village in Oaxaca.

As we sat and talked, Ignacio's brother said that he, too, had worked in the United States, but that he moved from field work to garden work. His last job was in Beverly Hills. He brought out a picture of himself with one of the Gabor sisters and her husband, for whom he had worked as a gardener. I could not help thinking of the symbolic distance between Colonia Obrera and Beverly Hills and how this Oaxacan Indian's experiences had bridged the two.

For the families left in Tijuana by the Oaxacans working in the United States, life can be difficult until money arrives. The women and their children sell gum and little toys in the downtown tourist areas of Tijuana. They sometimes beg for money. Tijuana residents look upon the Oaxacan Indian women as giving the city a bad image, especially when they beg for money from tourists. Merchants resent the competition for tourist dollars. Both residents and merchants complain to the Tijuana police, who periodically try to roust the Oaxacan women from the tourist areas. Moreover, the people of Tijuana generally refer to all Oaxacan Indian women as "Marías." The fact that they give all Indian women the same nondescript name, erasing their different personalities and thus their humanity, reflects the low social status accorded Indians in contemporary Mexican society (Chavira, 1983; Friedlander, 1975).

DISCARDABLE WORKERS

Farmworkers in northern San Diego are generally employed as seasonal workers. All of the Oaxacan farmworkers I spoke with in the canyons said they were employed only temporarily and intended to return to Mexico. Once the harvest is in, there is little need for most of the farmworkers until early spring, when preparations for planting begin. For many migrant workers the seasonal nature of the work fits well with their personal goal of earning some money and returning home. I found, however, that the temporary nature of their work contributed to an amorphous feeling among the farmworkers that they are a discardable workforce.

Undocumented workers have been used in the area for the most physically demanding and dangerous jobs. For farmworkers, on-the-job accidents pose potential threats to the goal of earning money to send home to Mexico. When such accidents occur, many employers take the worker to a doctor at company expense. However, some workers complained that when they were ill or injured they were not helped by the company doctor. For example, one fellow said:

> The doctor said he could do nothing for me even though I had little strength left in my right hand. It didn't seem to me that he had my interest at heart. When I asked him a question he would shrug his shoulders and say he couldn't help me. When I asked him what would happen to my hand if I went back to harvesting oranges, he said I could work until I hurt it worse and then take a few days off to rest it and then return to work until I hurt it again. A good doctor doesn't say this to someone, they try to cure the problem.

Even though most farmworkers find their employers will take them to seek healthcare following an injury, not all are so lucky. Injured workers can easily be disposed of if they are temporary, undocumented workers. As one farmworker said,

> One time I was working very hard. We had to lift some heavy equipment and I was trying to please my *patrón* [boss]. I pulled so hard I hurt my back. For two days I could barely move. Then my patrón took me in his truck and I thought he was taking me to a doctor. But imagine my surprise when we arrived at the border and he told me to get out and go back to Mexico or he'd call the Border Patrol.

Undocumented farmworkers are often reluctant to seek health care for injuries or illnesses. Since they rarely venture far from the farm, the workers often do not know where to find a local health clinic or doctor's office. Then, too, paying for health care further diminishes their savings. As a consequence, many farmworkers either take their health problems back to Mexico with them or simply suffer with them.

Part of the reluctance to seek care is related to the workers' vulnerability and powerlessness in the workplace. They are often afraid to tell the employer of an accident for fear of losing their jobs. For example, a tree limb dropped on one fellow's head, and he was fired afterwards for working slowly. He left rather than admit he had been in an accident. Such fear and reluctance can have tragic consequences.

Manuel had been in the United States for 20 years at the time he was interviewed. Although he is now a legal resident of the United States, for most of that time he had no documents from the INS. He has always worked on farms, and although he complains constantly of feeling sick—a state he attributes to exposure to pesticides and fertilizers—he has never received medical attention for those complaints. On the one occasion that he did complain to his employer, he received the same treatment as the person whose story was related above: His boss took him to the border and told him, "Now go back to Mexico." But it was Manuel's wife's tragic experience that exemplifies how undocumented workers fear complaining about illnesses or injuries.

Manuel's wife died after a trailer fell on her and some of her coworkers. But, as Manuel said, at the time neither his wife nor the other workers mentioned the accident to the foreman

> because of fear of losing their jobs. Soon she began to complain that she couldn't move her arm or leg, but she never liked to go to a doctor in the United States. When she couldn't take the pain any longer she went to Tijuana to stay with her mother, and there she died.

Miguel, the 16-year-old from Oaxaca, provided a personal example of how farmworkers often take their health problems to doctors in Tijuana. One Friday night at about 11:00, Miguel showed up at my apartment with Alberto Hernández. They stopped to rest and eat a little before continuing on to Tijuana. Miguel had broken his wrist on Wednesday and yet continued to work. But now, he said, the pain was too much to bear and he had decided to accept Alberto's offer to take him to Tijuana, where he could see a doctor. Miguel was back at work on the following Tuesday.

Shortly after this incident, I returned to the fields. As I approached the canyon where the men I knew had their camps, it became clear that things had changed dramatically. The canyon had been scraped clean of brush and the workers' campsites. I approached a worker and asked him what had happened. It appears that the farmer (for whom they worked) had bulldozed the area to force the men to move from the canyon, which was on his property. Farmers in the area frequently use this tactic to avoid responsibility for the farmworkers, especially for their proper housing and sanitation. Farm owners have said that one of the reasons they do not provide housing for the workers is that the workers prefer the canyons, which offer them protection from the INS and Border Patrol (Taylor & Montemayor, 1980). Others have said that they are under no obligation to provide housing, are not landlords, and fear they could be charged with harboring "illegal aliens" if they provided housing (Walbert, 1981). A representative for a grower offered this explanation for his client's bulldozing of an encampment: "We spend lots of money attempting to clean up debris or any kind of nuisance situation. They choose to live this way. We know of some workers who live in regular housing, but these [other] people are trying to save money to send to families in Mexico so they live this way" (Dennis, 1979). At any rate, it did not take me long to find the workers, who had already set up new makeshift shelters in a nearby canyon.

WOMEN AND CHILDREN IN THE CANYONS

When I first began visiting the canyons where the workers lived in the early 1980s, I did not encounter women. Perhaps women were to be found in some of the sites, but I did not happen upon them. By the mid-1980s, women were frequently found in some of the campsites in the canyons and hillsides near the nurseries and flower farms along the coast. It is difficult to assess how many women live under these conditions.

Women living in the canyons.   Don Bartletti

I interviewed two women living in shacks on a hillside just east of Del Mar. The hill sat in the shadow of the houses in Rancho Santa Fe, one of the most exclusive residential districts in California. I was led to the area by Rafael Martínez, a retired Presbyterian minister who has devoted a great deal of his time to providing assistance to the people living in the canyons. With me also was Paul Espinosa, an anthropologist and a producer at KPBS-TV in San Diego. We followed a dirt road past a large wholesale nursery. We had heard that undocumented workers had built 35 to 45 shacks on a hillside somewhere along this road. As we came over a hill the road forked. The principal road went down into a large ravine but the side fork led to a stand of trees and large bushes. Only a sharp eye could detect the top of a wooden shack in the brush.

We parked our van and made our way toward the shacks. It had rained recently, and the clayish soil was still wet, making walking difficult. We came upon a wooden structure a little more than five feet high. Tar paper, held on the roof by rocks and a few nails, flapped in the wind.

When we reached the shack Father Martínez called out for Benita. A woman came out carrying a 2-month-old boy.

Benita was 26 years old and had migrated from Michoacán. Her husband lived with her but was working in one of the nearby nurseries at the time. Her shack was dark, with the only light provided by the sunlight. It was small, and the roof was too low for us to stand straight. We sat on the bed talking and playing with the baby. Clothes were piled neatly in bags and boxes on the dirt floor. A small table held a camping stove and some food. A gas camping-lantern sat on the floor. The room was cramped, and wind whistled through cracks in the walls.

We asked her what had happened to all the other workers that we expected to find living in this area. She pointed to the hillside above her shack and said that the

Benita and her son in their shack.   Leo Chavez

workers' camps had been bulldozed by the owner of the land. She was told that the people living in the houses across the canyon complained of the workers' campfires. She said her shack had not been bulldozed because she worked as a housecleaner for some of the nearby houses. All of the other workers scattered into less conspicuous canyons.

As it turned out, there was not one shack, but two. Next to Benita's wooden shack was a metal shed, the type typically sold as storage for lawnmowers and garden tools. It, too, had a dirt floor and lacked running water and electricity. In it was a bed and a small camping stove. In front of the shed someone had planted flowers, giving it a cheerful and pleasant appearance.

Living in the metal shed was Rocio, a 20-year-old woman from Oaxaca, and her 8-month-old son. She had first gone to Los Angeles, but the brother-in-law of a friend of hers told her of work in this area and brought her to the hillside encampment. She worked 6 days a week for minimum wage at the nearby nursery, where, she said, "We nurture the plants so they will produce. We must harvest continually in order to continue producing this same kind of plants."

She and her male companion, her son's father, lost their campsite in the bulldozing, and then he was laid off from the nursery. Her companion left a couple of months ago when a friend suggested going to Los Angeles, where they believed jobs were available at higher wages. She had not heard from him since. Benita offered Rocio the metal shed when she found out she was alone and had no place to stay.

I asked Rocio why she lived in a shack rather than in an apartment. She said,

> If we paid rent there would be virtually nothing left. There is barely enough to live on now. But by living here, we can exist more or less. Apart from what we spend to live

[for food], we have a little left over. I send money to my mother because she is old and lives alone. She can no longer work.

The expense of rent and the need to send money back to her mother in Oaxaca left Rocio believing she had few alternatives to the way she now lived. But she compared her life here to her life in Oaxaca and found little difference:

I had imagined the United States very differently. I thought it was one big city. I never imagined it was the same as there [Oaxaca]. In Oaxaca, we live in a small village and we live the same as here. In our house there is no electricity, no water. We must haul water to the house the same as here. We use candles instead of electricity the same as here. There is no stove. We had to haul wood from the mountain just as we do here. Our house is wood like these. It is the same. The same living there as it is here.

Despite the living conditions, Rocio wanted to stay in the United States rather than return to Oaxaca,

because the wages there are very little. What one earns there is not even enough to eat. They pay very little and expect even more work than here. That's why.

Rocio had been working in the United States about a year when she found out she was pregnant. When it was time to have the baby she went to Tijuana. When the baby was about 6 weeks old, she made her way back across the border, walking over the hills during the middle of the day. She resumed her old job, but now Rocio has to pay another young woman $30 a week to take care of her son. Her main fear is that she will be picked up by the INS while at work and not be able to pick up her son. If that happens, she said she would return immediately to the United States.

After I interviewed Rocio, we walked down to the ravine below her shack. As we walked through a stand of trees and bushes we saw an old Chevrolet with two young men in it. We stopped to talk to them. They, too, worked at one of the nearby nurseries. They said that they had bought the car even though it did not run very well because they could drive it down into this ravine and sleep in it at night.

We returned a couple of weeks later. Reverend Martínez, Paul Espinosa, and I built Rocio a wooden shack that provided her and her baby with a little more space than the metal shed. I also brought her some toys and baby equipment that my son no longer used. When I saw Rocio again, she had just been robbed. Someone had broken into her shack while she was at work and taken the few toys and pieces of baby equipment. For families living in the canyons, life is precarious and tenuous, at best.

Finding an affordable apartment close to work in such an affluent area, however, is difficult if not impossible. To take advantage of the demand for shelter, some people rent out garages or buildings that are only slightly more comfortable than the shacks in the hills.

I visited one family that had moved from the hills to a more permanent wooden structure. Their home was down a hill behind a large house. It had once been a stable for horses, but the people in the large house converted it to human use and rented it for $250 a month.

Inside the converted stable was a small Oaxacan Indian woman. Her "house" consisted of one room. It had two beds, one for the woman and her husband, who was at work at the time, and one for their two sons, who were about 7 and 8 years old. On one wall a sink had been installed. The only source of light was an orange workman's lamp, the type used by auto mechanics because it has a hook at one end so that it can be hung easily. An extension cord ran from the lamp to the outside, presumably up to the house on the hill. That was the sum of the "conversion" from a horse's stable. The floors were rough wooden planks and the walls were uninsulated plywood.

Such housing does not conform to government codes, but it exists. Although the move from the canyons to residential life does not always lead to substandard housing, those who attempt such a move often find it difficult to locate an affordable apartment or house. Undocumented immigrants respond to this problem using various strategies, as we explore later.

MARGINALITY AND INCORPORATION

When the migrants whose living conditions I have described here crossed the border, they separated themselves from the social structure of their home country. They removed themselves from family and friends and suspended many obligations that may have been expected of them as a result of their social status in the community. In exchange, they became migrant workers who, because of their isolation, undergo few experiences that might move them out of their liminal status. The farmworkers living in the canyons interact little with the larger society. They rarely leave the campsites except to work or get food. They generally do not attend church services, go to the movies, go to school, or seek health care. They try to minimize the situations that draw attention to their presence. For all intents and purposes, they remain outside the social structure in the communities where they work.

The workers living in the canyons are socially marginal even though their work makes them an integral part of the local economy. Indeed, work provides them with the principal, and in some cases only, contact with the larger society. As a result, they remain in an extended period of transition, far from full incorporation into the larger society.

The farmworkers' social marginality stems from the conditions of farmwork in the area, as well as the negative view some members of the local community hold of the people who live in the canyons. In addition, their marginality stems from their own motivations and objectives. They migrate with a specific purpose: to earn some money and then return home to family and community in Mexico. They did not necessarily leave one community to become part of another community in the United States. They remain rooted in their home community and view their stay in the United States as temporary.

SETTLED FARMWORKERS

I emphasize that I am talking here about temporary migrants with relatively little time in the United States. Most undocumented farmworkers return to Mexico after a season in the United States. However, not all do so. Some farmworkers stay and become long-term residents of the United States. Ramón Carrillo's case illustrates the changes that occur and points out the differences between migrants and settlers, the subject of later chapters.

Ramón and his family live in a neatly kept mobile home on a hill surrounded by fields of oranges in a remote area near Valley Center. Ramón lives where he works. On this particular Sunday, he had invited me out to his home so that I could interview him at length about his life. With me was Paul Espinosa, who was interested in Ramón as a possible participant in the documentary "In the Shadow of the Law." When we arrived, we found that his wife had prepared a meal for us. Despite feeling guilty about accepting such a generous offer, we ate heartily, chalking it up to one of the benefits of fieldwork.

Ramón first came to the United States in 1974, when he was 30 years old and single. He followed a seasonal pattern of migration, leaving his hometown of Ibarra, Guanajuato, to work as a farmworker in San Diego for 6 months and then returning home for 6 months. His life during these early years in the United States was very similar to that of the temporary farmworkers discussed in this chapter.

Since coming to the United States, Ramón has worked for a company that owns a number of citrus and avocado farms in northern San Diego County. His brother, who had migrated a few years earlier, worked for the company and helped Ramón get the job. Another of Ramón's brothers, who also migrated to the area, was killed when the pole he was using to pick fruit accidentally touched an electrical wire.

In 1976, while back in Mexico, Ramón met Lucila, a young woman from San Felipe, Guanajuato, and they soon married. He continued his routine of temporary migration until 1978, at which point he brought his wife and 6-month-old son to live here with him. Ramón reflected on the change this way:

> Actually, I had never thought about staying here in the United States. But when I worked here I would hear talk that there was a law that if you had a child here you could fix your status. I thought maybe we could do that, but I didn't take it seriously. And then the law changed and there is now nothing like it. But it didn't matter, we still stayed here to work. . . . You know how it is. One wants to improve the living standard and well-being of the family. Here it is much better than over there [in Mexico]. It also depends on what kind of person you are. If you are not educated it is possible for you to fail in a good job over there. You are then obligated to find the means to live.

Although Ramón has worked at different company farms, he has now been working at the same farm for a number of years. He received this position because "after some time I told them [the company] that I was here to stay if they had a ranch to assign me to. They sent me here because they needed someone." His steady work has given his family—which now includes a son and daughter born in the United States—a sense of stability.

Ramón is the only full-time employee at the farm, with another eight to ten workers employed during the harvest. Ramón is responsible for the daily operations of this specific farm, reporting to a foreman who oversees various farms. Ramón describes his work in the following way:

> I'm like an administrator, I think, because I'm responsible for everything. People come to pick at harvest time and I have to keep track of what is picked and who is here and

give that information to the foreman. I see what supplies are needed and request them from the company. I also make sure the trees are watered.

Ramón's life is similar in some ways to that of temporary farmworkers in the area. He, too, has relatives in Mexico with whom he feels a strong connection. He regularly sends money to his parents, sometimes on a monthly basis. But in other ways, his life is very different. His wife and children are with him now, and he speaks in a way that gives one a sense of his confidence in dealing with U.S. culture. Unlike the seasonal farmworkers, he is not restricted to life within the boundaries of the farm:

There are people who have suffered by not being able to go out. They have to buy food that is very expensive [from a lunch truck] or they don't have a lunch when they need one because they can't go out. They are afraid.

In contrast, Ramón and his family know their way around:

When we need something we go to Valley Center. Every Friday we go to Escondido to the store to get our groceries. We go to the swap-meet on Sundays and there is no problem. If we need something during the week we go to town.

Although Ramón Carrillo and his family may feel they know their way around, they still share with the temporary workers the possibility of being apprehended by the authorities. In February 1986, Ramón and his family were driving to Texas to visit his wife's brother when they were stopped by the INS near Yuma, Arizona. At the time I interviewed them, they were in legal proceedings to determine whether they should be deported or allowed to continue living in the United States.

Ramón Carrillo has had many experiences that have helped incorporate him into society. He has brought his family to the United States, obtained full-time, permanent employment, assumed a position of responsibility on the job, sent his children to U.S. schools, and learned to move about in the larger society. Yet Ramón is still undocumented, which impedes his and his family's full incorporation into U.S. society.

The experiences of Ramón and the other farmworkers discussed in this chapter point to an important feature of their territorial passage in contrast to more typical rites of passage. In ceremonies that mark the transition between social categories, such as the ceremonies marking the transition from childhood to adulthood, there is every likelihood that the participants will be incorporated into the new category. Participants in a territorial passage to a new country cannot be assured that their transition will come to an end and that they will become fully incorporated into the new society.

In the next chapter, we examine the case of relatively recent migrants to the United States who built makeshift housing discreetly nestled among the trees and bushes of a hillside in Carlsbad, California. What occurred is a drama of rejection that clearly reveals the obstacles to incorporation faced by immigrants. Ironically, this case also includes individuals who have participated in one of the most important rites of incorporation: They have become legal residents of the United States.

5 / Suburban Shantytown and Refuge

On September 27, 1988, an inspector for San Diego County's Environmental Health Services signed an abatement order for a camp of makeshift shelters known as Green Valley (Walker, 1988). This was routine practice for the inspector, whose duty was to ensure that living conditions for the county's residents meet health and safety standards. Indeed, it was merely one of six such orders she had signed that day (Owens, 1988). But this particular action eventually led to the camp's dismantling and unleashed a heated controversy that focused unprecedented attention on the plight of migrant workers and their families in San Diego.

The story actually begins much earlier. The events leading up to the abatement order and the nature of this specific camp provide insights into why the camp was torn down and the health department's involvement in the matter. The controversy surrounding the existence of the Green Valley camp also reveals the obstacles to the incorporation of immigrants into the larger society. These were the issues that led me to Green Valley.[1]

Green Valley (Valle Verde in Spanish) is the name of a squatters' settlement that at the time of its destruction was home to about 200 immigrants from Mexico and Central America. During part of the year, however, as many as 450 migrants could be found living there (Rodgers, 1988). Their makeshift houses (or *cantones)* were hidden in the hills off El Camino Real, a major road running north and south through the county just a short distance from the Pacific Ocean. Green Valley sat on a narrow peninsula of land belonging to the City of Carlsbad, but was flanked by the communities of Encinitas and La Costa, where nearby condominiums and homes cost $250,000 and up.

The Green Valley camp had been around for a number of years, at least since the early 1980s. At that time, the area was still largely agricultural. Migrant workers were an integral part of the local agricultural workforce. Their presence was not as noticeable to the residents in the then-distant communities in Encinitas, La Costa, and Carlsbad. But the region has experienced rapid development. New homes and shopping centers have brought the suburbs to the very edge of Green Valley. The migrant workers no longer lived out of sight and out of mind. They were now seeking jobs by standing along busy streets in the middle of suburban development. Problems have accompanied these changes: "As new housing tracts and custom homes sprout from erstwhile flower fields and farmlands, the region

---

[1]These issues also prompted me to work with Paul Espinosa on a Public Broadcasting Service documentary, "Uneasy Neighbors," that tried to tell Green Valley's story.

has increasingly experienced a clash of cultures, a collision of socioeconomic circumstances" (Bailey & Reza, 1988).

Some, if not many, residents near Green Valley expressed their distress with what one newspaper headline called "The Alien Presence" (Bailey & Reza, 1988). They complained that they had moved to the sunny climes of San Diego County's coastal area in search of their suburban dream, only to find the landscape marred by migrant workers. One new resident of Carlsbad seemed to strike a common chord when she said that she was wary of the strangers and escorted her young son to the nearby grammar school. She added that when she went out for walks migrant men harassed her by calling out and whistling at her. "It's like we're living in the Third World here. It doesn't seem to me that this is part of the American Dream" (Bailey & Reza, 1980).

However, not all local residents viewed the migrants with suspicion. Many felt sympathetic to the migrants' plight. As one new resident said, "I feel so sorry for them, I just don't understand how they can live like that. If conditions in Mexico are worse than this, then heaven help the whole country" (Bailey & Reza, 1988). In fact, diverging opinions on these issues, including the destruction of the Green Valley camp, were expressed in news stories and at hearings held by task forces set up by the Cities of Carlsbad and Encinitas. The opinions of unofficial spokespersons for these differing points of view provide insight into how the larger community reacted to the presence of undocumented and legal migrants in the local community. In exploring these statements (what might be called "discourse" in contemporary cultural analysis) I am less concerned with their veracity, that is, whether the behavior attributed to migrants is true. I am more interested in the meaning of what is being said, that is, the message such statements contain, the impression they give, and their underlying significance for understanding how the larger society perceives undocumented and legal immigrants. These perceptions provide important insights into the controversy surrounding the Green Valley settlement and its destruction.

THE MIGRANT PROBLEM

John Johnson, the owner of a mobile home park next to Valle Verde, has lived in the area 28 years. When asked about the migrant workers, he said,

> We didn't notice them until in the early 1970s. In the early '70s they were good, honest, hard-working people. There's a lot of them out there now who are good, honest, hard-working people. There's a lot of them who are not. . . . There used to be none standing around here [on El Camino Real]. It's just been in the last probably four to five years that they have congregated here and waited for work.[2]

It was also about the same time that Mr. Johnson began to notice workers congregating on El Camino Real, in the mid-1980s, that the tension between migrants and other local residents in the Carlsbad and Encinitas area became a public issue. One of the most important episodes occurred in September 1986, when migrant workers were accused of asking young students for money as they

[2]Interviewed December 8, 1988, for "Uneasy Neighbors."

walked to elementary school *(San Diego Union,* 1986). Although none of the charges were ever substantiated, this episode seemed to galvanize resentment against migrant workers (Bailey & Reza, 1988). It was also about this time that a candidate for the County Board of Supervisors held a press conference in which he commented that illegals "line our streets, shake down our schoolchildren, spread diseases like malaria and roam our neighborhoods, looking for work or homes to rob" (Weintraub, 1986). Frequent news stories and gossip about migrant workers accused of burglaries, rape, and other crimes fanned this growing resentment and spurred a demand for action. In response, the city councils of Carlsbad and Encinitas each appointed a task force to study issues raised by the presence of undocumented workers.

Monica Tortelli, an attorney in her early thirties, lived in Encinitas near the Green Valley camp. She attended public hearings called by the Encinitas task force on the migrant problem and eloquently expressed what she termed a "humanitarian approach." As she noted, her views represent one of two opposing perspectives presented at the hearings:

> There were actually two camps. One camp was obviously the camp of the residents that live right next to a place where the workers are using it as a home. And they were obviously very much concerned with getting the undocumented workers out of the city. The other camp were those looking for a more humanitarian approach.[3]

Monica Tortelli explained that the reason the men stood on street corners was because of the abundant work in the area. "There's a lot of building, a lot of landscaping, and that's typically the work that they're being hired to do. There are a lot of 'yuppies' in the neighborhood that don't have time to go out and do the weeding, but they all want the nice properties." She also expressed her concerns about the presence of migrants, but suggested that the solution is not trying to force the migrants out:

> I have some concerns as a homeowner, as a parent, that there are a group of men that are, you know, without money or assets so close to an area that's obviously affluent. . . . I kind of take the approach that if we make it harder and harder for them to be employed then it's going to be more and more likely that they're going to find some other ways of getting money. You know they're not going to stop eating. There's no way we're going to stop their basic human needs for food, and finding food and clothing for their kids.

Even Tortelli's sympathetic view lists the problems generally associated with migrants: They are a drain on property values, their basic needs make them potential criminals, and their economic position contrasts sharply with the economic class of the surrounding communities. These and other problems come out strongly in the comments of Larry and Emma, a retired couple in their sixties, who have spoken at length in public hearings and to the press about the presence of "illegal aliens."

Larry and Emma live on the edge of a canyon not far from Green Valley. They have lived in Encinitas since 1953. Until about 1983, they said, they had no problem with migrant camps, which began to become noticeable in 1985. By 1988, the

[3]Interviewed December 8, 1988, for "Uneasy Neighbors."

camp had grown to as many as 50 residents. As Larry walked through the canyon, he poked at the debris with a golf club, his yellow jacket and blue-gray checked pants contrasting sharply with the green brush. He called this a "high-class" camp because the migrants had built a latrine. As he walked, he pointed out that some of the nearby houses had been burglarized, and that one day he found four or five men stealing oranges from his orange tree. As Emma said,

> We've had two and a half years of hell, and it was about 40 or 50 living down here. It got so we couldn't even sleep at night. And the last thing that really got me after my things in the paper didn't do any good, I went down to the city council. They had banged on our door and thrown oranges on our house and everything. City council told me to go to the undocumented task force. That was more or less a joke.[4]

To Emma and Larry's surprise, the task force suggested that the fire department teach canyon dwellers how to build safe fires and that portable toilets be installed. Even though Larry had complained about small fires having been accidentally started by men cooking over open fires and the "Border Patrol land mines" (piles of defecation) the men left on canyon trails, he and Emma disagreed. As Emma said, "Over our dead bodies, we wouldn't let them do that."

After complaining to the city council, the county sheriff, and the local school district (because the canyon land was school property), Larry and Emma finally saw their problem solved. "The sheriff, the Border Patrol, and the school maintenance force all got together one morning about five o'clock and made a sweep. Cleaned them out. . . . We haven't been bothered since." Larry walked around the deserted canyon as an archaeologist might do at a recently excavated site, pointing to evidence of a past that no longer existed. He said,

> They put in all this cardboard you find here. We tore the cardboard off, but this is where they were, right in here. This is where they had their fires. There's the paper, and we tore their rug out, took it down here and put dirt on it. That rug was up in here and this was the camp. . . . They're not here anymore. They've gone someplace else. But this is a camp that she [Emma] and I tore up about two weeks ago.

At the time Larry and Emma were interviewed, the Green Valley camp was set to be dismantled. Their fear was that the canyon next to their house would prove inviting to the displaced residents of Green Valley. Emma said, "One of the things that we're afraid of is that when they tear that other camp down up here on El Camino Real, we're afraid they're going to come down here. So now we're going to have to watch that."

John Johnson also had a list of problems associated with camp dwellers. His mobile home park is next to El Camino Real, where men lined up to wait for offers of work from passing cars. He said that 25 to 30 men stood along the road during the day. His main complaint was that the men used a drain that sits back off the road, and on his property, for a toilet. He said he also had to take out a water faucet that was used to wash out trash containers because they used it to bathe with. "They'd go up there and strip down in the trash containers and take their showers."

[4]Interviewed on December 12, 1988, for "Uneasy Neighbors."

This, he said, led to complaints. "The people in the mobile home park here, we get complaints from them. We get complaints from the women in the shopping center. They come out here to dump their trash and here they are taking their shower."

The mobile home park owner also said women are afraid to walk in the park after dark, even though there have not been any instances of criminal activity: "There's been no attacks in the mobile home park, just the presence of them. They come upon them in the dark and it scares them. . . . They've actually caused no damage in the park other than tearing down the fences and going through it and scaring the people."

Mr. Johnson also said he knew of problems other businesses near Green Valley were having. He said that retailers in the nearby shopping center "are very shook up with them and they drive other business away that they want." He noted that the center's liquor store, in particular, did a lot of business with Green Valley residents. But the liquor store, he said, "is not looking for their type of business." According to Johnson, the liquor store employees tried to discourage Green Valley residents from shopping there:

> They catch them trying to walk off with the beer and different things like that. He's having a lot of problems with them. And he tries to run them out and they come back and break his windows. So he's replaced several windows, and he feels that it was those people that are doing it. Every time he cracks down on them, that's when he has problems. He tries to discourage them from coming into the store. . . . I imagine he refuses to sell to them or something. He won't sell to them if they're drunk.

The City of Encinitas's undocumented workers task force heard many of the local residents' complaints concerning Green Valley and other migrant encampments. An Encinitas councilwoman[5] and task-force member summarized the complaints that they received as concerns about (1) people in the country illegally standing on the roadside soliciting work, (2) people camping illegally in the canyons and on hillsides, (3) the use of cooking fires in dry areas, and (4) burglaries believed committed by migrants. The task force also received numerous reports of excessive noise, drunkenness, fights, defecating in public, use of other people's property for outdoor toilets, and trespassing in various forms.

Besides this litany of complaints about migrant workers in general, the councilwoman cited accusations specifically regarding Green Valley residents. She noted that nearby shopping centers complained of many "illegals" loitering and intimidating customers. A beauty salon complained that men were intimidating its women customers. The owner of a liquor store on El Camino Real complained that he was assaulted in the store, and that customers avoided his store because of the men loitering outside. The liquor store owner also said that men used the water taps outside his store to bathe with, and that they were using his storage area as a toilet. Older people at the mobile home park next to Green Valley complained of migrants trespassing on the premises. The councilwoman added that two "illegal aliens" had attempted to burglarize her own house, but were caught.

The image of men standing on streets waiting for work was particularly disconcerting to local residents. The men were typically dressed in rumpled and dirty

[5]Interviewed December 8, 1988, for "Uneasy Neighbors."

work clothes, which set them apart from the new, modern, clean developments in the area. As the councilwoman said,

> Wherever there are groups of unkempt men hanging around together, it's intimidating to people who walk by. That one thing alone is frightening to people to have that on the streets. It's not something they've seen before. Maybe in the Depression years there were things like that, but not since the Depression.

The councilwoman went beyond the complaints of local residents in her characterization of the residents of Green Valley and other encampments. She pointed to their flouting of laws in their behavior and illegal entry to the country as important to understanding "the problem." "Actually, the problem is that they're not obeying our laws here and that they know when they come across the border that they're not obeying the law." Moreover, she emphasized their lack of permanence in the area, whether they are legally in the country or not, as a fundamental part of their character. In her opinion, they were simply passing through the area on their way someplace else. As she said,

> The ones that are living in the encampments are here on a temporary basis and they're moving north. . . . People move in. People move out. I think there is only so much work here and the saturation point has been reached, probably was reached a long time ago for permanent workers of any kind. And it's probably true that people in this camp are transient and they're moving on.

By stressing illegal behavior and transiency, the councilwoman represented the residents of Green Valley and other such camps as outsiders to the law that legitimate members of the community live under. Moreover, their lack of permanence is presented as a willful choice to remain outside the community's established and enduring social system. Their representation as outsiders, as illegitimate and temporary residents, includes denying their contribution to the local economy, and therefore, to the welfare of the local community.

It is easy to understand, then, how squatter settlements and men standing on streets waiting for work present an incongruity for members of the larger society. These situations do not fit into the image local residents have of themselves, as members of a modern, affluent community. This incongruity is expressed through exasperated denunciations of the outsiders, that is, the migrants and their encampments. The focus narrows to that of the problems they cause, with less attention paid to the conditions that lead to the very existence of such camps and to men seeking employment on street corners. Many local residents seem less concerned with the "why" of the situation than with the need to "do something" to get rid of the problem. As the councilwoman said,

> Why should people be afraid in their homes? Why should a lady have to call her councilwoman to tell her that there are men who come into her backyard and steal her fruit and defecate and burglarize the house. You know it's not fair. It shouldn't happen. And I believe we have an obligation and a right to regulate. And I think we should.

The events described up to this point set the stage for the health department's action that led to Green Valley's destruction. But why the county's health officials rather than the INS, which one might expect to be the central actor in such a drama?

And why did the destruction of yet another migrant camp lead to a large controversy? To answer these questions, we need to examine the development of the
Green Valley camp and the effect of the 1986 immigration law's legalization program for farmworkers.[6]

A COMMUNITY AT GREEN VALLEY

In its early years, the Green Valley campsite differed little from other camps of
makeshift shelters. Mostly single men lived there. That began to change, however,
in the mid-1980s, as women and children also began to live at Green Valley. What
developed was a community with a family atmosphere that gave Green Valley a
distinctive ambience. The first time I visited Green Valley, I was struck by its
village-like appearance. There were two restaurants, a soccer field, and relatively
neat and unlittered campsites. A number of 50-gallon drums served as trash cans. I
remember thinking at the time that this was surely the most developed camp in all
of San Diego County. This development of a community and the presence of families added to the controversy surrounding the camp's dismantling.

Gloria Martínez was the first woman to live at the Green Valley camp. By November 1988, Gloria had been living in the camp for 2 years. She left Oaxaca City
in 1984, at the age of 39, and migrated with her common-law husband to work in
Oregon. But when work ran out in Oregon, they decided to move to Encinitas,
where friends had said there was work. Besides, Oregon winters were too cold for
her liking.

When she first came to Green Valley, Gloria worked in various jobs, such as
maid and gardener in some of the well-manicured homes near the camp. But on
many occasions she was without work and had to stay in camp without her husband.
On these occasions, Gloria felt secure.

> I was the only woman but nothing ever happened to me. Sometimes he [her husband]
> would go to work and I would stay in my house and nothing ever happened. I feel there
> are no people who misbehave because if there were bad men and they saw a woman
> alone, something would happen. But never. And now, since many women have seen
> that I've been here and nothing happened, now there are more women here.

Gloria was worried because her lack of steady work left her unable to send
money to her children back in Mexico. At the same time, she noticed that the Green
Valley camp had a lot of men living in it, and that these men often came home from
work too late or too tired to cook for themselves. The situation was ripe, in her
mind, for an entrepreneurial venture. As she said,

> When I lived in Mexico, I once had a restaurant business. So then there was a time
> when there was hardly any work. So I said, "You know what, there are a lot of people
> here on the hill, why don't you let me set up a little business to see if we can do better

[6]The 1986 immigration law contained a special provision for farmworkers, called the Seasonal
Agricultural Workers Provision, that provided legal residency for individuals who had worked 90 hours
in agriculture during a specific time period, among other criteria.

Gloria cooks in her restaurant.   Don Bartletti

and are able to send money to our children." So he said, "Okay, let's set it up." We set it up and little by little people started coming by.

In November 1987, Gloria started her restaurant. When I first visited Green Valley in December 1988, the restaurant was difficult to see. It sat at the foot of a hill, well-hidden in thick brush. The interior was sealed off by a wall of leaves, palm fronds, and branches that matched the live plants quite well. In front of the hill is a flat, green valley that extends about 300 yards to El Camino Real. A person standing along the highway more than likely would not have been able to tell a restaurant was nestled cozily in front of their view. To one who knew, however, a light smoke drifting up from the open-fire kitchen marked the restaurant's exact location.

Upon entering Gloria's restaurant, I immediately noticed its coziness. The walls of leaves and palm fronds sealed off the restaurant from the outside world. The entryway opened into a room with a number of handmade benches and two tables made out of plywood and two-by-fours that, I was told, had been discarded at some construction site. Gloria had covered the tables with plastic tablecloths and stocked them with condiments (pickled jalapeño chiles, salt, pepper, mayonnaise, sugar). The dirt floor was clean and the room had a neat appearance. On the wall opposite the entrance was a sign roughly in the shape of a deflated American football that read "El Restaurante Los Pollos" ("Restaurant of the Illegals").

The dining room was separated from the kitchen by a low plywood wall. A firepit had been dug out of the hillside and a large grill placed over it. The fire was fed with wood taken from a large stack that sat in front of the restaurant. Three cooking pans typically sat on the grill, one filled with rice, one with beans, and one with the main dish of the day, often a chicken stew or soup *(caldo de pollo)*. Gloria said she varied the menu, sometimes making chicken mole, or steak with chile. Tortillas were also warmed on the grill.

The kitchen had a cooler for cold sodas, a table for preparing food, and a couple of chairs. The end wall of the kitchen was a room used for storage, where Gloria, her husband, and two younger children also slept. Her 14-year-old son slept elsewhere. Chickens occasionally ran into the kitchen and back outside again.

Gloria or her daughter prepared breakfast, lunch, and dinner. The price for a plate of food was $3 a plate or $3.60 with a soda. A beer was $1. On an average day, at least 20 people ate at Gloria's restaurant, with at least 30 people arriving on a Saturday. Keeping a kitchen stocked with food can be a problem for a restaurant without electricity or refrigeration. Gloria shopped daily, her husband often riding her on the handlebars of a bike to the nearby Von's market in La Costa, where she shopped side-by-side with her affluent neighbors. What she spent varied daily, with typical expenditures ranging as high as $70 to $110, with the larger purchases for Friday nights and Saturdays. She said,

> For example, Monday, Tuesday, and Wednesday I buy three chickens and six pounds of meat to fry. I bring six pounds of meat for steaks. Then three or four cartons of 18 eggs, but the eggs aren't necessarily for one day. Since it's something that doesn't spoil, I have them here for two or three days. I do buy meat daily. The maximum I've bought, which is on Fridays, is five chickens. And besides that I buy plates, glasses, spoons, a lot of things. Since there are a lot of different people, we prefer to buy everything disposable.

Business went well for Gloria. She also obtained permission to stay in the United States through the legalization program for farmworkers. This led her to bring her three sons from Mexico. Her daughter and son-in-law, who also has legal residency, and their son had already joined her at Green Valley. Gloria believed life in Green Valley had its drawbacks, but was not too bad compared to life in Oaxaca:

> As for our economic situation that we had in Mexico, we've done well here. We aren't accustomed to anything more elaborate. So we feel just fine. On the contrary, where we come from some live in even worse conditions because of a lack of work or they don't have any means by which to move. So here we can go down and work. We go to sleep knowing that the money we have we have earned.

Gloria faced competition at the Green Valley camp. A few months after she started her restaurant, another family started their restaurant on the southern end of the hill. José and Marta Fernández, also from Oaxaca, opened their restaurant in March 1988, 3 months after arriving in San Diego. Their restaurant was smaller and cruder than Gloria's and offered less general comfort. It was completely open, with the makeshift table under a canopy to ward off the sun. The Fernández restaurant offered fewer dishes than Gloria's, but sold a plate of food a bit cheaper, for $2.50, or $3 with a can of soda. Unlike Gloria, however, José and Marta were undocumented, which made running the restaurant even more perilous. As Marta said,

> I never thought that I would be cooking for so many men, but when we decided to come try our luck in the United States I never thought that we would end up living in *el monte* (the hills). In Mexico, we had a house, humble as it was, but nothing to eat. Here we

have enough to eat, but look at how we live. The conditions are terrible, and we have to worry about the *migra* all the time. (Reza, 1988a)

There appeared to be enough business for both restaurants. Each had its steady customers. In fact, both did enough business to attract the attention of a tortilla salesman for a tortilla factory in Los Angeles (Reza, 1988a). The salesman had once lived in Green Valley and included it on his delivery route because of the large number of tortillas the residents consumed. He arrived at the camp at 7 A.M. on Sundays, Tuesdays, and Fridays, bringing each restaurant 150 dozen tortillas per visit, or 450 dozen tortillas per restaurant a week. Not only was stopping at Green Valley profitable, but it gave the salesman a chance to see old friends. He said,

> Each of these restaurants buys more tortillas from me than most of the stores and restaurants on my route. . . . Besides, I used to live here and still have friends here. When I come on Sundays to make my deliveries and collect for the week, it gives me an opportunity to meet and talk with my friends. (Reza, 1988a)

The existence of restaurants added immeasurably to the quality of life at Green Valley compared to other workers' camps in northern San Diego County. Living conditions were also improved by the manager of the land on which Green Valley was located. The land is owned by a partnership that includes a Texas tycoon, but is subleased by Fred Bright (a pseudonym), who farms the land and runs a construction company on it (Rodgers, 1988). Bright was generally sympathetic towards the residents on the hill behind his business. He had set up a rudimentary shower, washing facilities, and a faucet for drinking water on the edge of the camp.

As news of Green Valley's relatively pleasant conditions spread among the migrant network, Green Valley attracted more single women and families, as well as

Green Valley residents taking a shower.   Don Bartletti

other male migrants, who had friends or relatives in the camp. Also, Green Valley's location in the middle of suburban development attracted women to jobs in hotels, in homes as housekeepers, and other service jobs. A conversation I had one Sunday with two women illustrates how and why women came to Green Valley.

I met Luz and Marisa on a cool, crisp Sunday afternoon in early January 1989. The camp was virtually deserted, as most residents took advantage of an offer by parishioners of a nearby Catholic church to take them to Mass and then provide them with a lunch afterward. But Luz and Marisa had stayed in camp. They were both in their early twenties. We sat on a log and some large rocks in one of the campsites. Marisa was dressed in shorts, a light blouse, and tennis shoes, like some-one out for a jog on a summer's afternoon. We joked about the cold weather and her attire, and she said she was used to the weather. Then we talked about when they came to Green Valley. Marisa had come first, about 7 months earlier. Her brother and cousin had come before her, saw that it was a place women could live, and then her brother returned to Tijuana and brought Marisa back with him. According to Marisa, he said, "Let's go over there, they don't charge rent. Let's go make a little house."

Luz had been in Green Valley but a short time. She migrated a few years earlier to Oregon, where she worked in agriculture and as a housekeeper. Her work in agri-culture allowed her to obtain a legal permit to reside in the United States under the legalization program for farmworkers. While in Oregon, Luz heard that her friend Marisa was living in Green Valley. Both their parents were originally from Guadalajara but were now living in Tijuana, where Luz also had two children. This made moving closer to the border appealing. Luz said,

> She's also from Guadalajara, so am I. We've known her since childhood, and that's
> why I follow her a lot. And I want to be near Tijuana since I have children in Tijuana.
> So then I can go see them and take them things. When I was in Oregon, it was very dif-
> ficult to go there very often.

Marisa added that she came to Green Valley because she believed jobs were plentiful and because the employers in Mexico pay poorly and expect a lot of work. She said that just the month before she went to Guadalajara for a vacation and while there took a job in a restaurant because "I Didn't want to be without something to do." She said,

> I only worked 15 days and they were already mistreating me. They don't do that in the
> United States and that's even though they're white. Over there they're your own race
> and they mistreat you. Just because I dropped an onion they mistreated me in Guadala-
> jara. I said, "This may be my land but I can't stand it. Let's go back [to Green Valley]."

In addition to the people who came because of a connection to a family mem-ber or friend in the camp, Green Valley also received a number of people who were pushed out of other camps. Fred Bright noted, "Everytime that they've razed an-other property we've had an influx, and this [camp] has been sort of a sanctuary for a while."[7] For example, a few months earlier, John Johnson tore away the brush on the hillside behind the mobile home park in order to get rid of the camps. He said,

---

[7]Interviewed January 15, 1989, for "Uneasy Neighbors."

"The only way to get rid of them is to clear the land, because they have no protection from the weather at all when there's no brush. So then they leave. I imagine they moved on down the valley here [to the Green Valley encampment]."[8]

As Green Valley developed in the late 1980s, it became known as a relatively tranquil place, where women and families could live. Green Valley also took on a distinctive social system. The difference between Green Valley and other worker camps was evident and was described in one newspaper account as "one of the cleanest and [most] crime-free in North County" (Rodgers, 1988). The same article noted that police investigated just two violent crimes at the camp in 3 years, a shooting and an assault. A Carlsbad police officer, who had been patrolling the encampments for 11 years, attributed Green Valley's few problems to its "family atmosphere" (Rodgers, 1988).

It was this characterization of Green Valley as a community, a place where women and families lived, that caught the public's imagination and resulted in a controversy over its demise. At the time of the first notice that Green Valley was going to be dismantled at least 11 families with children lived there, as well as many single women such as Luz and Marisa. Another encampment just 5 miles from Green Valley, in Macario Canyon, swelled to as many as 1,000 men during the peak agricultural season of the year. And yet, its destruction did not generate a fraction of the attention focused on Green Valley.

Many of the residents of Green Valley had also obtained permission to legally live in the United States under the Seasonal Agricultural Workers provisions of the Immigration Reform and Control Act of 1986. It was difficult to estimate the proportion of Green Valley residents that were now legally in the country. One estimate by the Border Patrol was as high as 75% (Bailey, 1988). My own sense, based upon conversations with people about how long they had been in the United States and descriptions of how many people ran when the INS appeared, was that somewhere around 40 to 50% may have been legal residents. For example, AnaMaría (whose husband Ignacio wanted to apply for legalization as a farmworker but had trouble obtaining his birth certificate from relatives in Oaxaca) said, "I'd say about 50% [of Green Valley residents] are working on it [legalization] and the rest aren't because they've been here less time or because they don't have all the necessary requirements. That's what I think, because when the immigration comes, a lot of us run."

But all of these numbers are estimates. Importantly, though, the presence of legal residents in the makeshift shelters meant that the issue was broader than that of "illegal aliens," which added to the controversy and made the problem of getting rid of Green Valley's residents more difficult than merely having the INS round them up.

LIFE IN THE CAMP

Having a sense of life in Green Valley may help us understand the residents' responses to the eviction notice and the larger society's view of them. Life was difficult in Green Valley, but offered a measure of comfort, predictability, social interaction, and access to jobs.

[8]Interviewed December 8, 1988, for "Uneasy Neighbors."

The day began early in Green Valley. Even before the sun rose, Gloria and Marta would awaken and begin preparing the cooking fire at their respective restaurants. As dawn broke through the darkness, people began making their way down the hillside. Some stopped for coffee and a plate of beans and eggs at one of the restaurants. Others made their way to the faucet to splash some water on their face, wash their hands, and comb their hair. Still others made their way along the trails toward the highway, hoping to be among the first on the street for a possible employer to pass by. The lucky ones who already had a job hurried to be there on time. By 6:30 or 7 A.M., a lunch wagon was usually parked down at Fred Bright's business, and some of the Green Valley residents stopped there for coffee and a donut on their way to the street.

At the time I visited Green Valley—the winter months of November, December, and January—the morning air was clear and cold. Water left outside in dishes froze. Moisture on the plastic toppings of the houses frosted over, turning the roofs a glistening white. I was at Green Valley one morning before dawn.[9] Even though I was dressed in several shirts and a ski jacket, I had to constantly move around to stay warm. Even after the sun had come up, I felt chilled to the bone. Imagine my surprise when a young fellow I knew came walking down out of the hills with nothing on but thin pants and a sport shirt. As he passed, he called me the Spanish equivalent of a "sissy" for being so cold.

Each person made his or her own canton out of plywood and discarded two-by-fours, with plastic or tar paper thrown over the top to keep out the rain. The wood was found lying about, or taken from other shelters not being used. AnaMaría, a woman in her late twenties and obviously pregnant, lived in a one-room shelter with her husband and 3-year-old son. They had constructed the shelter about 2 1/2 months earlier, when they came to Green Valley after their makeshift house in another camp was razed to make way for construction of a housing tract. She explained where her family obtained the wood for their new home: "This wood is from a woman who had it. She had two rooms, but since she wasn't there we took the wood to make it. But now that she has returned, she knows I took it, and when she needs it I will return it."

Given the makeshift quality of the shelters, the seal against the elements is not perfect. AnaMaría said, "It's very cold. A lot of air comes in and when it rains, sometimes when the plastic breaks, the water comes in also and then we have to fix it again." AnaMaría's principal concern at that moment was the baby she soon expected to deliver: "Since they're small, they don't resist like we do. They can easily get sick because of the cold and rain."

Luz, one of the young women mentioned previously, said that inside her shelter it was warm thanks to the blankets she received from a local church group. "In church they gave us sleeping bags, blankets. Everytime I go they give me a blanket. They already gave me three blankets and a sleeping bag. So it covers me."

The restaurants served as the social centers of Green Valley. Wandering down to eat or buy a soda or beer offered individuals an opportunity to see other residents. Otherwise, residents spent most of their time in their own canton and interacted mainly with those who shared their specific site. In addition, residents tended to group by region, so that those from Oaxaca, or even a certain area in Oaxaca, built

[9]I was there with Paul Espinosa and a film crew to record morning events for "Uneasy Neighbors."

their cantones near one another. Most of the people in Green Valley were from Oaxaca, but many, if not most, were mestizos (Spanish-speaking and part of Mexico's national culture) rather than Mixtec or Zapotec Indians. I also met migrants from Zacatecas, Jalisco, Michoacán, Hidalgo, Guerrero, and other states. There was even an area in the northern part of Green Valley where Central Americans (mostly Salvadorans but also some Guatemalans) clustered their cantones. One day I met a man in his mid-forties who had served as a captain in the Guatemalan army before migrating. The restaurants provided a place where all these different people could meet and share experiences.

Established residents liked to eat at the restaurants, even though they sometimes ate a hamburger or some other American food at nearby fast-food restaurants. As one fellow said, "The food [at Gloria's] is very good. She tries to make the meals Mexican-style, which is good for us since we're used to it. We also have an American meal once in a while."

The restaurants served as a convenient place for me to meet people. They were also sought out by other newcomers. The first time I was in Gloria's restaurant, two young men sheepishly asked, "What's to eat today?" as they walked in. Gloria responded, "Caldo de pollo," or chicken soup, and then she set a plate of food in front of the hungry customers. Their clothes were disheveled, and they had a disoriented look. I struck up a conversation with them and found out they were actually two teenagers (ages 16 and 17) who had just arrived from Zacatecas a few days earlier. They laughed and said they came to the United States as the result of a sudden, impetuous decision. They just had a sudden urge to see for themselves what the United States was like. They had not found work and were completely without money. The only food they had eaten, which was very little, was what Gloria gave them on

The author at Gloria's restaurant.

credit. When I saw them a month later, they looked better, having earned some money and acquired newer clothes and jackets.

The restaurants offered newcomers a place to find other people from their region or state. I met Isabel at Gloria's restaurant. She was there with a couple of friends she had made in the camp. She had been in Green Valley only a month, having come to join a girlfriend, and leaving her children in Oaxaca. She had been afraid to come, but had found that other Oaxacans befriended her. "There are a lot of people from Oaxaca, which I wasn't expecting. Since I have no family here, at least this awaited me here. So I don't think it's too bad." Her new friends also helped her to find work cleaning houses, which she was able to do on an irregular basis.

One of her new friends at the restaurant, Antonio, had formerly lived in a campsite behind the trailer park with his sister, two cousins, and another friend. But when that hillside was cleared out, he moved to this site. Antonio told me that he liked living in Green Valley because he was able to stay there for most of his needs. Except to work, he said, he did not feel safe leaving Green Valley.

> I feel very happy here. Since I have always lived [in these hills], I don't know where to go. I don't even like to go to the market because if I go out, right away it's back to Tijuana [because of immigration authorities]. So we pass the time around here roaming around enjoying the scenery. We can't do anything else.

Antonio also found Green Valley to be a refuge given that he had been unable to find steady work in the 2 years he had been in San Diego. He said, "I came because I needed to work and I told my mother that when I got a job I would send her money to help them out. Right now I have helped them very little because there is no [steady] work." Given his economic circumstances, Antonio believed he could not pay rent someplace else.

On another day, Margarito stopped in to eat at Gloria's restaurant. He had just arrived in Green Valley after a 48-hour bus ride from Oaxaca. He had been in Green Valley before and returned to try to obtain legal residency as a farmworker, but found he had arrived after the filing deadline. He pointed out how Green Valley serves as a place to retreat when jobs are scarce. As he said, "When we don't have work, we come here. When we have a lot of work, we move and go to apartments."

AnaMaría and her husband Ignacio also found Green Valley's lack of rent made the difference between survival and an ignominious retreat to Mexico. They had three other children in Mexico whom they sent money for their support. Unfortunately, the jobs Ignacio had been able to get were not steady. AnaMaría said,

> Right now, he's looking for work. He sometimes goes out there and gets a job in gardening, but not every day. One day yes, one day no. Sometimes he gets one only twice a week, three times a week and with that we eat and send some [money] to the ones over there [in Mexico].

AnaMaría balanced the negative aspects of life in Green Valley against her family's economic situation and goals. "We suffer a lot because of the weather, the rain, the cold, especially for the little boy, but we withstand it to save a little more to give the rest of our children [in Mexico] and my family [here] also." In the meantime, AnaMaría found Green Valley relatively pleasant thanks to the other residents. Their campsite was near enough to others for easy social interaction. She said, "Since there are other people we don't feel bad. I can see that we would feel bad if one couple was here, another a distance away. There are three couples here [close by] and one man has some brothers, so at night there's noise and conversation, so we don't feel bad."

AnaMaría expressed hope that after she delivered her baby and became able to work again, she and her husband might be able to pay rent. But given her ignorance of the local medical system, and her lack of private medical insurance and an obstetrician, she acknowledged that the impending delivery posed a problem.

> A lot of [women] go to Tijuana or they give birth in the hospitals here, but it's only if they have money to pay. But since we have more children to send the money to, we don't have any money. . . . If they admit me to a hospital to have it, fine. If not, well, I'll see what I do to give birth. I'll see who helps me.

For children, camp life offered daily adventures. One day I roamed around with Gloria's two young sons, Roberto and Alejandro, aged 7 and 11. They had been in Green Valley about 8 months, entering the United States without documents. Both attend elementary school, catching the bus on El Camino Real. We spent some time poking around the discarded litter and wood in abandoned shelters. They showed me a little trap they had set to catch squirrels. They had caught two squirrels and several birds.

Roberto and Alejandro liked going to school. Roberto said, "It's pretty. There are lots of toys. It has swings and a football field." The boys sometimes went out with their mother shopping, but mostly they stayed at Green Valley. Though they enjoyed playing in the campsite, they felt hemmed in at Green Valley. Alejandro said, "In Mexico, I felt more comfortable because I could go out. And here I'm closed off." To which his little brother added, "Because of the migra." We then engaged in the following dialogue:

LC: Are you afraid of the INS?

Roberto: Oh no.

LC: What do you think when you see a green van?

Alejandro: That they're going to take my friends away.

LC: Who?

Alejandro: The migra. I'm not afraid of the migra. They won't do anything to me. I have my card showing I go to school and take the bus. My mother said that with that they wouldn't do anything to us. Later my mother will work out our permits.

LC: What about the others?

Alejandro: Well, they should run and not let themselves get caught.

Although it gave him a sense of security, a card showing that he attended school offered no protection against apprehension by immigration authorities. Gloria's oldest son, Rafael, age 13, did not attend school. As it turned out, Gloria's husband's application for legalization under the farmworker's legalization program was not granted at the same time as Gloria's. Although he had an appointment the following month with immigration authorities, he became depressed. As Gloria said, "He felt very anxious, very anxious because they hadn't given him the permit. He didn't want to be here as an illegal anymore." And so in early January 1989 he left. Gloria didn't know if he went to Oregon or Mexico, or if he would return for his appointment with the immigration authorities. In the meantime, Rafael did not go to school. "He's the one who helps me here. When I leave he sells sodas or coffee or something. So, he's my companion here." Rafael, therefore, spent almost all his time in Green Valley.

Most of the people living at Green Valley, if they had children, left them back home with family rather than bring them to the United States. The money earned in the United States could buy more things in Mexico, and the parents did not have to also worry about their children's safety and possible apprehension by the immigration authorities. Margarito also emphasized that his children's inability to speak English concerned him. As he said, "Sure it's great to live in the United States, but my children are starting to grow. They're 12, 8, and 5 years old. They'd be lost. Not lost but disoriented. So, if I brought them here into a world of English, they wouldn't know where to start."

As we see in the next chapter, although the residents of Green Valley had formed their own community, an island of refuge within the surrounding affluent communities, Green Valley did not exist in isolation from the larger society. Its residents set out daily to work, or at least to look for work, in the local area. Their conspicuousness intensified the larger community's resolve to "do something" about their presence, which ultimately led to the camp's demolition.

6 / Green Valley's Final Days

For Green Valley residents, work was of prime importance. These people were classic examples of *homo economicus*. Many had left family behind to pursue well-defined economic goals, and even those with families in the campsite viewed earning money as their prime objective. They came to the United States to work and actively sought it out. For men, this most often meant standing along El Camino Real waiting for an employer to stop and request their services. Felipe, a man in his mid-twenties who wore his hair in a long ponytail with a scarf tied around his forehead, pointed out how important work was as he and some friends ate at Gloria's restaurant: "When you work, it makes you happy because at least you have enough to buy food. That's what makes us the happiest here. Can you imagine, if we don't have money we can't have anything to eat."

Felipe was sitting and eating with Ernesto, who had been in Green Valley about 4 months and who intended to return to Mexico after a few more months. Ernesto spoke philosophically about work. "There will always be some [jobs], even though the worse ones are for the Mexicans. An American isn't going to take on a pick and shovel and get big blisters; that's the Mexican's job." Ernesto used his understanding of Mexico's geography and of the demand for Mexican labor in the United States to explain why anti-immigration laws will not stop Mexicans from coming to work. "It's impossible [to stop] unless you build a wall like in China, and even that way there's still the helicopter. If we lived in Brazil, then we wouldn't come. But here, we're neighbors."

STREET-CORNER EMPLOYMENT

The jobs found by workers who lined up on the street varied with who offered them on any day. They were hired most often to do gardening, clean up construction sites, clean up private yards, landscape, perform nursery work, dig trenches, and just about anything else that requires manual labor or can be taught quickly. Although the streetside job seekers were usually men, Marisa also joined them. Young and strong, she believed she could do most kinds of the work typically offered, especially gardening.

Most women, however, tried to find jobs cleaning houses, or as domestics. Rather than standing on the street, most used their social networks to find work. As Isabel said, "I ask others if their employers know someone who needs a live-in housekeeper and that's how I hope to find a job so I can stay." Others found jobs outside of homes. For example, Luz obtained legal papers under the farmworkers' provisions, which helped her to get a job as a maid in a hotel. Every morning she walked to the highway and took a bus that left her a block and a half from the hotel.

Men waiting for work along Encinitas Boulevard.   Don Bartletti

After work, she left the neatly arranged hotel rooms and returned by bus to her shanty on the hill because "Right now I can't pay rent, since I just started working."

The work Margarito found while standing on the street paid more than he could make in Oaxaca. He had left behind his wife and three children, and a car that needed a new motor. As he said, "In Mexico there's always a need. Well, there's

Suburban work includes landscaping. His cap reads: My life is great.   Don Bartletti

work, but not enough money. So you see yourself obligated to come here for the dollars that are very beneficial for us in Mexico."

According to Margarito, minimum wage in Oaxaca was 10,000 pesos per day—about U.S. $3. Here, he tried to earn $5 an hour for his labor. He said he would turn down an employer who offered him only $25 for a full day's work. After 1 month in Green Valley, Margarito was able to send his family $600. Margarito intended to return home after another 6 months of work.

Undocumented Central Americans living in Green Valley also seek work along El Camino Real. María Favala and her husband joined her father-in-law at Green Valley in July 1988. With no money to their name and María pregnant, they were not able to rest after their perilous journey. The day after they arrived, her husband found himself standing along El Camino Real. "We got here on a Sunday morning. On Monday, he went to work. He would work some days, then he'd have days that he didn't work." By the time I met her in December, her husband was having very good luck finding work. He had carpentry experience in El Salvador, which enabled him to work in construction. "He's been working this past week. He worked three days and the employer told him he was going to work there daily, so he wouldn't have any problems."

María's husband and Margarito were fortunate in that they were able to find work often, despite their undocumented status. Some employers offer work only to legal immigrants. As Margarito said, "Sometimes they come and ask for workers with documents, so the ones that don't have any don't come forward. When some come and take anyone with or without papers we have no problems. But they only request one or two people so everyone gathers to see who will go."

Frequent patrols by immigration authorities disrupted Green Valley's residents' search for work. When the INS or Border Patrol agents arrived, those without documents ran. Even when caught, many made their way back to Green Valley as soon as possible. Felipe said, "They take us to Tijuana. From Tijuana we have to come back. That's the way it is." Those with documents remained on the street. As Raimundo said, "Sometimes they [immigration authorities] ask us [for papers], sometimes they don't ask us because they know that those who don't run have papers."

The immigration authorities did not confine their activities to the street, but often continued on to the Green Valley campsites as well. When this occurred, which was often, the first person to see them would shout "la migra," and all those without documents would run. AnaMaría told me, "When they come, we have to run as far as we can so they won't catch us. They came about a week and a half ago. It was raining and they came all the way in here, except that they didn't catch us." About a week after she made this comment, she and her husband and son were apprehended and deported. That AnaMaría was in the last stages of her pregnancy reduced her ability to outrun immigration agents. AnaMaría and her family did not return to Green Valley.

The same morning that the immigration authorities apprehended AnaMaría and her family, they also picked up Lupe Carrillo's young son and daughter. Lupe had gone early that morning to a nearby flower shop whose address many of Green Valley's residents use for postal delivery. Leaving her children in camp, "I went in to see if there was any letter, and when I came out the INS was there and they must have taken them." Lupe's daughter suffers from epileptic seizures, and had recently spent 3 days in a local hospital. Her arrest left her without her daily antiseizure medicine, which Lupe herself carried.

Temporary day work has drawbacks besides the patrols by immigration authorities. Work is not consistent, leaving workers with days of inactivity. In addition, employers sometimes pay less than the agreed price for a day's work, sometimes not paying at all. Antonio, Isabel's friend at Gloria's restaurant, had an experience all too common among day laborers. He had worked for a woman for a number of days and been paid with a check, but the bank would not cash it, claiming the account had insufficient funds. Antonio returned to the woman and asked her to pay him in cash. She said the check was good, and apologized. "I didn't want apologies, I wanted my money," said Antonio. "And to date she still hasn't paid me. She owes me about $250, and I don't know what to do to get it from her. She doesn't want to pay me."

The attraction Green Valley held for its residents went beyond camaraderie. The residents of Green Valley came to work in an area that has limited housing for low-income people. The available apartments, condominiums, and houses are relatively expensive for people intent on saving money to help support family back home. And irregular work and earnings make paying rent difficult.

Raimundo Ventura underscored the link between the temporary work he is able to find, his undocumented status, and his inability to afford the high rents in the area. He pointed out that finding an affordable apartment was difficult because he worked an average of three days a week. The streetside employers, he said, "pay us very little, and sometimes they take advantage of us since we're illegal and they pay us whatever they want. . . . There are no permanent jobs and, like I told you, they don't pay minimum wage. For example, they pay $4 an hour, that's why its hard to pay [rent]." Raimundo's unsteady income and high rents in the area made Green Valley attractive.

Raimundo had lived in Green Valley for 2 years. Over the years, the competition for jobs had increased, making it more difficult to obtain regular work. "As time goes by, there are too many people. They come from other countries to the hill, and that's why there are more people and less work. And that's why it gets a little hard." Notice that Raimundo's comment betrays a tinge of resentment against the even newer arrivals from Central America.

Life in Green Valley proved too difficult for Raimundo's wife. About a year after they arrived, his wife decided to trade in the wind, rain, cold, and cooking over a fire for the life of a live-in baby-sitter. She moved to a house in nearby Encinitas, leaving Raimundo and two sons in Green Valley. Raimundo's sons also looked for work along El Camino Real. They hoped to pool their resources to rent an apartment, if steadier employment could be found. But Raimundo's uncertain future was an obstacle to planning. Although he had obtained a temporary permit to stay in the country as part of the 1986 immigration law's legalization program, he doubted his ability to qualify for permanent legal residency. He said, "They tell us we need to learn the laws and language of the United States. But I think it's rather difficult for everyone to learn English. It's going to be a little difficult to get permanent residency."

All of Green Valley's residents faced a tenuous future daily. Not only were those without documents subject to apprehension, but everyone faced the possibility that no work would be offered on any given day. After long hours watching as hundreds of cars passed by, many of the workers would finally give up and return to camp, where they would find something else to occupy their time. Sometimes the men would engage in a game of soccer, especially early in the week. They rarely played on Fridays or Saturdays, since most seemed to find work on those days. Gloria said, "The days they play [soccer] are Mondays about noon, when they see that no one has picked them up. That's when they come back here. They don't play on Saturday or Friday because that's when work is usually more available than on any other day." Ernesto added that "Some of us play some [soccer], others in some houses might play dominoes. Those are the only things we have here."

There were other activities at the camp. On most Sundays the residents could make their way to an area where cement pilings had been laid down as seats, and attend church services offered by either a priest from a local Catholic church or Rafael Martínez, a retired Presbyterian minister. The Reverend Martínez also occasionally taught English classes to Green Valley's residents, and a church-related volunteer offered rides two or three nights a week to anybody who wanted to attend those classes. These activities added to Green Valley's sense of community.

In sum, life in Green Valley had its own routine. The people living there had learned to make do with what they had and to feel comfortable there despite the living conditions and the ever-present raids by the INS and Border Patrol. The hillside offered them a small, tenuous island of security, a base from which to look for work, and a place to return after work. The residents of Green Valley may have behaved as *homo economicus,* but they were also *homo socialus,* social beings who had developed a sense of community. As they soon found out, however, their days at this place of refuge were numbered.

Catholic Mass at Green Valley.   Don Bartletti

THE HEALTH DEPARTMENT

Frustration grew in the surrounding community over Green Valley's presence. Even though the INS and Border Patrol were a constant presence, Green Valley would not go away. Local residents came to view the immigration authorities as ineffective in dealing with this problem. Part of the reason for the inability to disperse the Green Valley community had to do with the fact that many of Green Valley's residents were legal residents (Bailey, 1988). Emma's comments displayed this sense of frustration: "We see some of them going down that way, but you can't tell [where they're going]. . . . It's a revolving population. But now they're all legal, I guess. So, I don't know what you can do about it."

The Encinitas councilwoman also projected this sense of frustration as she listed the various agencies called upon to deal with the migrant problem. "If you ask the fire department to go into an encampment and have the fires put out, they can do that. But then they light the fires again. If you ask the Border Patrol to come in and collect the people who are living there illegally, they can do that. But they scatter in all directions, and maybe the two or three that they take are gone for a while, but the rest come back." She also laid part of the blame on the 1986 Immigration Law and its legalization, or amnesty, program. As she said, "The amnesty program was a form of a compromise which was to supposedly solve the problem. But it hasn't, and we still have the same problem. . . . It may have solved some of the migrants' problems, but it hasn't solved ours."

As these agencies proved ineffective in getting rid of the residents of Green Valley and other camps, another strategy was emphasized. As the councilwoman said,

> We do have agencies that have the right to solve some of these problems. We have the County Health Department. . . . We have laws about substandard housing. So there are

things that can be used to solve some of those problems. I think that we need to start with the possible.

The opportunity to focus the attention of the health department on Green Valley occurred as the result of an article in the *Los Angeles Times* on July 17, 1988 (Reza, 1988a). This relatively positive article actually meant to show the resourcefulness of Green Valley's residents. It focused on the two restaurants and how their owners provided a service to camp dwellers. The headline read "Home Cooking Among the Hooches of La Costa: Two Restaurants Provide Familiar Flavors for the Residents of Hidden Migrant Camp." It was accompanied by photographs of Gloria cooking in her kitchen, Gloria and her husband riding a bike home from the store, the restaurant as it appeared hidden in the undergrowth, and a map of Green Valley's location.

The response was immediate. The San Diego County Department of Health Services began receiving a number of complaints concerning the existence of restaurants in the hills. The assistant director of the department noted that these complaints were, in large part, what drew the health department into this specific case. His explanation of the events leading up to the department's involvement conveys the frustration other agencies were having with Green Valley and the public's general fears about migrant workers. Although such concerns may not be part of the health department's operating code, they were part of the implicit reasons for their actions.

> Last summer [1988] there were a whole series of articles in the newspapers. Two of those articles had to do with the Green Valley camp, and there was a fairly significant write-up on two restaurants that were operating out of Green Valley. And subsequently, there were two outbreaks of malaria in the Carlsbad area. Sort of parallel to that, there had been a lot of complaining up in the north county area, in particular about crimes perpetrated, I guess that is the word, by migrant workers against kids, children, school age kids up in that area. . . . Coincidental with that activity, in early summer, was the fact that the Border Patrol was increasingly reluctant to cite any of the migrant workers. And the reason for that was that the immigration reform act had some dates, and those dates were going to kick in, and there was some concern on the part of the Border Patrol, INS, that they might be charged by different legal groups representing or advocating for the migrant workers, at some point, with discrimination.[1]

The assistant director said that the *Los Angeles Times* article had provoked this response: "The complaints we got were, 'Well, how is it that these folks up here can have a restaurant?' 'Are they permitted?' 'Are the same standards of health and safety being adhered to?'"

The Environmental Health Services office of the county health department responded to the complaints with an investigation. They found numerous violations of the health codes, as the assistant director noted:

> Essentially violations dealing with water, lack of adequate water, sewage, as an example, lack of potable water for drinking, structures that just didn't meet any building-code provisions whatsoever. There was a lot of debris on the ground. A lot of fecal

---

[1]Interviewed February 8, 1989, for "Uneasy Neighbors."

material on the ground. Just generally a very, very poor, I should say, unhealthful living environment.

A health department inspector then signed the abatement order mentioned in the previous chapter. At that point, the property owner had the responsibility to either correct (or *abate)* those violations by bringing the conditions and structures up to code, or else remove the structures and people. The health department took this action even though there was no evidence of a specific health problem at Green Valley. As the assistant director said, their action was

> more of a preventive approach. I don't know of any information, data, or statistics that support that there was an eminent health danger [at Green Valley]. Our approach was that continued living under those circumstances in that environment could lead to a health threat, probably the greatest health threat, and I'll put that in quotes, was "the fire hazard". . . . A lot of what we were directing ourselves towards was the safety for the migrant workers themselves. There was always that potential, that some illness could spill over into the broader community.

The irony was not lost on the assistant director that the migrant workers would undoubtedly face worse conditions in some other canyon. As he said, "I don't want to be viewed as the agency that basically is going to play a shell game with these people. And that's what it's going to amount to until more definite solutions are presented."

The owners decided to dismantle the Green Valley campsite rather than provide toilets, supply running water, and improve the buildings to comply with building codes. A representative for the owners said that although they intended to comply with the abatement order, their actions would not solve the "migrant problem." As he said, "As you push them from one piece of land, they simply migrate to another" (Walker, 1988a). Immediate implementation of the abatement order, however, proved difficult.

The health department allowed the camp's demolition to be delayed a number of times. The delays stemmed in part from pressure by community and religious groups concerned with the future of the camp's residents. The timing of the closure conjured up images of families with children dislodged during Thanksgiving and Christmas. As the Reverend Rafael Martínez said in a newspaper article at the time, "Why did they wait until winter and the holiday season? The main concern on the part of the county seems to be to enforce the rules by the book, apparently not realizing that they're dealing with human beings" (Bailey, 1988).

Although not admitting it had bowed to such pressure, the county health department delayed demolition on October 3, 1988, ostensibly to wait until most of the workers returned to Mexico for the holiday season (Walker, 1988b). It was later delayed again, ostensibly to give some of the families living in Green Valley time to apply for housing assistance from the City of Carlsbad (Rodgers, 1988). Demolition was to begin in mid-November, but was delayed once again after the Coastal Commission interceded (Owens, 1988b). The hills where Green Valley stood were also home to willows and sycamores that grow near freshwater and saltwater marshes. If any mechanized equipment were used in the demolition, the Coastal Commission stated, the environment was potentially endangered, and a permit would be required. With this news, instead of bulldozing the campsites out of existence, the landowners decided to have Green Valley's residents dismantle their own shelters, paying them for delivering the materials to a trash truck set up on the premises. Demolition was then set for January 1, 1989 (Reza, 1988).

A number of newspaper stories, with headlines such as "Migrant Families Left with No Place to Call Their Own," focused on the impending demolition of Green Valley (Pierce, 1988a). On the evening of December 13, 1988, about 70 people held a candlelight vigil at a clearing on El Camino Real in front of the Green Valley camp (Pierce, 1988b). The vigil had been organized by the North County Coalition for Human Resources, a watchdog group for immigrants' rights, to dramatize the plight of homeless migrants in the area, and specifically the eviction of Green Valley's residents. The organizers cited the serious shortage of low-income housing in the area as the main problem. The Reverend Martínez, who spoke to the mainly Anglo crowd at the vigil, put the issue this way:

> I believe all problems have a solution, and all solutions have a price. And society has to be willing to pay that price. We just spent, this winter, two million dollars to save a couple of whales from being killed by the ice in the North Pole. And to tell me we can't house a few low-income people who work for us seems the greatest of absurdities. It's a matter of priorities. A matter of values in the society. Is it that we value whales more than human beings?

The candlelight vigil was widely covered by the local news media. Following this event, a number of newspaper stories on migrant workers and the Green Valley camp appeared. Some were human interest stories, such as "Breaking Camp," and a multipart report on Oaxacan migrants titled "The Invisible Workforce" (Bailey, 1988; Walker, 1988a, b). Other stories focused on immigrant rights activists' efforts to stall the camp's impending destruction and the frustrating efforts of local government officials to find funds to help displaced migrants (Rodgers, 1988; Owens, 1988b). An editorial in the *San Diego Union* (1988) pointed to the dire need for housing for the county's migrant workers, and a commentary in the *Carlsbad Journal* (Sumner, 1988) argued that it was perhaps better to let Green Valley exist, to "Let Well Enough Alone." The timetable was delayed again, and destruction of Green Valley did not begin on January 1, 1989. The final notice of the camp's destruction, however, did appear in early January 1989.

THE FINAL DAYS

The mood at Gloria's restaurant was somber the day I talked to Gloria, Ernesto, Felipe, and others about their imminent departure from Green Valley. It was mid-January, and Fred Bright had distributed, about a week earlier, flyers announcing the final notice of eviction. Gloria stood as she talked, often returning to her cooking between statements. She said, "All this week was quiet. It was very sad for us to all of a sudden be told that we have to move out." Felipe agreed. He sat at the table and read the notice aloud (in Spanish) for dramatic effect:

> "Everyone who is found living here or using this property is here without permission, and as such is trespassing on this property. This is to notify you that you should leave

the property before February 1, 1989. You can take with you your personal belongings, such as your construction materials. Any belongings or construction materials left on the property after February 1, 1989, will be considered abandoned and will be confiscated. After February 1, 1989, anyone who continues using the property may be subject to legal action and in conjunction with section 2L of the penal code of California, it is requested that you clean your living area, and leave in an orderly manner. Trash bins will be available to deposit all kinds of trash. You must leave the property. . . . The property owner."

A personal letter from Fred Bright, in which he apologized for this action and called the residents of Green Valley "good neighbors," accompanied the formal notice. Even though they had anticipated being forced to leave Green Valley for more than 2 months, the final notice came as quite a blow. Felipe spoke in disbelief. "We received this notice with sadness since we have lived here a long time. It's as if we were to leave our home anew and to start over." Ernesto quietly added, "This notice? It only hurt our feelings. We feel sad and depressed."

I asked Gloria if she was angry at being forced to leave. She said, "I don't think anybody is mad. What happens is that everyone is sad because we're going to be removed from here. That's the only feeling. It's not anger. We feel a sadness because we don't have enough money for rent. And then you see that you have to give a deposit or they won't give you the house. If we rent a house, say at $800, we have to put down $1600 and to get that money, where will it come from?"

I asked them why they thought this was being done, why the camp was being closed. Their answers reflect their acute sense of how negatively the larger society views them. Ernesto, in his philosophic manner, said,

There are some Americans who appreciate us from their heart as humans. Then there are others who see us as animals. Even when they look at us. We have worked all day with pick and shovel to buy food to eat and they work all nice and clean and perfumed. We just try to get home and try to buy food. We can't rent an apartment and buy some $80 or $100 perfume and smell real nice. . . . Maybe they think that everyone who lives here doesn't like to work, or that we spend our time doing something else. But the majority who are here are here to save money.

Marisa also noted the bad impression she thought the larger community held of Green Valley's residents. "All the *gabachos* [Anglos] say that drunks live here, killers, and a bunch like that. No. It's just needy people who come here to earn a living."

At the Fernández restaurant I encountered Anatolio Herrera. He was also from Oaxaca and the oldest resident of Green Valley I had met. He must have been in his mid-fifties. When I first saw him, he was sitting on a log, drinking a beer. His beard had about 2 days' growth. He had picked apples, melons, and other fruits and vegetables throughout California, and his skin was darkened from laboring in the sun. He resented being evicted from Green Valley, and spoke quite eloquently about his feelings, about history, and about how he thought Americans treated those who migrate to work in the United States.

Why do the Americans detest the Latin Americans, the Mexicans? . . . The North American invaded all of California. They colonized it. . . . [Now] we come here to look for a job in what you could almost call our native land. . . . We come in search of dollars. Your precious commodity. With one of your dollars we've earned our living for the entire day. You're selfish. You treat us like dogs. And that's what hurts because we're human, and hard workers because we're determined. We come here honorably.

All of my companions live like squirrels, like rats, like rabbits, like lizards, and the like. While you have rugs, and heaters for the winter, and we sit shivering, wiping off the ice. It's ridiculous. Is that what you call human rights? No, it isn't.

The North Americans have no feelings. They don't understand. Don't they have a heart? Now they kick us out.

Where will we go? Will we continue hovering in corners like coyotes, like dogs, lizards, like I just told you? . . . They chase us away. We go over there. They chase us away over there, we come back here, and it continues. . . . We must take flight like the migrant birds. The ones that go from one country to another, the swallows.

Anatolio's future was now even more tenuous and unknown than before. As Green Valley's residents discussed their immediate future, they imagined they would merely find themselves on another hill or in another canyon, and the conditions would be worse than at Green Valley.

For Gloria, the move meant an end to her business, her sole means of supporting her family. She said, "I think I'll go to another hill and take everything I can. I'll dismantle it [the restaurant] and take it with me." Antonio said that when he left he would take "all my clothes and my suitcase, and I'll see where I go. Maybe behind a tree on the road." Isabel feared she would have to return home, with little money to show for her trip. "If they kick us out of here and I don't find a job where I can live in, then I will have to go back. What can I do here without a job and without a place to live?" Margarito took it all in stride: "We can settle anywhere. For example, if they kick us out of here we can go over to that side or anywhere. But we always try to find a way to settle in some place to live."

Gloria's reflection on the immediate future turned out to be prophetic of later events. She said,

In some other place I'll have to get to know the people there and I don't know what kind of people they'll be. Here the majority of people are from Oaxaca and so am I, so there's no problem. But I will start over some other place risking that after arriving there we will be evicted immediately just as they've done here. But I hope not.

GREEN VALLEY'S DEMOLITION

Dismantling Green Valley's shelters began in mid-January. A large trash bin was hauled out to the campsite. Under Fred Bright's management, residents of Green Valley were paid 50 cents per bag of trash, 20 cents per kilo of steel and wood, and $3 dollars for each mattress (Reza, 1989a). The dismantling went on for about 2 weeks, up until the last day residents were allowed to stay.

Green Valley's residents undertook the task of taking apart their homes in an orderly manner (Walker, 1989b). Gloria took apart her restaurant and bundled it up, determined to find a new place for it somewhere else. Her nephew began digging

Green Valley's residents dismantling their campsites. They were paid by the pound for the materials they collected.   Don Bartletti

out a foundation for the new restaurant beneath some manzanita bushes in a nearby canyon (Reza, 1989b). Others took everything they could carry to be weighed and paid for. Some earned a couple of hundred dollars for their efforts (Reza, 1989a).

Tensions mounted, however, as Green Valley residents felt set upon by the media and immigration authorities. At one point, María Favala's husband claimed to have been harassed by the Border Patrol. On January 25, two agents arrested him as he stood waiting for work along El Camino Real with several other men. He was forced inside the Border Patrol vehicle, even after he tried to show the agents his petition for asylum. María's husband said the agents then took him to a remote, hilly area, where

> They took me out of the vehicle and [the agent] grabbed me by the shirt and threw me to the ground. I landed on my knees and took the immigration papers out of my pocket to show them. [The agent] grabbed the document and tore it up without looking at it. He said, "This piece of paper is no good." (Quoted in Reza, 1989d)

The agents then left him on the ground, he said. A few minutes later, he continued, four cholos robbed him of $300 at knifepoint (Reza, 1989d). He later filed a formal grievance against the Border Patrol (Sherman, 1989), and the telling of this event among camp residents reinforced their already strong feelings of being unwanted outsiders.

As the final day approached, community activists proposed using an old landfill in Encinitas to provide temporary housing for Green Valley's displaced residents.

Local homeowners opposed the proposal, citing their concern for the health and safety of the migrant workers. Representatives of local homeowners' associations indicated that even if it were shown not to be a health risk, they would still oppose the proposal. The health department also undermined this proposal, noting that obtaining the required permits would take too long to make it an effective alternative (Owens, 1989a).

Green Valley's residents had no clue to where they would go. Ten families with children applied for housing assistance from the City of Carlsbad (Reza, 1989c). The funds for the assistance program came from a federal program called Section 8, which assists only families with children, which meant that most of Green Valley's residents did not qualify (Owens, 1989b). At the end of January, however, five families did receive housing assistance, including Gloria Martínez and her family and María Favala and her family. Under this program, families such as Gloria's and María's pay 30% of their income for rent, with the rest then paid for with government funds.

This was a tremendous relief for Gloria in the short run. But she realized that her long-term means of earning a living was taken away. She now had to find a new way to earn money for rent, utilities, and food. How long would she be able to stay in an apartment, even with assistance? Yet for the others who did not receive assistance, the immediate future looked even bleaker. Gloria said,

> As for ourselves, they're going to give us some help, which seems good. But for others who are very poor and come from Oaxaca, they feel very sad because the few earnings they'll make they'll have to use for rent. So they prefer to leave [for another hillside]. They don't believe their earnings will be adequate to pay the rent.

Ironically, one family that had earlier received housing assistance found that life outside Green Valley presented perhaps even greater risks. A man and his wife, who had fled Guatemala when rebel soldiers burned down their six-room house, had been in their apartment only 2 days when somebody picked the lock on their front door as they slept on their bedroom floor. The burglar stole the husband's wallet, which contained $428 and, more important, his immigration papers. He had applied for political asylum, but without papers to prove it he was subject to deportation if he were apprehended by the immigration authorities. Afraid to go out, he felt a prisoner in his new apartment (Owens, 1988a).

AFTER GREEN VALLEY

By the end of January, many of Green Valley's residents had scattered to other campsites in Encinitas, Carlsbad, La Costa, and the surrounding area. Many, carrying pieces of plastic, cardboard, and their belongings in trash bags, found their way to the nearby abandoned landfill in Encinitas. By February 2, the Border Patrol had already raided this new site (Walker, 1989b). The news media also followed the migrant workers, with headlines announcing that the migrants had set up new camps at the Encinitas landfill. Nearby residents immediately began to express their concerns about the possibility of migrants trespassing on private property and stealing their belongings (Walker, 1989b). Officials also raised the possibility of danger to the migrants from methane gas at the old landfill (Walker, 1989c).

Between February 1 and February 3, Encinitas City Hall and the health department had received 36 calls and 16 formal complaints about the migrant camp (Gandelman, 1989a). A representative of a homeowners' association asked the council to "provide the necessary means to immediately remove the encampments and transgressors" (Gandelman, 1989a). Another resident said, "We're worried about the health threat. . . . They [the migrants] have lived in squalor. They're used to it" (Gandelman, 1989a). Responding to these complaints, the Encinitas City Council agreed on February 8 to hold a special meeting to discuss the new campsite at the abandoned landfill (Gandelman, 1989a).

By February 10, the health department had begun tracking down the owners of the landfill to cite them for allowing migrants to settle there and to notify them of health violations (Reza, 1989e). At the special meeting, held on February 13, a series of speakers addressed an overflowing crowd (Gandelman, 1989b) on the new migrant camp. A few were supportive, but most were hostile to it. The council voted to find a way to have the new migrant camp at the landfill dismantled (Gandelman, 1989b). One headline suggested, however, "If Camp Shut, Migrants Will Find New Canyon" (Kozub & Valencia, 1989).

The migrants were finally given a March 6 deadline to leave the abandoned landfill (Himmelspach, 1989). This deadline was briefly delayed when a local lawyer brought a lawsuit on the migrants' behalf, claiming that their rights were violated because the city council had targeted them as Hispanics, while no action was taken against homeless whites who camped out at beaches or in parks (Gandelman, 1989c). The judge, however, refused to block the eviction on these grounds (Bailey, 1989). By March 7, the landfill had been cleared of migrant workers (Davis, 1989).

The "problem," however, did not go away. Migrant camps continued to vex communities in Encinitas, Carlsbad, and throughout northern San Diego County, and headlines continued to chronicle events in the ongoing "migrant problem" (McDonnell, 1989a). In Oceanside, a private security firm raided migrant camps built on private property, arriving with armed guards, dogs, and helicopters (McDonnell, 1989b). New camps formed primarily by Guatemalan migrants raised new fears for Encinitas residents, who also resorted to a private security firm to clear their campsites (McDonnell, 1989c; Trotta, 1989; Glionna, 1990). As one newspaper article noted, there are two major obstacles to solving the housing dilemma in this part of San Diego County: high land values and residents who do not want low-income neighbors (Wisckol, 1989). This point was driven home at a meeting in Oceanside to discuss siting a number of trailers near the old Mission San Luis Rey to house homeless, two-parent families who are legal residents, since no shelters in the area take two-parent families. The meeting began with one resident referring to migrant homeless families as "hazardous waste" and continued in a similar vein. One resident suggested the homeless be housed at Camp Pendleton "so the Marines will be around to smash a few heads if need be." A young woman who lived in a condominium complex on a hill above Mission San Luis Rey said, "These are lower-level-life people, Mexicans who don't even belong in the United States and I don't see why we should be supplying them with anything" (Himmelspach, 1989). Green

Valley may no longer be home to migrants, but the situation has changed little locally. Mexicans, and increasingly Central Americans, still come seeking work; jobs are still offered, there is still little affordable housing, and they are still viewed as outsiders by the larger society.

FINAL THOUGHTS

Green Valley is a story rich in insights about the status of relatively recent Mexican and Central American immigrants and about the community that receives them. In this case, they settled in a relatively affluent area, where they clashed with local residents out of culture and class differences. And yet, an important lesson emerges. It is difficult to create a community consisting strictly of well-to-do residential developments. Given the division of labor in a complex society such as ours, there is still the need for people who provide services to more affluent residents. Construction workers, landscapers, gardeners, restaurant workers, hotel workers, domestics, housecleaners, baby-sitters, to mention but a few workers, are needed to maintain a middle-class and upper-middle-class life in these suburban communities. Individuals desiring to perform these services are drawn to the communities and become part of them, economically if not socially.

The residents of Green Valley and the residents of the surrounding neighborhoods did not communicate directly, although they lived in close proximity to one another. Perceived differences did not allow them to engage in dialogue. Rather, they were like two trains passing each other on parallel tracks, completely missing each other's viewpoint. But, to make the metaphor reflect the uneven power relationship, the views of the larger society passed overhead on a trestle, while those of Green Valley's residents passed in the valley below. The relatively powerless camp dwellers were never really heard. They were members of what Edwin Ardener (1975) calls "muted groups." Muted groups consist of less powerful members of a society who, as Henrietta L. Moore has summarized, "are silenced by the structures of dominance, and if they wish to express themselves they are forced to do so through the dominant modes of expression, the dominant ideologies" (Moore, 1988, p. 3). Green Valley's story was always told by the media; rarely were Green Valley's residents able to talk directly, and express their views themselves, to the larger community.

There was really no doubt as to the final outcome. The "problem" Green Valley's residents presented to the larger community would be "solved" by simply removing the campsite, which was ultimately no solution at all. But it was a solution that corresponded to the perception the larger society has of recent immigrants and their lack of integration into the community. One of the advantages of being the more powerful group is that, as Foucault (1979, p. 194) has noted, "power produces; it produces reality; it produces domains of objects and rituals of truth." The larger community defined the residents of Green Valley as "illegal aliens" and "migrant workers," giving them an identity based upon negatives: illegal residents, transients, homeless, poor, unemployed or temporarily employed, criminals or potential criminals, all of which contrasted with the identity of legitimite residents. Green Valley's residents were cast as outsiders.

Finally, Green Valley's migrant camp illustrates the role of health professionals in controlling society and its members, especially those considered out of the mainstream because of poverty-related behavior or cultural differences. According to Irving K. Zola (1978), there is an ominous and growing trend in our society toward such "medicalization." As he suggests, (1978, pp. 90–91), "Any proposal is immensely enhanced, if not justified, when it is expressed in the idiom of medical science." This trend has led to increasing social intervention by the health professions into everyday life:

> Medicine is becoming a major institution of social control, nudging aside, if not incorporating, the more traditional institutions of religion and law. It is becoming the new repository of truth, the place where absolute and often final judgements are made by supposedly morally neutral and objective experts. And these judgements are made, not in the name of virtue or legitimacy, but in the name of health. (Zola, 1978, p. 80).

What occurred in Green Valley fits well with Zola's view of medicine as an agent of social control. The health department became the de facto agency to which the larger community turned to rid themselves of unwelcome neighbors. Health issues may have drawn the health department into action, but their involvement had as much, if not more, to do with the general "migrant worker problem" as with health and disease. The health department was the agency of last resort to get rid of the Green Valley encampment. As the assistant director of health services said:

> It wasn't our intention in the Green Valley encampment controversy, if I can call it that, to be an enforcement arm to anybody. It did happen that way, and in retrospect, I look back at what did evolve and it certainly looked as though there was some concerted effort to make us the people, the health department, the people responsible for dealing with this problem because no one seemed able to deal with it. It was not intended that way. But the outcome, I think, was very much that way.

I have spent a great deal of time reconstructing the last days of Green Valley because it offers important lessons about the life of undocumented immigrants in American society. Relatively recent migrants, chased from temporary camp to temporary camp, have little opportunity to form links to the surrounding community. Other recent migrants may not live on hillsides or canyons and their dislocations may not be as severe as those experienced by Green Valley's residents. But recently arrived Mexican and Central American immigrants are the most conspicuous of the undocumented immigrants, and the image the larger society has of the "illegal alien" is based upon an interpretation of the recent migrant's experiences.

But what of undocumented immigrants who are no longer recent migrants? In the chapters that follow, I examine the experiences of undocumented immigrants and their families who have been in the San Diego area for many years. They face problems different, yet similar, to those of Green Valley's residents as they work, raise children, and try to avoid detection by the immigration authorities.

7 / Families, Domestic Groups, and Networks

Separating oneself from family and friends is not without costs. Migrants leave behind the emotional support gained by daily contact with relatives and friends in their home and community. They leave behind jobs, sometimes even after years of experience. And they leave behind, if only temporarily, whatever prestige and social status they may have in their home community. In short, migrants are separated physically and geographically from home, even though emotionally they retain a strong bond.

While migrants may not sever family ties, those ties are stretched across time, space, and national boundaries. I refer to families with one or more members in the United States and one or more members "back home" in another country as *transnational families*. Such split families experience emotional, financial, and physical stress as a result of the migrant's absence. Undocumented migrants are subject to many life-threatening experiences in crossing the border and then in working in the United States. As a consequence, parents in transnational families wait expectantly for the migrant's return, as do spouses and children. Wives not only fear for their husbands' safety, but also often worry that their husbands will meet other women, causing them to forget their families back home, so far away.

Family members left behind often must assume tasks and roles belonging to the missing spouse. Although this can be quite burdensome, many families left behind do not reunite with migrants in the United States. Others, however, find the pressures too great to bear, and choose to join the family member in the United States.[1]

TRANSNATIONAL FAMILIES AND REUNITED FAMILIES

Felicia and Héctor Gómez remember vividly why Felicia and her children joined Héctor in the United States. Héctor has the immense hospitality of most of the people I interviewed and then some. Even when pressured by work on the avocado farm, he took time to talk with me, and then send me off with a box of avocados. He would usher me into his small living room, adorned with a well-used sofa and pictures of Jesus and the Virgin of Guadalupe, and then patiently tell of his family's migration. Héctor had a slow, thorough manner of speaking, as if he wished to ensure that this piece of history not be lost.

---

[1]One hundred of the Mexicans I surveyed in 1986 had a spouse and/or children, but only about half (53%) were living together in San Diego. More (61.7%) of the 107 Central Americans with a spouse and/or child were living together in San Diego.

Héctor left Mexico for the United States in 1972, when he was about 26 and Felicia about 21, with two children and another on the way. Héctor and Felicia lived, at that time, in a rancho called Cabellito, in the state of Aguascalientes. Héctor had always worked in agriculture. Both his and Felicia's parents were farmers. Although his father owned a piece of land, it provided the family with little income. Héctor said, "We were very poor. I never had schooling. My father was poor and the work I had to do was to help him." Héctor did not have his own land after he married Felicia. His father's land was given to his brother. "I didn't have land. I was just a field hand," Héctor noted. "Sometimes I worked and sometimes I didn't." Faced with irregular work and the economic demands of a family, Héctor decided to migrate to San Diego County, where his cousin worked.

> I worked very much, very much [in Aguascalientes]. And we tried to save to buy things, a chimney for the house. We didn't have these things. We didn't have anything to buy them with. So, I had a dream to come here because I knew that here one could earn a little more. So, I said to myself, "I'm going to the United States. I'm going to try."

For five years Héctor migrated back and forth between an avocado farm in Escondido and his family in Aguascalientes. Héctor would see his family in Mexico once a year, as he said, "for a month, or a couple of weeks, or 15 days, depending upon when there was little work. Then I'd return to Escondido when there was more work." Felicia and Héctor had two more children during this period of brief encounters.

As Felicia remembers it,

> The first time he came here I was left alone [with two children] and pregnant. Then he came back when my daughter was born. Then he returned [to the United States] while I raised her. During the time I was raising her he came back again and I got pregnant again. He returned when the boy was 2 months old. Then I raised the boy and he returned and I got pregnant with the other girl.

Héctor's absences meant extra work for Felicia. The rancho she lived in was very rural. Felicia had to perform physically demanding chores daily, such as carrying water from a well or nearby river to the house. She had to take care of all household responsibilities alone, as well as care for their growing family.

> My life was full of a lot of work, cutting wood, hauling water to bathe my children, and all of the work. Well, I had to do my husband's work and mine, too, because all of the men there would gather the wood and haul water to the house. But because he was absent, I had to do it. And I had to do my work, which was caring for my children, making tortillas, and preparing food for them. So, it was too much suffering for me to have to carry the whole weight, fetching the water, gathering wood, washing. Because I couldn't carry a lot of water at once, I had to bathe them [the children] with what little water I had and with the remaining water I washed the clothes. All day long, this went on. One day I would fetch five or six buckets of water. The next day I would wash, because it wasn't possible to do everything at once.

Héctor's separation from Felicia and their children was a physical strain on Felicia. But his absence also created an emotional gulf between Héctor and his children. Since he saw them for only one short period during the entire year, his children were growing up without his presence. As Felicia noted,

The children didn't know him because he could only stay 2 weeks in Mexico. So, when he arrived the children cried because they didn't know him. They didn't know their father. For them, their father was only a picture.

Héctor felt saddened by the emotional distance between himself and his children. He lamented the lack of affection his children held for him. They were almost like strangers.

> The first years, I was fine. But then the time came, after 4 years, that I would go to visit my family and my children didn't know me. I would try to hold them and they wouldn't allow it. They would cry. They weren't comfortable with me. I noticed that they didn't have any affection for me, nor I for them.

Despite these problems, Héctor did not consider bringing his family to the United States. His work on an avocado farm earned him only about $1.50 an hour, and he did not have housing suitable for a family. It was his employer who kept insisting that Héctor bring his family. Over the years, the employer, who did not live on the farm, gave Héctor increasing responsibility for its daily operations. Héctor noted that when he would suggest going back to see his family, the employer "didn't like it because I was in charge of the trees. He said, 'I don't like it that you go so often. Look, send for your family.'"

After his pay was raised to $2.50 an hour, Héctor finally decided to bring his family north. "I thought I must make a decision. It was very hard for me to continue living here alone. My family occupied my thoughts; when would I be able to see them on a continual basis?" In 1977, Héctor returned to Aguascalientes and brought his family back with him to Escondido. "I brought them and they were all very happy. My children and I could finally be together."

For the Gómezes, Héctor's life as a migrant meant that he lived more in San Diego than at home in Mexico. They viewed the effect of this separation on Felicia and the children as a major problem facing the family and its future. Their solution was to move the entire family to San Diego, where they would face new problems as undocumented immigrants. But for the Gómezes, these were challenges they could face together, as a family.

When Wives and Mothers Migrate First   When women migrate, leaving children and husband behind, they often worry about their children's daily care, something men rarely worry about since the children are typically with their wives. Andrea Portrero, whom we met earlier, worked continually in San Diego County after her first trip to Fresno in 1971. For many years she lived in with and cared for an elderly Indian woman. Since this was much closer than Fresno, Andrea was able to return to her family once a month, arriving on Friday evening and returning to work on Sunday afternoon. Andrea believed this was a better arrangement than when she worked in Fresno, where "I didn't see [my family] at all. And this way, if they had problems they could call me." But the separation still proved trying for Andrea.

> My life was very difficult. Sometimes, in fact, I would go see them and the little ones would be sick and I'd think, Well, I'll stop working and try to find work here because my children are sick and unattended. Then I'd start working in Tecate, but we just couldn't make it.

With Andrea back in Tecate, she and her family barely earned enough to support their large family. Then, in 1977, Andrea's husband lost his job at a maquiladora. It was then that he decided to migrate to Los Angeles where he had a friend. Andrea joined him in Los Angeles and their friend found her a job as a seamstress. But Andrea's anxiety over her children's welfare heightened now that she and her husband were both away from their children.

> The worrying was even worse because no one was with them. So I told my husband that maybe we should try to bring the entire family over here. He didn't agree, but I didn't want my family to be on its own. We both had to work, though, because it was a large family.

The anxiety became too much to bear and so later that same year Andrea, her husband, and their 11 children moved to San Diego. They joined their oldest son, who had migrated to San Diego in 1974, and found work as a dishwasher. Andrea's daughter, Ester, was 17 when the family decided to move to San Diego. She had also worked in San Diego previously. During the summer vacations of her fifth and sixth grades of elementary school, she worked taking care of children whose parents were friends of her parents. As she said, "I contributed to our support in that way." Ester also noted that her family's decision to move to San Diego involved all family members:

> It was a decision we all made at home, because every year things got more difficult. As the kids got older, they were no longer children. They were adolescents and wanted to go out, and we were always worried about their whereabouts. Those kinds of problems came up and it was then that we all decided to be together.

Andrea and her family recognized a need for parental supervision of their children. At the same time, they had become dependent upon work in the United States to support their family. Their solution, to move the entire family to San Diego, has allowed the family to reside together continuously since 1977.

Single Mothers   Single mothers, most of whom initially leave their children in Mexico with their mother, sister, or some other relative, have to decide whether to bring their children to live with them. Some women I interviewed worked as live-in maids during the week and returned to their children on the weekends, crossing the border with their local border-crossing card. They preferred to keep their children in Tijuana, where they would grow up with Mexican values and culture rather than what they considered the negative influences of American culture, especially drugs, disrespect for parents, and promiscuity. In addition, they believed that the money they earned could provide much more for their children in Mexico than in the United States. For these women, life in a transnational family was preferable to reuniting their family in the United States.

Other single mothers, such as María Delgado, desired to have their children join them in the United States at the earliest opportunity. María started working in San Diego as a live-in maid in 1977. She left her four children with her mother in Tijuana and returned every weekend when possible, or at least every two weeks. She would visit her children for an afternoon, sometimes staying a whole day before returning to work. But María found the separations too emotionally draining: "It didn't seem right, however, to see them and then leave them. The little boy [8 years old] would cry and stare at me, saying 'Mommy, Mommy.' And I'd tell him that I was going to come back very soon. So that didn't seem right to me." Two years later, three of María's children joined her in San Diego. Her oldest son, who was nearly 18 at the time I interviewed her, preferred to stay in Mexico. She said he went to school in Tijuana, had friends there, and worked as a carpenter building kitchens. Even though he visits his mother in San Diego, "He never thinks about staying. He likes it better over there."

Some women leave their children with family members who live deep inside Mexico, making it unfeasible to see them on weekends. Moreover, those without border-crossing cards would have to reenter the United States illegally every time they visited their children in Mexico, an experience many wished to avoid at all costs (see chapter 3). This results in long absences from their children. For example, Estela, 35 years old, worked as a live-in maid. She left her three children with her parents in Tomatlán, Jalisco, after her husband abandoned her. "Life in Mexico is hard and I am taking advantage now that my children are young to earn money." When I spoke to her, it had been 3 years since she left her family, and she intended to return soon. At that point she did not intend to stay in San Diego. When she reunites with her family, it will be back home in Mexico.

Leaving children with family in Mexico sometimes creates problems with overburdened caregivers. In addition, the unpredictable nature of undocumented immigrants' lives can make matters worse. Angelina Ortega, whom we met earlier, had found herself in a difficult situation when I interviewed her the first of many times in 1986.

Angelina is a relatively large woman whose round face speaks of sincerity and friendliness. But it is also a face that expresses the ordeals she faces in her life. She lives in a small duplex apartment that sits behind another house in a relatively low-income neighborhood. The houses and apartments around her show the wear of years of occupancy and neglect. Her apartment is furnished with the essentials, nothing extravagant. The living room holds two couches and an old black-and-white portable television. Though somewhat shy, Angelina is nonetheless articulate and open about her experiences.

When she left Santiago, Guanajuato, in 1978 she left her two children, a son age 6 and a daughter age 3, with her sisters. She was about 30 years old at the time. Even though she had never worked outside her household before, she left Mexico with her husband to work as a housecleaner in Los Angeles, while her husband worked in the agricultural fields. They had two more children in the United States; the second, a daughter, was born with cerebral palsy in 1984.

After the girl was born, Angelina and her husband moved in with her sister in Chula Vista, in south San Diego. Six months before I met her, Angelina's husband had left to work in the agricultural fields in central California. Angelina feared he might not return because of their handicapped child.

> Some friends invited him to go north and because the girl was already sick he felt it was better if we stayed here with my sister. But it will be 6 months since he's left and

we don't know of his whereabouts. Some acquaintances in Los Angeles were deported about 4 months ago and he was with them to find work. I don't know if he's up there or over here.

Since her husband left, Angelina has been the sole provider for their children. Because of the demands placed on her as a result of her daughter's sickness, Angelina could no longer work. Rather than return to Mexico, Angelina decided to stay in the United States because she believed the medical care her daughter was receiving for her illness surpassed what was available in Mexico. She said,

> I was living with my sister and I had my son also and there were many expenses for them. It was a desperate situation for me. I did not have many choices. When my daughter was 8 months old she had no physical movement. None at all. They told me to take her to Children's Hospital. The doctor told me that possibly she would walk, but she would need a lot of therapy.

It had been about 8 years since Angelina had last seen her older children. They were very young when she left, and now they were 15 and 11 years old. The price Angelina paid to work in the United States was to miss seeing her children grow up. Angelina considers this separation to have been a major sacrifice in all their lives. But it was a sacrifice that she decided was for the better.

> It was 8 years since I had seen my children. The first years were difficult. Later, I had adjusted by rationalizing that Los Angeles was troubled by things, like trouble between Mexicans and other people, the schools were having trouble, and other things. I figured it was better there [in Mexico]. There they were able to study, and they were with their aunts.

Unable to work because of her daughter, Angelina could no longer send money to the sisters who were taking care of her older children. Angelina decided at that point that she could no longer burden them. "That is when I decided to bring the rest of my children." When the two children arrived from Mexico, Angelina moved into her own apartment, but she still relies a great deal on her sister in Chula Vista, who visits her often. But Angelina reunited her family under difficult conditions. She was unemployed, a single mother, lacked legal immigration status, and her disabled daughter required intensive therapy. When offered government assistance for her daughter, a U.S. citizen by birth, Angelina believed she had no other choice but to accept it to survive economically. It was not the best of times, and yet Angelina quietly persevered.

Central Americans and Family Reunification   Many Central Americans also desired to reunite their families in San Diego. But among those who left their native country because of a fear of violence, family reunification was a matter of great urgency. Umberto was 20 years old when he left his wife and two children in San Salvador. He migrated to avoid being drafted into the army because "I didn't want to fight against my own people." For the 2 years since he had arrived in San Diego he had taken English classes and had worked as a carpenter in a furniture factory. He believed that, with only 6 years of education, carpentry work offered him the best opportunity for earning "good" money, even though he had earned minimum wage for 2 years. Umberto will return to El Salvador only when the government changes or to bring his wife and children to the United States if they are afraid to make the trip without him. He intends to bring his family to join him as soon as possible.

In 1983, Filomena left her rural community of San Eduardo, in La Union, one of the departments (states) in El Salvador that has experienced intense political conflict. She was 33 years old when she left. Her husband had recently abandoned her, leaving her with three children to support. Then, in their search for rebels, government forces burned her house. "They attacked my house, leaving me in the street, and I had to leave because of the poverty." She left her children with her parents and joined a friend in San Diego. She found a job cleaning houses, and a second job 2 years later as a seamstress in the garment industry. She works as many hours as possible to send money to her family and to save enough to go back to El Salvador for her children and then return to San Diego. "I work hard in order to reunite my family, that is indispensable." Umberto and Filomena, like many migrants with family left in politically turbulent regions, believe that the longer their families remain the greater the possibility of their being endangered by the conflict.

MARRIAGE

Bringing family from back home is one way to form a family in the United States. Another way is to meet someone here and then get married. Since many undocumented migrants are single, this is an ever-present possibility. Single women who do domestic work or clean houses usually know at least one other person in the area. Often it is someone they knew before they migrated. Then again, they meet other young women working in nearby houses. Men make acquaintances at work as well. Through these social contacts a network of relationships develop, so that friends introduce friends to other friends.

The young undocumented immigrants with whom I talked also said they met people at sporting events, such as the soccer games the men frequently play on weekends. Such events help to reduce the sense of isolation individuals feel away from home. San Diego also has a couple of dance clubs specializing in Latin music such as *cumbias* and *salsas*.

A favorite place for young women who worked as live-in maids in La Jolla, Pacific Beach, Del Mar, and other coastal cities to congregate on summer Sundays was the grassy park area near the popular La Jolla beach known as The Cove. Young undocumented men working in the area would also assemble there, in hopes of meeting old friends and making new ones. There, amid the rich and famous, and other San Diegans, young undocumented women and men would mingle and enjoy each other's company.

The story of Enrique and Beatriz Valenzuela's meeting is illustrative. After Beatriz arrived in San Diego, she stayed with the sister of a friend she had come with. After finding a job as a live-in maid, Beatriz would visit her friend on weekends. Her friend worked for an older American woman in a large house with a swimming pool. "This woman would drink a lot, night and day. On the weekends, those of us who didn't have a place to stay would get together there and the lady didn't mind."

Beatriz's friend would sometimes invite male friends over to go swimming. On one of these occasions, Beatriz met Daniel. "Later, on the beach in downtown La Jolla, it's called The Cove, Daniel introduced Enrique to us. From there, we started to go out together. He would invite me to go out to eat, and to just be out because we didn't have money. He didn't and I didn't. I sent my $27 a week [all her earnings] to my mother." Enrique and Beatriz did not have much time to spend together. She worked as a live-in maid during the week and on some Sundays cleaned another house in order to earn an additional $10, which she would keep for spending money.

Their relationship grew despite having little time to actually be together. As Beatriz tells it: "When I met him I didn't live with him. I only went to see him on weekends because I lived at my job and he with his friends, until I got pregnant with Carolina. That's when we looked for our own place, apart from our friends." They married in 1977, a year after their son was born.

Enrique and Beatriz Valenzuela are not alone. A survey I conducted in 1986 suggests that many undocumented immigrants meet their future spouses in the United States. Out of 73 married undocumented Mexicans, 23 (31.5%) met their spouses in San Diego, and 3 others (4.1%) met them somewhere else in the United States. Similarly, 16 (20.5%) of the 78 married Central Americans I surveyed met their spouses in San Diego and 4 others (5.1%) met them somewhere else in the United States.

Not all undocumented Mexicans marry other Mexican nationals. Three of the Mexicans I surveyed were married to Salvadorans, another was married to a Nicaraguan, and seven (4.8%) were married to spouses born in the United States, who were thus U.S. citizens. Moreover, while only one Central American was married to someone born in the United States, 14 (9.9%) of the Central Americans were married to Mexicans. Marriage between Central Americans and Mexicans reflects an important level of inter-group interaction, which surfaces again when I examine domestic groups (see below).

BINATIONAL FAMILIES

Undocumented immigrants who stay and form a family in the United States, either by bringing family to join them or by marrying someone they met here, are typically young and in the family-formation period of their lives. Part of the reason for this is that migration is selective; it is primarily young people who migrate. Most undocumented immigrants, for example, are between 19 and 29 years of age.

The accompanying charts show how relatively young immigrants are compared to nonimmigrants by using age-sex pyramids. The first pyramid reflects San Diego's population as found in the 1980 U.S. Census. The other two pyramids represent all the people living in the households of 145 undocumented Mexicans and 144 Central Americans I surveyed in 1986.

It is easy to see that the pyramids for the Mexican and Central American interviewees have quite a different structure from that of the pyramid for the general San Diego population. San Diegans generally are found evenly distributed throughout

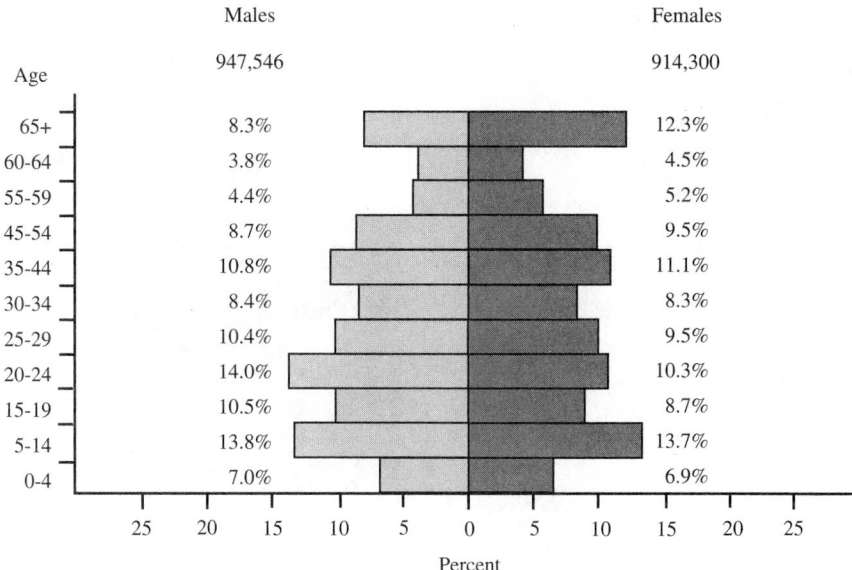

AGE AND SEX OF THE
SAN DIEGO POPULATION

Males 947,546 — Females 914,300

Age	Males	Females
65+	8.3%	12.3%
60-64	3.8%	4.5%
55-59	4.4%	5.2%
45-54	8.7%	9.5%
35-44	10.8%	11.1%
30-34	8.4%	8.3%
25-29	10.4%	9.5%
20-24	14.0%	10.3%
15-19	10.5%	8.7%
5-14	13.8%	13.7%
0-4	7.0%	6.9%

Percent

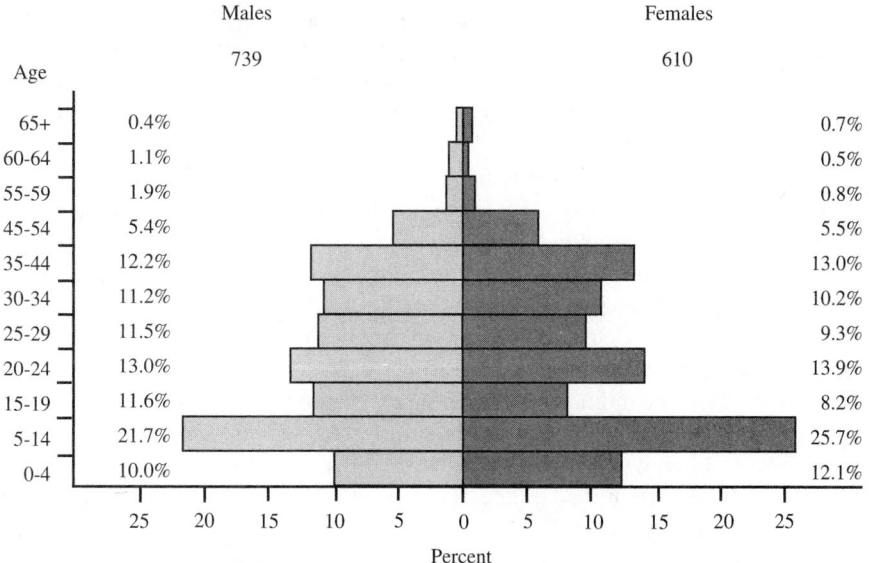

AGE AND SEX OF
ALL HOUSEHOLD MEMBERS,
UNDOCUMENTED MEXICANS

Males 739 — Females 610

Age	Males	Females
65+	0.4%	0.7%
60-64	1.1%	0.5%
55-59	1.9%	0.8%
45-54	5.4%	5.5%
35-44	12.2%	13.0%
30-34	11.2%	10.2%
25-29	11.5%	9.3%
20-24	13.0%	13.9%
15-19	11.6%	8.2%
5-14	21.7%	25.7%
0-4	10.0%	12.1%

Percent

most of the categories. But notice how the relatively large number of 65 and older residents distorts the top of the pyramid. This distortion is partly caused by San Diego's attraction as a retirement area and partly by the fact that the Anglo population is growing older, at least in contrast to Blacks, Asians, and Latinos.

AGE AND SEX OF
ALL HOUSEHOLD MEMBERS,
CENTRAL AMERICANS

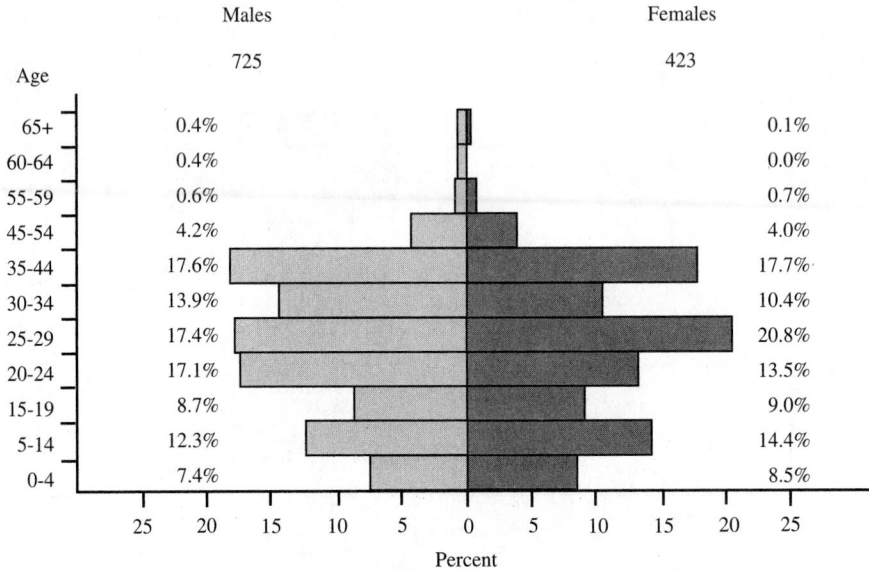

In contrast, the Mexican pyramid is relatively large at the bottom, reflecting the presence of children. This tells us that many of the undocumented immigrants have formed families in San Diego, and since they are relatively young, they are also in the childbearing years of their lives. The age categories from 20 to 44 are about equal in distribution. These are the prime working years and are the ages associated with migrants. After 45 years of age, the pyramid narrows dramatically, which means there are few older people living in the households of undocumented Mexicans. Older people are often less willing to uproot themselves from their family and friends to migrate, especially when it involves the risks associated with crossing the border illegally and then living the clandestine life of an undocumented immigrant. The population pyramid for the Mexicans I interviewed is what you might expect for a migrant population that has begun to settle and form families.

The pyramid for Central American interviewees is more like what you might expect for a group that has only recently migrated. The adult categories, that is, those of working-age migrants, hold the largest distribution, causing the pyramid to widen in the middle and narrow at the bottom and top. Compared to Mexicans, they have fewer children with them and even fewer older people.

Because they are in the childbearing period of their lives, undocumented immigrants who marry here or who are joined by their spouse are likely to have children born in the United States. Among the undocumented immigrants I surveyed in 1986, 30.3% of the Mexican and 19.4% of the Central Americans already had at least one child born in the United States.[2] Having children born in the United

---

[2]Over time, however, interviewees were much more likely to have a U.S.-born child.

States means that an undocumented immigrant's family now contains a U.S. citizen. This fact alone points to the problem of calling this family an "illegal alien family" or an "undocumented family." All members of the family are not undocumented immigrants.

We have seen that some undocumented immigrants, in addition to having a child who is a U.S. citizen, are married to a spouse born in the United States. Moreover, one or more family members may be a legal immigrant. What sometimes happens is that the first person to migrate may have obtained legal residency and then later other members, such as a spouse and children, joined him or her in the United States. In some cases, undocumented family members may have applied to become legal immigrants themselves, using as the basis for their application their position as the spouse or children of a legal immigrant. Rather than wait for their case to work its way through the INS bureaucracy, which could take many years, they join their legally immigrated relative. Once again, these examples point to the erroneous usage of a general term like "illegal alien family" to refer to families consisting of a mix of legal statuses. I use the term *binational family* when speaking of a family that consists of both undocumented immigrants and U.S. citizens or legal residents (Chavez, 1988).

DOMESTIC GROUPS

I have encountered undocumented immigrants in an incredible array of living arrangements: in canyons, in camps of makeshift shelters, in garages, and in apartments and houses. They live alone as live-in maids, in nuclear families, in single-parent households, and in extended families. Some crowd into apartments with other single friends and relatives, and sometimes two families share an apartment or house.

When I first encountered this seemingly chaotic pattern of living arrangements, I was at a loss. Is there a sense of order and rationality here? If we shift our focus from the family per se to a different unit, the domestic group, a sense of order does come forth. Domestic groups consist simply of the people who live together. Domestic groups are sometimes referred to as "those who share a roof." But this definition can be a bit tricky. Those who live together in one apartment constitute a domestic group, but those who live in separate apartments in an apartment complex are not a domestic group. Other times they are referred to as a household or a coresidence group, in other words, the people who reside together.

Importantly, domestic groups or coresidence groups often contain individuals related through kinship; that is, they are family. But that does not have to be the case. Individuals who are friends or even recent acquaintances can also share a domestic space, as can combinations of friends and relatives.[3]

Domestic groups are typically discussed in terms of composition and structure. For example, a domestic group might be composed of a woman, a 6-year-old boy, and a 4-year-old girl, or of four working-age adults. The organizational structure of those individuals refers to their relationships: The first example is a single-parent family consisting of a mother and her son and daughter. The second example is that

---

[3]I have examined domestic groups in great detail elsewhere: Chavez, 1985, 1990.

TABLE 7.1 DOMESTIC GROUPS AMONG UNDOCUMENTED MEXICANS
AND CENTRAL AMERICANS IN SAN DIEGO

		Percent in This Situation (%)	
Household Situation		Central Americans (N = 144)	Mexicans (N = 145)
I.	Solitaries	9.0%	12.4%
1.	lives alone/boarder	3.5	4.9
2.	lives at work	5.6	7.6
II.	No Family Households	18.8%	24.8%
10.	coresident siblings	0.0	0.7
11.	coresident relations, not sibs	0.0	2.8
12.	persons not related	13.2	20.0
13.	combo of 10 + 11	0.7	0.0
14.	combo of 11 + 12	0.0	1.4
15.	combo of 10 + 12	4.9	0.0
III.	Simple Family Household	43.1%	49.0%
20.	married couples alone	1.4	6.9
21.	married couples with child(ren)	25.7	23.4
22.	single parent with child(ren)	3.5	7.6
23.	combo of 20 + friend(s)	5.6	4.1
24.	combo of 21 + friend(s)	4.2	3.4
25.	combo of 22 + friend(s)	2.8	3.4

of four friends unrelated by kinship. These are just two of many possible compositions and structures. The total range of domestic groups I found in my 1986 survey is presented in Table 7.1.

By focusing our attention on domestic groups we can get an appreciation for how undocumented immigrants use social organization to help them meet both their goals and the challenges they encounter as "illegal aliens." Rather than viewing the variety of domestic groups formed by undocumented immigrants as random or chaotic, I believe we should view it in the way anthropologists view other forms of social organization. Their domestic groups reflect rational and strategic decisions on how to organize their lives in a way that helps them to accomplish their goals. As we shall see in chapters 8 and 9, undocumented immigrants find themselves in a politically and economically tenuous situation in the United States. They have limited economic opportunities. The jobs they find are relatively low paying, offer few benefits, and are often impermanent. They also have limited access to government resources (for example, welfare) and face possible apprehension and deportation by the authorities. These are the realities undocumented immigrants confront and their objectives and behavior are influenced by these realities.

TABLE 7.1 (CONTINUED)

Household Situation		Percent in This Situation (%)	
		Central Americans (N = 144)	Mexicans (N = 145)
IV.	Extended Family Households	14.6%	6.9%
30.	extended upwards	0.0	0.0
31.	extended downwards	1.4	1.4
32.	extended laterally	6.9	2.8
33.	combo of 30, 31, 32	0.7	0.7
34.	30 + friend(s)	0.0	0.0
35.	31 + friend(s)	0.0	0.0
36.	32 + friend(s)	2.1	0.0
37.	33 + friend(s)	0.0	0.0
38.	single-parent fam (SPF) exten up	0.0	0.0
39.	SPF extended down	1.4	0.7
40.	SPF extended laterally	2.1	1.4
41.	38 + friend(s)	0.0	0.0
42.	39 + friend(s)	0.0	0.0
43.	40 + friend(s)	0.0	0.0
V.	Multiple Family Households	14.6%	6.9%
50.	Int = primary family, 2nd unit up	0.0	0.7
51.	Int = primary family, 2nd unit down	1.4	0.0
52.	Int = primary fam, 2nd unit lateral	0.7	1.4
54.	Int = secondary fam and is down	0.7	0.0
55.	Int = secondary fam and lateral	0.7	0.7
57.	Int = primary and SPF, 2nd unit up	0.0	0.0
60.	Int = secondary, SPF and lateral	0.0	0.0
63.	Int = primary, 2nd fam SPF + lateral	0.7	0.0
65.	Int = primary SPF, 2nd unit SPF down	0.0	1.4
67.	Int = SPF, 2nd unit SPF lateral	0.0	0.7
69.	nonrelated families	5.6	0.0
70.	nonrelated families, int = SPF	3.5	1.4
95.	55 + friend(s)	0.0	0.0
103.	63 + friend(s)	0.0	0.0
109.	69 + friend(s)	0.7	0.7
110.	70 + friend(s)	0.7	0.0

Different types of domestic groups help undocumented immigrants meet some of their objectives. As their goals and objectives change over time, so do the domestic groups in which they live. Recent migrants, who are here without spouse and children, have one set of goals—typically, to earn money, avoid detection by the immigration authorities, and return home. Undocumented immigrants who have been in San Diego many years share these goals, but often have additional goals influenced by the fact that family members now live with them.

Let me lay out some of the major goals of undocumented immigrants. Although these goals often overlap and may occur at any time during a particular migrant's stay in the United States, generally the relative emphasis given each goal proceeds in the order presented here. In other words, imagine that time in the United States increases as we go down the list of goals.

Goals of Undocumented Immigrants

- Find someplace to stay, if only temporarily
- Work
- Live cheaply
- Survive economically
- Send money back home
- Reduce loneliness and boredom
- Live more comfortably, with more space, fewer people, and less crowding
- Satisfy domestic needs: care for children, socialize children; cook and do other domestic chores
- Minimize disruption caused by apprehension
- Assist others in migrating

Living with Other Single People   Living with friends and other single relatives, such as siblings or cousins, offers a convenient way for singles to share the cost of housing and thus meet the goal of living cheaply. For example, Teresa shared her $525 monthly rent evenly with the three other women with whom she lived. As a consequence, Teresa's share of the rent came to about 13.4% of her monthly earnings. Living with other single friends is also convenient for individuals who intend to stay in the United States for only a short while and do not intend to bring their families to join them.

Living at Work   Since the primary goal of undocumented immigrants is to work, they sometimes take jobs in which they live at the place of work. Maids and baby-sitters who live in the home of their employers are one example. While they may share a roof with their employer, they are not part of the employer's family. From the maid's point of view, they are more like renters, since they exchange their work for a place to live.

The farmworkers living in canyons on or near the farms they work are also in this category. Immigrants who live at their place of work perform other jobs as well. One fellow lived at the place where he took care of fighting cocks. Another, Juan, lived in the storage shed of the company for which he worked installing irrigation systems for landscaping along freeways. One major problem with these informal living arrangements is that they are often uncomfortable, make-do arrangements. And, as in Juan's case, they are sometimes unhealthy. The storage shed where Juan has slept for 4 years also houses the company's store of pesticides, fungicides, fertilizers, and other chemicals. Juan believes his health has suffered as a result.

Living Alone   I have encountered only a few undocumented immigrants who live alone. Sometimes they rent a room from another family. They become boarders; they do not "share" the rent and, thus, do not share responsibility for the residence. Because they are often desperate for an inexpensive place to rent, some undocumented immigrants even rent garages. Two people I met in 1986, one a 43-year-old Mexican man and the other a 27-year-old Salvadoran woman with children back home, each paid $175 a month to live in a garage. Although cases of undocumented immigrants living alone exist, living with other people who can share expenses is the frequently found alternative. I believe that it is the concern that the high cost of living will undermine the initial goals—saving money to send home—that results in few undocumented immigrants living alone.

Single-Parent Families   A few single parents, mostly mothers with their children, live alone. Those who do are in the minority. For example, out of 145 Mexicans I interviewed in 1986, 24 were single parents or lived in a domestic group that included single parents. Of the 24, only 11 lived alone. More often they live with other family or friends, which helps them meet their goal of economic survival.

Single mothers are especially hard pressed to live with others who can share the cost of rent. For example, Genoveva was 20 years old when she left Mexico in 1981 to join her boyfriend in San Diego. They married shortly thereafter and had two daughters. About a year before her interview in 1986, however, Genoveva left her husband and moved into a one-bedroom apartment with her children. The rent was $480 a month, which would have been about 52% of Genoveva's earnings as a waitress. To reduce her costs a friend of Genoveva's, a 32-year-old woman also from Mexico, lives with her and contributes $100 a month to the rent. Her friend earns money caring for children in Genoveva's apartment, including Genoveva's children, for which she pays her friend $50 a week. Genoveva's friend has a husband and children in Tijuana, whom she helps support. Genoveva views this arrangement as beneficial because even though she has to work hard, "I can go to school in the afternoons to try and get ahead *(superar)*."

For single parents, living with others also helps to minimize the disruption that could be caused by the parent's being suddenly apprehended by immigration authorities. As we shall see in chapter 9, this is not an idle fear. Other adults can take care of the children until the mother or father returns. For example, Genoveva has been apprehended and deported once before. Having another woman living with her provides her with a sense of security for her children should she be detained again and suddenly find herself temporarily out of the country.

Two-Parent Families   Sometimes a couple and their children live alone, without other friends or relatives in their domestic group. However, they sometimes have a friend living with them who also pays part of the rent.

I found that the longer Mexicans and Central Americans lived in San Diego, the more likely they were to live alone in two-parent families. Those who stayed and settled were much less likely to live with other single migrants after a few years in San Diego. Either they went back home or stayed and eventually formed a family in San Diego.

Extended and Multiple Families   Sharing domestic space with a friend is one strategy to lower the cost of living. More often, however, families had another relative living with them, in which case they lived in an extended family. Extended families are two-parent families or single-parent families that also include at least one other relative, for example, a spouse's sister or cousin. This other relative is single, or at least migrated without spouse and children.

Extended families offer another strategy for including adults who will contribute to expenses such as rent. Bringing in relatives, such as sisters or nieces, also helps with the problem of child care, which often allows adults to work outside the home. Other adults in the household can also share some of the domestic work and responsibilities. Isela Díaz and her two sons share their two-bedroom apartment with two of her young male cousins. They help with the rent, but more importantly for Isela, they are there to help pick up the children from school or take care of them when she is late from work.

Extended families also reflect new migrants joining established settlers. In this sense, additional family members reflect not only possible economic contributions, but also familial responsibilities to kin in the place of origin. Both Mexicans and Central Americans expressed the need to help other family members who desired to migrate to the United States. But for many Central Americans it was not just to assist them to find a job or higher income, but also because of fear of the dangers in areas experiencing political conflict. Inez, a 35-year-old unmarried Salvadoran, came to the United States in 1971, at the age of 20, because she wished to learn English. When she arrived she stayed with friends from El Salvador. She began work as a seamstress in a garment factory, but has managed to acquire better jobs until now she develops photographic film and earns $8 an hour. She has stayed in the United States "because my country always has conflicts and I am afraid to return; here I am very happy."

These sentiments led Inez to assist family members in El Salvador to migrate to the United States. Her niece was the first to join her about 5 years before the interview. Now 23 years old, her niece works as a secretary. Two years later her mother and her nephew also joined Inez. Her mother is 65 years old and earns money babysitting; her 20-year-old nephew is continuing his education. All three women contribute to the rent and expenses of a three-bedroom apartment. But aside from such economic cooperation, Inez has found that having family members to live with has alleviated the sadness and loneliness she felt before they came. In addition, Inez articulated the difference in her motives for helping family join her compared to the motives of undocumented Mexicans:

> All the undocumented suffer, but those from Central America suffer more; we are very far [from home], and the motives for coming and to feel free are greater than those [motives] for those from Mexico; my country is in war and Mexico is free and there is peace.

Finally, sometimes more than one family shares domestic space. This happens as children grow and marry, or have children, and continue to live with their parents. Other times, it happens when an established family helps a newly arrived family by allowing them live with them. Occasionally, two unrelated families decide to live together in order to rent a larger, more comfortable house.

Since many of these permutations of domestic groups are related to the goals of working and saving money, it's not surprising that I found domestic groups often had many workers in them. Out of 145 Mexicans, less than one in three (30.3%) lived in a domestic group that had only one worker. The rest had two or more workers, and many (31.7%) had three or more workers.[4]

Given the objectives of undocumented immigrants, they typically experience a number of different types of domestic groupings. As they are confronted by different economic and social demands, they enter into a living arrangement. Then as these demands change, they dissolve the domestic group and form another one. Domestic groups reflect the adjustments immigrants make to the high cost of housing, low incomes, child-care demands, social responsibility to family members who are also migrating, and many other factors. Over the course of an individual's life in the United States, different types of living arrangements may be necessary, or desirable, as a way of coping with limited incomes, minimizing disruption caused by apprehension and deportation, and alleviating personal loneliness and social isolation.

Importantly, crowded conditions may be tolerated by undocumented immigrants, especially recent arrivals, but such situations must be viewed as part of a process of migration and settlement, not as a fixed and enduring condition of life among undocumented settlers. They are more likely to live in family units the longer they reside in the United States. Moreover, the incredible array of domestic groups entered into by undocumented immigrants must be seen as they are: creative strategies for mustering social resources.

NETWORKS, CLUSTERS, AND "DAUGHTER COMMUNITIES"

Domestic groups are not the only source of social resources developed by undocumented immigrants. Undocumented immigrants, and immigrants in general, create layers of resources and strategies for dealing with the larger society. These levels are based on the individual, on the family, and on a social network of *parientes* (relatives), *camaradas* (comrades), *paisanos* (fellow countryfolk), *amigos de confianza* (trusted friends), and *vecinos* (neighbors). By forming a network of family and friends in an area, undocumented immigrants increase the numbers of people who can be turned to for help during times of unemployment and when other crises strike, especially apprehension by immigration authorities (see chapter 9).

For undocumented immigrants, and migrants generally, family and friendship relations serve as the means through which migration takes place.[5] That is why

---

[4]Central Americans were even more likely than Mexicans to live in domestic groups with multiple workers. Out of 144 Central Americans, only 15.3% lived in a domestic group with one worker, and 53.5% had three or more workers.

[5]Out of 143 Mexicans who responded to this question in my 1986 survey in San Diego, 39.2% were helped upon arrival by a relative and 48.3% by a friend the first time they migrated to the United States. Only 9.8% said they did not use a social contact for assistance. Similarly, out of 143 Central Americans, 37.8% relied on a relative and 42.7% on friends after arrival, with 14.7% saying they did not receive help from a family member or friend.

anthropologists and other social scientists speak of migration as a social process. More often than not, as we have seen in many of the examples up to this point, a migrant knows someone in the area to which he or she is migrating. This contact typically provides shelter, information on where to find a job, and information on how to get around in the area. Sometimes, as in Enrique Valenzuela's case, the relative or friend is not in a position to help (see chapter 2). The ranch where Enrique's father worked did not need any more help, which meant Enrique had to look elsewhere for employment.

More often, however, when recent migrants join more established immigrants, they are provided with a place to stay and their host often helps them find work. The case of Leonardo is a good example. Leonardo shared an apartment with seven other friends, all paisanos from Sinaloa. Seven of the eight friends worked as gardeners. The first two friends had been in the area for 5 years and provided referrals for employers for each of the subsequent migrants, the last of whom migrated 2 years earlier.

This relationship between the immigrant's social networks and job referrals provides an important benefit for both immigrants and employers. Employers are saved a great deal of time and money by using workers' social networks for recruiting new workers. When a job becomes available, a friend or relative of an existing worker suddenly appears, ready for work. The employer not only gets a fast replacement for a departing worker, but that new person has friends and relatives at the place of work who help instruct him on what needs to be done and even the forms of identification required as a result of the 1986 immigration law. These relationships also provide a measure of social control since the new worker's behavior reflects on the person who made the referral to the employer. All in all, social networks provide a very efficient system of migration and labor recruitment.

After a while, recent migrants move out of the house or apartment of their hosts. Quite often they find a place to live nearby. As children mature and marry, they often live near their parents, as was the case with Andrea Portrero. Six of Andrea's 12 children are married and live close enough to get together most Sundays. Andrea and her family are fairly typical. Over half (56%) of the undocumented Mexicans I surveyed in 1986 had relatives living in the area, as did 45.6% of the Central Americans. This results in a clustering effect in that people from a similar place live near each other.

This clustering effect often results in many members from a village or community living in the same apartment complex, or in the same neighborhood, or at least in the same city. For example, when I interviewed someone from Mascota, Jalisco, they would sometimes add, "There are many people from Mascota around here." In some cases, all the people from a particular community can be traced to the original migrant who established residence in the area and then helped others to migrate, find jobs, and then find a place to live nearby. Through this process, immigrants form "daughter communities" that consist of people who are all from the same "parent" village or town back home (Massey et al., 1987). Migrants from the same community sometimes even form organizations to help the village back home, for example, to build a church or improve a road.

Social networks serve as a source of emotional support and help dispel the loneliness and sense of isolation migrants often feel in a new land. For example,

Estela, a live-in maid, said that the greatest difficulty she has faced in her 3 years in San Diego has been the loneliness and sense of isolation. But when she gets together with her friends, "We go out and talk about things in our places of origin and this helps us a little."

Having a trusted *amigo de confianza* can serve as an important resource. Indeed, having a trusted friend or relative with more experience dealing with the institutions of the larger society is an important survival strategy found among undocumented immigrants. For example, Enrique Valenzuela has found that a friend of his who is a U.S. citizen has been an essential resource when he feels he is being cheated, ignored, or discriminated against.

> Within the family we resolve our problems. But there are problems, like about the house, if they're not billing me correctly. Then I complain. But I think that these people overcharge not because they know for sure that you are illegal, but simply because you're Mexican. I've seen it and experienced that. They simply ignore you. So you feel that you have to have a friend who is Mexican but [also] a [U S.] citizen. And we have one who has helped us a lot. We always go to him.

Networks often extend across ethnic lines. I found that many (42.1%) of the 144 Central Americans who provided me with information on their living arrangements in 1986 lived in a domestic group that included Mexicans. On the other hand, few (only 5.5%) of the 145 Mexicans lived with Central Americans. That Central Americans should turn to Mexicans for help finding living arrangements is not surprising. Undocumented Mexicans and Central Americans have similar experiences. They must both find ways to survive given the constraints of their immigration status and limited economic opportunities. They also share a common language, although with regional variations. But Central Americans lack the long history of migration and well-established communities found among Mexicans in San Diego, and so Central Americans turn to established Mexican immigrants for social and cultural resources. Although this makes sense, I did not anticipate I would find this level of social interaction between Central Americans and Mexicans before I undertook this study.

Lest it sound as if I am romanticizing the relationships undocumented immigrants have with family and friends in the area, let me add that personality differences and conflicts abound. I met both Mexicans and Central Americans who bitterly complained that a relative or friend was unwilling to help them when they arrived. Or, one relative may provide a great deal of help while another is unwilling, or unable, to do so. For example, Angelina Ortega lives near two married sisters. One, who is also undocumented, provided a place for Angelina and her family to stay when they first moved to the San Diego area. Since then this sister has been extremely helpful. Her other sister is helpful, but less so. Although this sister and her husband came as undocumented migrants, they have since legalized their status. The greatest help her sister could provide, in Angelina's perspective, is to help her to also legalize her status. Angelina blames her sister's husband for this lack of help.

> She has a husband who is very Mexican. He rules the house and he doesn't want her to help us. In that way, no. He thinks that if I can't make headway on my own, too bad. He thinks everyone has to look out for themselves. He thinks that if my sister helps me

immigrate, the help won't be for me but for my husband. He thinks we will get better jobs, I think. So he won't help. He feels each man for himself.

Undocumented immigrants, like most other humans, are subject to cantankerous social relationships. Social interactions are not always harmonious. And yet, undocumented immigrants must develop a network of friends and relatives they can depend upon given their lack of other resources, for example, their low incomes and their inability to use most social services because of their undocumented status, as we see in the following chapter.

8 / Work

Work is a constant theme in the lives of undocumented Mexican immigrants who have managed to stay many years in the United States. It cuts across all aspects of their lives, from why they migrated to why they stay. Their work experiences give us insights into why families reunite in the United States and their subsequent living arrangements. Their daily activities revolve around work, and I heard many stories about their early experiences seeking work. These stories were variations on a theme; they told of an odyssey in a strange land where the ultimate quest was to find secure and stable jobs.[1]

Undocumented immigrants I have met are often quite willing to take any job, even when it is something for which they had little or no previous experience. Some people suddenly found that their qualifications and experiences mattered little in this new context. They were "illegal aliens" who found few employers willing to offer them anything other than menial jobs. For example, a single mother with a law degree in Mexico came to visit a son in California in 1980 and stayed when her daughter expressed an interest in attending high school in San Diego. After a few jobs baby-sitting, the woman found a job in a cafeteria and was earning $4.50 an hour in 1986. A 31-year-old woman who was a school teacher in Mexico first worked in a restaurant's kitchen in San Diego in 1982 and 4 years later, when interviewed, she was preparing food for airline flights, earning $6 an hour. Another teacher was working as a carpenter for $10 an hour in 1986, but his first job, 10 years earlier, was cleaning offices for $50 a week. A private accountant in Mexico worked in construction during the entire 6 years he had been in San Diego and had worked his way from $3 an hour to $10 an hour in 1986. A 51-year-old man was a colonel in the Nicaraguan National Guard who fled his country in 1979. He first worked as a parking lot attendant, and in 1986 he managed an apartment in exchange for rent and $300 a month. Although most undocumented immigrants from Mexico and Central America have not achieved this level of education—most have around 6 or 7 years of education, or a primary school education—these examples underscore the willingness of undocumented immigrants to do practically any job.

THE QUEST FOR WORK

Federico Romero's story humorously reveals the frustrating juxtaposition between his first jobs in the United States and his past training and experiences in Mexico. Federico was 25 years old when he first came to San Diego in 1978. Federico had

[1]Of the undocumented 87 Mexican men and 55 women I surveyed in 1986 most (94.3% of the men and 83.6% of the women) were employed at the time. Similarly, of the 94 Central American men and 50 women most (95.7% of the men and 94% of the women) were also employed.

studied hotel management at a technical training center in Mexico City. He then worked in a tourist hotel and later began his own business selling jewelry, which meant he had to travel to various tourist sites, such as Merida and Acapulco. His experiences in Mexico did not prepare him for the work he found in San Diego.

Federico joined a friend of his who was working in the eastern part of San Diego County. Although his friend's employer did not offer Federico work, his friend had another friend who helped Federico find work on a ranch.[2] He was hired to do general maintenance of the plants and landscape, which included a lake. But Federico was not used to such physical labor. "It was a world completely new to me." In addition, Federico realized he was being grossly underpaid—$7 a day—for his labor. To offset the low pay he was given meals, which he also found wanting:

> I knew what they were paying me and I knew that it was impossible for me to live with that. But they said that they gave me meals. Yes, they did give me meals. They gave me dinner and breakfast and two small sandwiches. One of peanut butter and the other perhaps of salami or something like that, something we are not accustomed to eating in Mexico. After working some 6 hours, I then went to lunch. But that wasn't nourishment for me. We Mexicans have a different system of nourishment. So, when you arrive here and you eat a little sandwich, well, that's nothing.

Federico found himself laboring away at this job, wondering what he was doing there. After 3 days, he wanted to leave: "I knew it wasn't for me." His frustration continued, but he was unable to do anything about it. His first earnings he sent to his wife in Mexico City. Without money, he didn't know how he was going to leave the job on the ranch. Finally, salvation came in the form of a green van. About two weeks after he started working on the ranch the Border Patrol arrived, asking workers for their immigration papers. Federico was close to the house chopping down a tree when he saw them coming. When the immigration agents asked for his papers, "I said I had none. [The agent] said, 'Get aboard [the van].' I said, 'Wait. Let me get my things!' And I got them."

Federico saw his deportation to Tijuana not as a setback but as a way to get off the ranch. Federico had already decided to return to San Diego that night, since he did not have any money with which to return to his family in Mexico City. He telephoned his employer at the ranch from Tijuana and told him he would call him the next day to arrange to get his second week's pay, but that he would not be returning to work. No matter what, Federico was determined to find some other type of work.

At the Soccer Field that night, Federico met another fellow bound for San Diego. Both pretended they knew the way across the border, and they became friends as they blundered their way to San Diego. His new friend was on his way to the house of a friend who had an upholstery shop. Federico told his traveling companion that he had some experience in upholstery. "He said, 'Let's go then and

---

[2]Most undocumented immigrants find work through referrals from friends and relatives. For example, 76.9% of 78 Mexican men and 70.8% of 48 Mexican women I interviewed in 1986 said that a relative or friend either introduced them to their current employer or recommended them to the employer for the job. Most Central Americans I interviewed also obtained jobs through social contacts: 83.9% of 87 men and 84.1% of 44 women.

maybe he'll give you work.' I got there, but I didn't know the first thing about upholstery."

Federico offered to do any type of work the upholsterer, who was also from Mexico, might require but said it would be for a temporary period only. Federico planned to look for better work. "He said, 'If you don't have anywhere to go, stay here for a week. You don't have to pay me anything. You can stay in the shop. If you want you can clean it, sweep it, and then you can leave after a week or two.'"

Federico agreed. He then prepared himself to look for work. The first thing he had to do was buy some different clothes. He had some other clothes in a small suitcase that he said had been confiscated by the Border Patrol agents. "So, I went to a thrift store, secondhand store, and I bought myself a different sort of clothes. What I was wearing were boots for working on a ranch." With that, Federico set out to look for work.

Federico found work as a busboy in a nearby Mexican restaurant. After two weeks he received a check for about $75. On the same day, the upholsterer invited him to share Thanksgiving Day dinner, after which he told Federico it was time to find a place of his own to live. Federico didn't know where to go and so he began walking to downtown San Diego. He arrived there at about 11:00 at night. He found an old hotel on Market Street and stayed the night for $20, or about a quarter of his earnings. The next morning he again looked for work. He found work in a restaurant, this time in a run-down Victorian hotel that would later be renovated to its former elegance. While there, he met another busboy who suggested a place to sleep. "They told me I need to be here by seven in the morning. I agreed. So one of the men there, one of the busboys, asked me if I had a place to stay. I said, 'No.' He said, 'See this address. That's where you'll stay. Tell him that I sent you and to let you stay, and if not then to show you a room they are going to rent.' They rented that little room to me for $70 a month. So they were my first friends that I met here in San Diego."

Federico worked at the hotel, but it was only part time, from 7:00 to 11:00 in the morning. "I knew that wasn't enough and that with that I couldn't live." About two and a half weeks after he started at the hotel, he was walking in the downtown area when he passed an electronic equipment store with a sign that said a Spanish-speaking person was needed for light work. Federico immediately entered the store to inquire about the job:

> I called a man there. I tried to speak English then, even though he had a mustache like yours [the author's]. Here, there are many people who are Mexican and, even so, won't help Mexicans. So I called him and asked him about the work. He said, "You need to talk to another man." So I went to him and then he told me he would give me the job and to be there tomorrow at 9:00 in the morning, and that he would pay me $80 a week. I thought that's very good. I was earning about $50 in the other place.

Federico quit his other job and began working at the electronics store. At last, Federico believed he had found his niche. "A store where they sold electronics. And that's what I wanted, sales." Federico was hired not as a salesperson, but as a general assistant to help move boxes and keep the store clean and tidy. But Federico saw this as his opportunity. "That first week he did not pay me $80. He paid me $100, because he saw that I tried hard. He saw that I helped him quite a bit. I said,

'Well good. I'll try even harder because I have to, that's all.'" Federico had learned a little English in his jewelry selling days in Mexico. He built upon his knowledge with studied observations while working at the store:

> I had to learn more English. I practiced more and listened. I had learned how to write the letters, [but] to spell I looked in front of me. There it said, "Long's Drugs." So, that's where I started to listen and look around, to see like S-O-N-Y, all those things. I knew a little [English] but here I practiced even more. Since I arrived here I've always had a paper, a book, anything to read, to learn more English, to know more and to know how to defend myself and my family. Since then I've done it, to practice more English, because I don't have time to study [in school].

Federico worked hard and gained more responsibility at the electronics store. After about 6 months, his employer started asking him to take care of customers. After about 2 years he was earning $240 a week plus commission on the sales he made.

Federico worked at the electronics store for almost 4 years. But events made working there difficult. First of all, the economic crisis in Mexico, and the severe devaluations of the Mexican peso after 1982, meant that fewer Mexicans were able to cross the border and shop in the San Diego area. According to Federico, the electronics store's business suffered as a result. Also, Federico said that his employer's wife's children from a previous marriage, who also worked at the store, became jealous of Federico's earnings and position. So, Federico left the electronics store. When I interviewed him in 1986, he was a salesperson in a store specializing in sports shoes—and he spoke almost fluent English.

Federico's early experiences reflect his determination to find both steady employment and work that suited his personal abilities. Among the many undocumented immigrants I have spoken with, it is perhaps the quest for steady employment that overshadows opportunities for economic mobility, at least at first. The desire to have a job that is regular and continuous is of paramount importance. Even among recent migrants, steady work, even if it is not permanent, is an important goal. Ironically, an important part of the reason those who had been in the United States for many years decided to stay was because they found relatively steady work. Moreover, once undocumented immigrants develop a relationship with an employer, they are typically very loyal workers. They will stay at the same job for years, even if they realize it has limited opportunities. In essence, they exchange economic mobility for job security. Enrique Valenzuela is one of the best examples of this.

THE STEADY WORKER

Enrique typically is the first one to arrive at the Chinese restaurant where he works. He unlocks the kitchen door, straightens up a bit, and begins preparing the vegetables and meats to be used in the day's Cantonese and Mandarin dishes. It is a routine he knows well. He has worked for the same employer since he arrived in the United States in 1970, some 16 years by the time I met him in 1986. "For 15, 16 years, it is the same schedule. I go in at 10:30 A.M., and leave [the restaurant] at 9:45

or 10 at night. I return home and I arrive at 10:10 or 10:15 P.M. I am away from home for almost 12 hours."

Although Enrique had come to join his father, the owner of the farm where his father worked did not need more employees. And so he had the coyote drive him to La Jolla, where his father had heard that there was restaurant work available. He walked into the first restaurant he saw and asked for work. He was hired as a dishwasher part time, which was enough for Enrique to survive, but barely. "When I began 16 years ago, it went very bad for me. I only worked 3 hours per day. I earned $1.50 per hour. The money was only enough to eat and pay the rent. There was no money for anything else. One year, exactly, I earned that salary. After one year, I earned $300 per month. For me, it was much better."

Full-time employment also meant Enrique had to experience a great American tradition: taxes. [3] At this time it was easy for anyone to obtain a social security card, a practice that would change in later years. "My boss told me that in this country one had to pay the government. So I went to apply for my social security card. I began to pay taxes in 1971 and I have done so ever since."

Enrique gradually learned to prepare Chinese food. "When I first began, I washed dishes. They graduated me to cut vegetables. Next to cut meats. Later to a position to fry foods. Then another position to prepare and cook. To date, I am at that same position." The evolution of his skills improved his position at work. He now works on a salary rather than by the hour, earning between $900 and $1,000 a month, depending on tips.

Enrique's acquisition of skills in the kitchen has helped him weather changes at the restaurant. In 1974, his employer opened a new Chinese restaurant east of downtown and eventually closed the La Jolla restaurant. Enrique continued to work at the new restaurant. Enrique has also managed to continue working despite personnel shifts at the restaurant. Once, the majority of kitchen help were Mexican. According to Enrique, "The Chinese bring their families little by little. So, they begin to employ their relatives and cut down on the number of Mexicans. Right now there are very few of us Mexicans, four or five." Enrique attributes his continued employment to hard work. "In all these years, I've never failed to go to work because of a stomachache or headache. They notice that and so they give me a chance. I'm the only Mexican there who gets a paid vacation. They give me a week a year."

Enrique realizes that he has little economic mobility left at his job. He is earning about the best he could possibly earn at the restaurant. He also realizes that despite having worked for so many years at this job, his job is not necessarily permanent. He also does not receive any other benefits, although he is able to buy medical insurance at a reduced rate through his work.[4] And over the years, he has

---

[3]Of those I surveyed in 1986, 56.8% of the Mexicans and 58.9% of the Central Americans had federal taxes withheld from their earnings. However, only about half (55%) of the Mexicans and a third (33.8%) of the Central Americans who had taxes withheld actually sent in their federal income tax forms; the others forfeited any withholding taxes they might have been refunded.

[4]Enrique is similar to other undocumented workers in that they typically do not receive benefits with their job. For example, among the Mexicans I surveyed in 1986 only 12.9% had pension plans, 31.1% had paid sick leave, and 43.7% received medical insurance with their job. Similarly among the Central Americans, only 5.3% had pensions, 16.9% received paid sick leave and 41.6% had medical insurance with their job.

experienced many personal slights and often has had to reduce his expectations. But he has endured all of this because at least the work was steady. He also believed he had only limited opportunities elsewhere due to his undocumented status.

> Without papers you have to tolerate everything at a job: humiliations, low wages, long hours. But if you leave that job and go to another, it's the same thing because you don't have papers. So for us, our papers are the most important thing in order to get ahead in this country. We want to progress. With papers we can open a cafeteria, for example, or a taco stand, where we can earn more, because we are not educated enough to find a good job. But we do like to work a lot.

A few months after Enrique arrived in San Diego, he met Beatriz, who was working as a live-in maid. They soon married and began a family. Beatriz's pregnancy presented Enrique and Beatriz with some important economic problems, especially as to where Beatriz would deliver the baby. As Enrique said, "I had very little money saved. You know how it is when you arrive here without knowing anyone. They don't trust you without having credit or anything. So we thought that she should have the baby in Tijuana because it was more affordable. She went to Tijuana to give birth and she returned about 10 days later with her [daughter]."

With the return of his wife and daughter, Enrique now had a family of three in San Diego. He became concerned with his family's future. Faced with limited economic mobility at their jobs, Enrique and Beatriz embarked on a strategy of saving what they could from their earnings. According to Enrique, "It was around that time that we started to save, not enough because we were now three. But because we were ambitious to accomplish something, we tried very hard." The concern with providing for a growing family and saving for a better future put added pressure on both Enrique and Beatriz to stay at their jobs, work hard, and not take the unnecessary risks associated with frequent job changes.

Beatriz's work history in San Diego did not begin when she met Enrique. After her tearful bus ride from her mother's home and the family bakery she had worked in, she too had to find work in San Diego. Undocumented Mexican women in San Diego work in many types of jobs, including manufacturing, the garment industry, and restaurants. Many, however, are engaged in domestic work, as live-in baby-sitters, live-in housekeepers or maids, and housekeepers who service a number of houses a week. Beatriz's story, and that of other Mexican women, suggests that this type of work is not "natural" in the sense that women may not have had any particular training for it. On the contrary, their past work experiences may have been as varied as that of men. But faced with limited opportunities in the San Diego job market, immigrant women turn to domestic work. And at times, they view it as having strategic advantages for them in comparison to other types of jobs they might find.

WOMEN AND DOMESTIC WORK

Beatriz arrived in San Diego on August 2, 1969, a day she remembers well. She arrived at the house of her traveling companion's sister. After a couple of days' rest, her friend's sister helped her find work as a live-in maid in La Jolla. The job paid little, the work load was heavy, and she had little time off. "I started working for a family that had three girls and two adults. But I was overworked there. All day, until 1 A.M., I would be ironing for only $27 a week. I got half a day on Sundays off. On Sundays, after feeding them breakfast, I would go out and then I would have to be back that same day because if I came back the next morning they would reduce my pay."

Beatriz left that job after 6 months. She found another that paid slightly better, $30 a week, but the lady she worked for moved to Colorado. Without work, she stayed with a friend until she found work again. She continued to work as a live-in maid until her daughter was born in 1972, after which Beatriz decided being away from home all week would be too difficult. Her friend, who also worked as a housekeeper, had already been in the United States about 13 years at that point and helped her find day work through her employer's friends. In this way she found her first daytime housecleaning job. This led to additional jobs.

> After I had Carolina, I went to work with [that family]. The lady liked the way I worked. I first started to work only 1 day a week with her because I had just gotten out of the hospital. She liked the way I worked so much that she gave me another day. I told her that I only had these 2 days of work and that I needed more. She got me work with an architect. That architect gave me 2 days, too. The lady next door to my first employer also asked me if I could work for her, and I said "Yes." She gave me 1 day, so I worked the 5 days.

After 5 years, Beatriz stopped working for the architect and the neighbor, and found two new employers to fill out her week. By 1986, she had worked for these two new employers for 10 years and in her original household for 15 years. Over this time she has seen her pay for a 5 1/2 to 6 hour day go from $10 to $12 to $14 a day, until finally she was earning about $27 a day in 1986 and 1987.

Over the years Beatriz has developed what she considers to be a personal relationship with her employers. Indeed, she has exchanged formal benefits and a contractual work relationship for this informal arrangement based upon personal relationships. Beatriz acknowledges that the lack of formal benefits, particularly medical insurance, is difficult. Although Enrique has medical insurance, it does not cover Beatriz and their children. "The day I get sick, it's expensive." She has come to depend upon an informal agreement for limited benefits.

> When I get sick and don't work, I get paid. Holidays I get paid. If I have a school meeting for the kids, I still get paid. Lots of times I've been sick and they've given me half the money so I can go to the doctor. And they treat me well. They don't give me too much work.

The fact that Beatriz has worked so many years for the same employers has allowed her to develop a personal relationship in which the informal benefits are understood and abided by. Other women do not develop such a relationship with an employer. Women who clean various houses a week typically get paid only on the days they work. They are, in essence, independent contractors. Their relationships with employers are more limited, and they often have many employers, some long-term but many on a short-term basis.

Women who work as housekeepers have different strategies for going about their work and charging for their services. Some women prefer to charge by the hour, while most others charge by the house. Let me give examples of both these strategies.

María Delgado cleans various homes in the San Diego area. When she first came to San Diego in 1977, she spent some time as a live-in maid, then returned to her children in Tijuana for a few months, then came back to San Diego and began working as an independent contractor. She has worked with some of the same people since 1978. She began charging $2.85 an hour and charged $6 an hour in 1986. She prefers to charge by the hour because she fears that if she charged by the house the employer would expect too much. "If I tell them that I'll charge them $35 to clean their house I can spend the whole day there."

María spends 6 hours cleaning one house, although she sometimes cooks rather than cleans. "Sometimes they'll tell me that they'll help me so I can make some tortillas for them, or some enchiladas, or some kind of food, and I do that gladly." After 6 hours, María leaves one house and spends another 3 hours cleaning another house. She does that 5 days a week, leaving the weekends to take care of her two high-school-age children who now live with her in a small house which she rents.

María does not pay taxes on her earnings. Like most undocumented immigrants in such informal working situations, María is paid in cash.[5] She once tried to get a social security card, but the regulations had been tightened by that time, and she was told she needed a U.S. birth certificate or a green card to prove her legal residency. María views her lack of a social security card as part of what makes her "illegal." "I'm a person that you can call 'illegal' because I don't have social security number, I don't file taxes. I am nothing more than illegal." Undocumented immigrants working in more formally structured jobs, typically those that pay with a check and withhold taxes from the employee's earnings, usually either made up a social security number, careful to use the right number of digits, borrowed a social security card from a friend or relative, or purchased a forged social security card. After 1986, with passage of the new immigration law, workers are now required to show identification, including a social security card, that proves their eligibility to work in the United States (discussed further in chapter 9).

Isela Díaz also cleans houses, but she charges by the house. When she first began cleaning houses she also worked by the hour. After her husband, Jorge Díaz, convinced her to migrate with him to San Diego in 1976, Isela did not work. Her husband, Jorge, wanted her to stay home and be a housewife, but after the birth of their first son in a local hospital, Isela had to work to help pay off their bill. Lacking relatives or friends to help her find a job, she put an ad in the newspaper and finally found her first job, from which she managed to get referrals to other employers. She remembers one of her first jobs well. It was in a large house in La Jolla, where she was paid the going rate of $2.50 an hour. "I remember that there were two kitchens. The kitchens had two refrigerators, two dishwashers. To get to her room I had to walk a distance like from here to the end of the block. I worked a lot and felt very tired."

---

[5]In my 1986 survey, 35.4% of Mexican men and 38.3% of Mexican women were paid in cash, as were 31.9% and 35.4% of Central American men and women, respectively.

Isela gradually phased out the clients for whom she worked by the hour and took on new clients whom she charged by the house. Isela spends 4 or 5 hours cleaning each house. In 1986 and 1987 she charged $35 for what she considered an average house. But for larger houses she charged up to $50. She considered this piece rate more suitable to her style of working. "It's not to my advantage to work per hour because I don't like to sit down and eat. I don't like to sit down and think. I like to work fast and get the job done, and if I sit down and think I'll get lazy and then I won't work. I need to work quickly, quickly, quickly and concentrate on the job alone."

Advantages of Domestic Work   For Isela, housecleaning had certain strategic advantages over other, more formal jobs. Although she has had different job experiences and training, she views her present work as preferable given her role as a mother. When she first left her home in Mascota, Jalisco, Isela migrated to Tijuana, where she lived with her cousin and his family. She found work in a maquiladora where her cousin was a supervisor and later an assistant manager. In addition to her factory work, she studied nursing at night. "I worked in the day from 7:30 A.M. to 5:00 in the afternoon. From 5:00 in the afternoon to 9:00 at night I studied nursing with the Red Cross. I got my diploma and did my service to the government. But I blew it in the end. That is, as soon as I finished serving for the government I got married and that was that."

With her work experience, training, and general enthusiasm for work, Isela believes she could find a job other than cleaning houses. But by cleaning houses she is her own boss and her hours are flexible. This is important to her because she believes her number one priority is to care for her two sons, the oldest of whom is in a program for gifted children. Housecleaning allows her to "take care of my children, because in those homes I don't have to be exactly on time. So if I'm late, 'I'm sorry, I couldn't get here on time, traffic.' But in factories and all other places, they have certain hours. Every minute is counted."

Many other women echoed Isela's comment. Women often believed that housecleaning allowed them to synchronize their working hours to the hours their young children are in school. On the other hand, factories demand inflexible hours and it is typically difficult to leave a formal job when a problem arises at home. As Beatriz noted,

> When my kids are sick, I tell the lady that my youngest child is sick and she'll tell me to leave right away, even if I've worked for only an hour. She'll say that it's more important to be with your son than work. So, that's why I'm happy working there. They never check when I get there or when I leave . . . If I worked in a factory or laundromat, my hours would be controlled. I would have to be there at a certain hour and leave at a certain hour. Work the eight hours. I like working in homes . . . I can go whenever I want and leave when my kids need me. In a factory I wouldn't have that advantage. If my kids were sick I'd still have to go to work.

Disadvantages of Domestic Work   Although domestic work has some advantages, it also has some distinct disadvantages. Recent arrivals typically take the jobs that offer the lowest pay with the most disagreeable employers. Women share with men (see chapter 6) this period of vulnerability, during which they must learn what to expect in work situations and what not to tolerate. As undocumented immigrants "learn the ropes," they typically change jobs frequently until they find jobs, and employers, they are comfortable with. But during this time, they sometimes experience work-related abuses. Both Mexicans and Central Americans face this possibility. I found that the individuals with the fewest friends and relatives to help them find jobs and explain American culture to them were the most susceptible to having such experiences.

Isabel, 38, and her husband, a 41-year-old accountant, left their children in Nicaragua in 1984 and migrated to the United States. She had worked as a secretary for the police in the Somoza government and left after the Sandinista revolution. Isabel and her husband came to California, where they stayed with a friend until they found work as a live-in maid and a gardener/handyman at a house in La Jolla. After 4 months of not being paid, they finally left, chalking up their losses as a bitter lesson. They decided not to work as domestics anymore.

Julia was 18 years old when she left El Salvador and found her first job as a live-in maid in La Jolla, 2 years before she was interviewed. The family offered her $90 a week. Rather than pay her each week, they told her they would save her money for her so that she would receive a large amount every so often. After 6 months, Julia asked for her money. According to Julia, the woman of the house said they were bankrupt and fired her. Her principal concern was that her loss meant that it would take her even longer to pay back the $1200 she had borrowed from her brother (who was already in the United States) to pay the coyote who had smuggled her into the country.

I have also encountered undocumented immigrants who do not even get paid for their work as domestics, but exchange labor for a place to sleep. A Salvadoran who had been in the United States for 6 years and his wife, who had been here only 1 year at the time, lived in this situation when interviewed. In exchange for a room, they must get up at 5:00 in the morning to do the yard work and clean the house before they leave for work as a gardener and housecleaner at other homes. They are practically indentured servants.

Many other examples could be provided, but the point is clear. Without a formal contractual agreement, domestic workers are vulnerable to job-related abuses. They are often desperate for work, especially just after their arrival, and have not yet learned how to avoid the worst situations or stop a negative situation before it continues too long. Only time and experience can provide such insights, but the development of a network of relatives and friends who share their experiences can help some undocumented immigrants become aware of abusive situations and even possible remedies.

Time can also take its toll on domestic workers. Women who work as live-in maids for many years complain of losing their ability to communicate. Their employers typically speak English, which they attempt to learn. But they have few opportunities to carry on full and continuous conversations in Spanish. One woman who had been a live-in maid for almost a decade said, "I believe I've forgotten many [Spanish] words because I don't get to use them." She also said she was not as outgoing as she used to be, since she no longer has the opportunity to socialize much. She believed she was becoming very "American" in that she was increasingly reluctant to leave the house.

Working as housekeepers places other stresses on women. Although house-cleaning offers flexible hours, which help women to juggle work and family respon-sibilities, it often increases the amount of work they are expected to do (a lament not restricted to housekeepers). For example, Isela suffered from what I call the housekeeper's dilemma. She believed that she was so tired from cleaning other peo-ple's houses that it caused her to neglect her own home. This became evident to me as we talked one day at her apartment. I was sitting in the kitchen as she continually moved about putting things away. As we talked, she saw that I was looking around the kitchen, which she took as a critical assessment. She said, "Don't look at my home because it is the dirtiest of them all! I never have time for my own home." The guilt she carried because of this self-critical determination was clearly evident.

Added to her own guilt feelings was the pressure of caring for her family after a tiring day's work outside the home. Although Isela and Jorge had been separated for about a year and a half in 1986, she still resented his lack of concern for the bur-den her double shift placed upon her:

> Jorge is very impatient . . . I worked and getting out of work I had to go get the kids, have a clean home, the meals made . . . That was hard. And that's what he said to me, "You can't handle it." And I really can't. Maybe when I get home I'm tired, nervous. When I get home from cleaning those homes, I see my home as very messy and it makes me nervous, and I can't do anything about it.

THE WORK ETHIC

The undocumented immigrants with whom I have talked, both men and women, typically express a great deal of pride in their ability to work hard. Moreover, those who have managed to stay in an area for many years sometimes point to the contri-butions they have made to local development. I will never forget the look of satis-faction on Héctor Gómez's face as he showed me around the avocado ranch in Escondido where he works and lives. He had helped to turn the rugged mountain slopes into a bountiful forest of avocado trees.

> I've been here at this [50-acre] ranch 7 years, and at the one below we planted 40 acres in February of 1973. When I came here, I couldn't even walk through here because of the bushes, a lot of brush, a lot of snakes, coyotes. . . . There was nothing. There were no roads. There were no trees. We had to bring water to drink here and everything was work.

Héctor's temporary migrations back to Mexico ended when his wife and chil-dren joined him on the ranch, partly because he missed his family and partly be-cause his employer insisted that he stay and tend to the ranch (see chapter 7). Not only domestics live at their workplace. Farmhands such as Héctor also live at work. Héctor speaks with pride about his rise to a position of responsibility. He has as-sumed management of the ranch for his absentee owner. In exchange for his work and dependable, 24-hour-a-day presence on the ranch, Héctor receives a place to live and a salary of $12,000 a year (as of 1986).

Jorge Díaz also expresses a great deal of pride in his craftsmanship. He lays ce-ment patios and is an expert bricklayer. He now works as an independent contractor, obtaining jobs primarily through referrals by satisfied customers. He began by working for various landscapers, but spent a number of years working for a particular Anglo landscaper, whom Jorge credits with befriending him and helping him learn to interact with American customers. Since he started working independently, he continues to get job referrals from this person. One day he took me to a house (on sale for some $9 million) on a hillside overlooking the ocean in La Jolla to see some of his work. For more than a year Jorge had worked on this house, redoing patios and putting in tile floors and stonework. Jorge, like almost every other undocumented Mexican I encountered, emphasized the value of work:

> I've dedicated myself to my work which is what I like most. Many come, work, earn good salaries, then they spend all of it on alcohol. They buy cars, they wreck them. They waste their money and never accomplish anything. I know many people who have good jobs and don't have any money. They throw it all away. If you come to this country, you have to come to work and save. The opportunity is here, right? All the people who come, work. Even if it is in a yard or washing dishes, but everybody can work, legal or illegal. I feel everybody should work, even if it's only two or three times a week.

I had many occasions to interact with Jorge and the only time I saw him agitated was when he spoke of the treatment laborers receive from well-off Mexicans. In his view, laborers in the United States, regardless of race, receive more respect than those in Mexico. These feelings came out as he talked about a recent experience he had with a woman from Mexico who had just moved into a house in La Jolla and called him for an estimate on some work.

> A month and a half ago a Mexican lady called from La Jolla. She had just left Mexico City, very rich people. A neighbor who I had worked for recommended me. I went and she opened the door. She said, "Wait a minute," and slammed the door in my face. A while later she came out and told me to go to the yard and wait for her. She peered at me through the windows. So I got mad. I told her that she was looking at me as if we were in Mexico. "Pardon me," I said. "I don't have time to be waiting for you. I have many things to do. If you are trying to scrutinize me it's better that you not call me for an estimate." Later she apologized. She wanted me to do the work. So I told her that she had to wait a month or two. You can feel the discrimination from the rich that come here from Mexico. They look at you like . . . the way they look at people there. In Mexico, they look at you like you're nothing.

Jorge's story reveals not only his resentment but his pride in his work and the respect he believes he is due. Respect, Jorge believed, as did most other Mexican immigrants, is not a value reserved for those with higher education and titles, but something given to individuals who are honest and hard working. Moreover, his confidence in his skills and ability to find other work allowed him to turn down the woman's offer of work. We really do not know if Jorge would have acted in a similar way if he was working in Mexico. But what seems clear is that Jorge believed he had come to the United States to seek a better life, had worked hard, and was not about to be treated in a manner that suggested he was undeserving of respect. These values are imbedded in what might be called the immigrant ethic, the system of beliefs that undocumented immigrants express when explaining their purposes and objectives in life.

Central to this belief system among undocumented immigrants is a strong work ethic. Over and over again I heard about how they came to work and how willing they are to work hard. They are quick to assert that they did not come for a government handout or to receive welfare. Isela Díaz's comment is typical of those I heard. She was speaking of paying off the large debt to the hospital for the birth of her children: "We never liked to ask anyone for help. We wanted to work, to struggle so that these boys would have everything that they need. So they would never have to say that they had to ask for help, like Medicare, while we were able to find jobs."[6]

Angelina Ortega received government aid. However, she received it not for herself or her other children, but for her daughter, who is an American citizen and suffers from cerebral palsy. Angelina's guilt for having no other recourse but to accept government aid brings into sharp focus how this contrasts with her values:

> I feel bad about receiving the assistance because we are not really used to something like this. At home we always paid for what we ate by earning it, whether it was the mother or the father who earned it. Not like this. In a way you could say that no sacrifices are made [because of the assistance]. But it is a very great sacrifice to see my daughter like this. I think that when my daughter recuperates and she goes to school, I will look for work. If I get a job that pays for my expenses, more or less, I plan to give up the assistance.

In sum, undocumented immigrants bring with them values similar to the Protestant work ethic. They tend to rely on their own resources, or on the assistance of friends and family. They are not accustomed to governmental assistance and view dependency on the government very negatively. Ironically, it is through the ambiguous process of acculturation, that is, the acquisition of American cultural values, that such values may become challenged and possibly eroded.

ENGLISH AND WORK

With more than 10 years of work experience in San Diego, Jorge is able to communicate effectively with his clients. Although still a limited English speaker, he is able to give bids, arrange work schedules, and buy his materials. It's this ability to communicate on his own, without having to resort to an interpreter, that Jorge believes gives him an advantage over more recent immigrants in the job market. Even though he sometimes loses jobs to people who will do the work cheaper, he believes there is work enough for everybody.

> There are people who come from Tijuana who work for $6, $7, or $8 an hour for work that is worth more than $18 or $20 an hour. They come to work like that because they earn more than they can earn in Tijuana. [But] I'm not afraid of the competition. The competition is among those who don't speak English.

[6]Studies have repeatedly shown that relatively few undocumented immigrants actually use government aid programs such as welfare (Cornelius, Chavez, & Castro, 1982). Among the Mexicans I surveyed in 1986, only five had ever received food stamps, two for Aid for Families with Dependent Children for their U.S.-born children and one person for a disability he suffered while working.

According to Jorge, those who do not speak any English at all are vulnerable to being paid whatever the employer wants to pay them because they do not know how much the work is actually worth. And they may find their interpreter does not translate well or is dishonest. These are lessons Jorge has had to learn the hard way.

Many of the thousands of undocumented immigrants in the studies I have been involved in had taken a class to learn English. However, few said they were able to speak English with any proficiency. Most often, they pointed to the fact that they worked with other Spanish speakers, which offered them few opportunities to practice speaking English.

Ester Portero's experience adds another facet to the theme of English and work. After Ester and her family migrated to San Diego, Ester attended 1 year of high school. She was 27 when I interviewed her in January 1987. For many years now she has worked for the same manufacturing company, which is almost directly across from an office of the Immigration and Naturalization Service, a fact that caused her much concern when she first started working there. "You can imagine. It was right across [from the INS]. We passed each other every day. At first I was afraid, but I also knew that it was worth it to work there because the benefits were significant." Her job is in shipping, taking orders. She actually had past experience working in a factory. When she was 13 she worked for a while in a maquiladora in Tecate. As for English, she said, "I know all the terms needed for my work, but outside my job some conversations are hard for me."

A problem developed at Ester's workplace because she and some of her friends were speaking Spanish to one another. "There are several of us who speak Spanish and because we're all Mexican, naturally, it's easier for us to communicate in our own language." Her employer received a complaint from another worker, after which Ester and her coworkers were prohibited from speaking Spanish at the workplace. "They threatened to give us a warning if there was another complaint that we were speaking Spanish among us, the Latinos. After three warnings, they would discipline us." This has had the effect of making her less communicative and somewhat isolated from her coworkers. She already understands enough English to perform her job well, but is too self-conscious to attempt to express more complicated ideas in English before her non-Spanish-speaking coworkers. And she now feels as if she is under surveillance by her coworkers because of the prohibition against Spanish. As she talked about this situation anxiety was written on her face, making her look like a person under siege.

EARNINGS AND MOBILITY

The type of jobs the people in these examples had were typical of those found by undocumented immigrants. They typically found unskilled or semiskilled jobs that paid minimum wage and offered few benefits, such as paid vacations, pension plans, sick leave, and medical insurance.[7] Over time, some undocumented

---

[7]In 1986, the average wage of 66 Mexican men was $5.62 an hour, and for 39 women it was $5.07 an hour. For 70 Central American men and 36 women, it was $4.76 an hour and $4.86 an hour, respectively. The minimum wage at the time was $3.35 an hour.

immigrants are able to find jobs that may pay more or offer some benefits. Or they are able to gain experience on the job and use that to increase their earnings. Most of the people in these examples, however, had been in the United States many years before the 1986 immigration law, which made it illegal to hire undocumented workers. The law's intent was to restrict the undocumented immigrants' ability to work in the United States and, thus, inhibit their mobility in the job market. One possible effect, then, is that changing jobs to increase earnings, as found in these examples, may no longer be as possible. At least that may be the case for undocumented immigrants working in formal jobs. Undocumented immigrants working in informal jobs, such as housecleaning or landscaping, are not as affected by regulations that require workers to show identification before being hired. But such workers often view themselves as limited in the types of investment they can make in their business. Jorge noted,

> If I'm going to invest money into tools and later I don't become legalized, it would mean a loss. I'd lose. I have to wait. I need it [legalization] very badly because I have a lot of work and I can't do it because I don't have the equipment. If I had my legalization, the first thing I would get is my license, study a course for contractors and get my license. Because like this I don't have the confidence to take on large contracts because if someone asked me for my license or something, I would have problems.

Interestingly, Jorge does not believe the same way when it comes to investing in a house: "I have plans to buy a house. Anyone can buy a house. There are plenty of illegals who have homes. In Los Angeles I have cousins who are illegal, completely illegal like me. One of them works a lot and has bought two homes." Buying a home is not only possible for undocumented immigrants, some have done it.[8] Despite their relatively low-paying jobs, Enrique and Beatriz Valenzuela managed to purchase a house in 1979. Although they had not considered buying a house before, Beatriz met a woman on the bus ride to work who suggested the idea of buying a house from her relative who sold houses for a living. Her relative contacted Enrique and helped him purchase the house they now live in.

Earnings and Settlement   Although their earnings may be low when compared to those of U.S. citizens, undocumented immigrants more often compare their earnings and lifestyle with what they left back home or with what they imagine the situation to be given the economic situation as they understand it. For example, Jorge Díaz cited Mexico's economic crisis as an important reason he would not want to return to Mexico:

> Let's talk about salaries. What one earns here in the United States in one day, even if it's minimum salary, you can clothe yourself. In Mexico, in order to clothe yourself you have to work one month and if you earn a minimum salary it's impossible. The crisis will continue. The crisis is going to increase and increase.

---

[8]Among the undocumented Mexicans and Central Americans I interviewed in the summer of 1986, 7.9% of the Mexicans and 2.1% of the Central Americans had purchased their homes.

For Jorge Díaz, the disparity in earnings between Mexico and the United States is an important reason he has settled in San Diego. But as we shall see later, his concern for his family also played a part in his staying.

Work and Education   I should add one more point here on the relationship between the value of working and education. In Mexico, especially in rural areas, there is a positive value placed on work. Perhaps because educational opportunities are limited, with families having to bear many of the costs of an education (for example, books and materials), many Mexicans in rural areas, and even in relatively poor urban areas, do not go beyond a sixth-grade education. By 14 or 15 years of age, many young men and women are working. When immigrants bring family members to the United States who are already teenagers, and who have learned to expect to enter the labor force at 15 or 16, both parents and the teenagers may feel a pressure to work.

Angelina Ortega migrated from a rural area in Guanajuato. As mentioned earlier, her two teenaged children joined her in San Diego after many years of separation and after her youngest daughter was born with cerebral palsy. Her oldest son was 15 years old in 1986 and had been in San Diego less than a year. Angelina discussed the economic pressure she is under and how it relates to her son's schooling:

> I would like my older boy to work and study. But because he is young, he needs many things that I can't give him. You know, young people today go to a store, see a display, they like a pair of pants and it costs $30 to $40 . . . He tells me, "I would like this," and I tell him, "Son, right now I can't give this to you. Maybe when we hear from your father." So he told me, "Why don't you speak with the counselor and ask her if I could work a few hours a week so that I could earn some money?" So I said, "Fine, I'll call."

The school counselor was against the idea of her son working because her son had just arrived and he needed to achieve a command of English. The counselor suggested waiting until next year, when she would help him find a job after school. Angelina believes some amount of work after school would help relieve some of her economic burden and teach her son important values.

> In Mexico, we say that's how a man becomes a man, and the women, too. They start working. If they want something they must make the sacrifices to buy that thing and then they will value it. It's not just that you say, "Son, here go and buy yourself something." . . . I was ten when I started working to help my mother. But times change. I'm not pressuring him to work [full time].

This reflection on economic demands and the value of work learned early in Mexico does not mean that little value is placed on education. But teenaged migrants may desire to work and help their parents by earning money, which may lead them to enter the labor force earlier than many Americans consider appropriate. However, I believe under these circumstances it is inappropriate to stigmatize these young people and their parents as not valuing education, as being "dropouts" and having raised "dropouts." Children born or raised in the United States from an early age learn a new value system and have different opportunities for schooling beyond primary school. And quite often, parents desire their children to achieve as much education as possible (see chapter 11). Before making value judgments, we must consider the age at which the child migrated and the values he or she brings.

FINAL THOUGHTS

Many, if not most, undocumented immigrants return home after spending a few months to a couple of years in the United States. Some of the people presented in this chapter also began as temporary migrants. Even though each person may have his or her own constellation of reasons for having stayed, there are some observable patterns. Steady work is important. Even if a person changes jobs frequently, or must rely on a steady supply of new clients (for example, houses to clean or yards to work in), those who stay have a sense that jobs are available. The people in these examples also had family in San Diego, which influenced their decision to stay. For example, Federico intended to stay 8 to 10 months when he first came. But after his wife joined him, he changed his mind. Having family with them in San Diego made these examples different from most of the temporary migrants discussed in chapters 4, 5, and 6, for whom the primary family responsibilities were back home. But we must remember that settlement is selective, which means we primarily know about those who stayed. Those who returned may have done so because they were unable to find steady work, or because of their responsibilities to their family back home, or because of some combination of these and other factors.

As this suggests, work, though important, was only one of the reasons that surfaced when trying to understand why some undocumented immigrants settled in the United States. Family considerations were also central. Attitudes about opportunities back home also played a part. Less tangible, but also significant, was a commitment to "learning to live" in the United States despite their undocumented status, a theme taken up in the following chapter.

9/ Learning to Live as an "Illegal Alien"

How does life as an "illegal alien" look through the eyes of those undocumented immigrants who have spent many years in the United States? First and foremost, undocumented immigrants are constantly aware that at any moment they could be apprehended and deported from the country. They use metaphors of confinement to explain what it is like to live in a state of almost constant fear. These explanations provide insights into how they perceive their status as outsiders, as defined by the larger society.

Federico Romero's activities have been circumscribed in a way he analogizes to life in a circle:

> We feel like all [undocumented] people who are here. We are trapped in this place, in a very small circle. If we break it [the circle] the migra will arrive and throw us back. That is what we have, a fear.

Alicia Herrera's movements are bounded by the borders of the San Diego area:

> The children ask me, "Mama, why can't we go to Disneyland or other places?" I respond that we just can't. . . . I say it's better not to take chances. It's better not to venture. You feel that fear, that fear that they impose on you here.

Héctor Gómez believes that he and his family live as if in a chicken coop:

> Right now we're, as they say, in a chicken coop. If we leave, we can't come back. So we have to stay there even if we don't want to. If we were legal, we'd have more freedom; freedom to go out, to visit Mexico, for recreation, and we wouldn't have problems.

Enrique Valenzuela describes his many years in San Diego as similar to being in jail:

> In all these 16 years I feel like I've been in jail. I don't feel free. I came to this country to work, not to do things on the street that you shouldn't do. That's not what I mean by freedom. I'm referring to the feeling of being in a prison because if you go out, like when we go out for fun, it's always in the back of your mind, will immigration show up? Or when you go to work you think all the time, from the moment you walk out of your home, you think, "Will the immigration stop me on the way or when I'm at work?" So I do feel like I'm in jail.

As Enrique and I talked about his feeling of being in jail, a song popular at the time, "Jaula de Oro" ("The Gilded Cage")[1], came up in our conversation. He felt the song echoed his situation and that of many undocumented immigrants who

---

[1]"Jaula de Oro," performed by Los Tigres del Norte, produced by Profono Internacional, Inc., 1985.

have been in the United States for many years. Two of the verses are particularly apt here:

Aquí estoy establecido en los Estados Unidos. Diez años pasaron ya en que cruzé de mojado. Papeles no me he arreglado sigo siendo ilegal.	Here I am established in the United States. It's been 10 years since I crossed as a wetback. I never applied for papers, I'm still illegal.
¿De qué me sirve el dinero si yo soy como prisionero dentro de esta gran nación? Cuando me acuerdo hasta lloro aunque la jaula sea de oro, no deja de ser prisión.	What good is money if I am like a prisoner in this great nation? When I think about it, I cry. Even if the cage is made of gold, it doesn't make it less a prison.

Enrique believed that the song described his situation to a degree. But he wanted to make it clear that when the singer speaks of "gold" it does not mean that he is rich. It merely means that he has a job and an income. "I don't feel free, but we don't have a lot of money, either."

All these statements have in common the idea of being encapsulated within a larger social system. Describing themselves as being in jail, living within in a circle or a chicken coop, and feeling confined within San Diego's borders are all ways of relating how their undocumented status places limits on their incorporation into society. Although they work and live in San Diego, their movements are ultimately constrained. Their agreement on a lack of freedom of movement emphasizes that even though they are inside a larger social system, they are not fully part of that social system. Their incorporation has not been complete.

HOME AS A REFUGE

To allay some of the constant fear of apprehension and deportation, undocumented immigrants attempt to create some security through a network of friends and relatives. They tend to live near relatives and friends who had previously migrated or by people who they themselves helped to migrate and become established in the area. But at the heart of this attempt to create some sense of security is their home, which becomes a retreat, a place of refuge, a sanctuary in which they are less visible than on the streets or at work.

For Beatriz and Enrique Valenzuela, being home offers some relief from their daily fears. Beatriz leaves home as the sun rises and walks about 10 blocks to the bus stop. She has been robbed of her bus money twice while walking along the road. She then rides a series of buses to arrive in La Jolla, a trip that takes about an hour and a half. She returns late in the afternoon. Enrique leaves for work at about 10 A.M. and returns home at about 10:30 at night. During the week, Enrique rarely is able to talk with his family. His daughter and son both attend school during the day. On Sundays, the Valenzuela family finally has the opportunity to interact with one another.

With their family outside of the home most of the time, Enrique and Beatriz constantly worry about one of the family being apprehended. Only when they are all at home do they feel a sense of security. As Beatriz said, "When one is at home, one feels secure. We are always concerned with the danger of the immigration [agents] on the bus. I'm always in danger. When I arrive home, it's then that I can rest and feel content. Because there is always fear of walking the streets." Enrique agreed:

> When we are all at home, [Sunday], is the only day that we are all happy, because it is that day that we all feel very secure, secure no matter what the danger. My wife is the first to leave. When she leaves the fear begins. Then, when my children leave, the same fear. Finally, when I leave, well all day long while I am at work, it is all I think about, that something could happen to us, because of the status that we have in this country.

Enrique and Beatriz carry these fears around with them during the day. Although Enrique has never been apprehended, he still becomes full of fear when he spots an immigration officer. Enrique and Beatriz believe that everything they have managed to acquire over almost two decades in the United States could easily be lost. In 1979, they purchased a modest two-bedroom home in a low-income area. They have appliances, a television, a car. And yet they realize that they live in a house of cards that could easily come tumbling down. As Enrique said, "At night I dream about it, that they catch me. That everything caves in." Beatriz added, "It's true. You're terrorized. I have nightmares!"

Once again, the song "Jaula de Oro" speaks to the fears held by undocumented immigrants and the security they often seek in seclusion:

De mi trabajo a mi casa. Yo no sé lo que me | From my job to my home. I don't know
pasa aunque soy hombre de hogar. Casi no | what is happening to me. I am a homebody.
salgo a la calle pues tengo miedo que me | I almost never go out to the street. I am
hallen y me puedan deportar. | afraid I will be found and could be deported.

For many undocumented immigrants who have formed a family in the United States, such as Enrique and Beatriz, one of their greatest fears is that a family member might be apprehended. When a spouse or child is late coming home, the fear quickly sets in that the person has been apprehended. Wives who do not work and who do not have a great deal of experience interacting with the larger society are particularly fearful of their husband's sudden apprehension. Dolores was actually in a state of panic when she was interviewed in September 1986. She had been in the United States for 2 years and had worked cleaning houses, but had quit work when her 6-month-old daughter was born. Her husband worked in the agricultural fields and had been apprehended just 3 days before the interview and had not yet returned. She was at a loss about what action she should take. Without a job, understanding little English, and without money, she did not know if she should wait or go to Tijuana to look for him. Patricia Romero expressed her feelings about being in such a vulnerable position:

> It is very difficult to be shut in here for years. He is exposed daily. I don't know if he is going to come home or not. It's something to think about. I also have to think about the children. He is the one who works. I can't do that because I don't understand English. I can't expose myself and go to a school [to learn English] and leave my family, my children.

Angelina Ortega, a single mother, wonders if her children will return from school. Her son often stays after school to practice running on the track. "I'm always wondering if he will make it home. Did they get him? Will immigration get him? That is my fear."

I heard such fears echoed many times by undocumented immigrants. Since the possibility of apprehension plays such an important role in their lives, it is a common theme that arises when people talk about their experiences. Undocumented immigrants I have interviewed all had their stories of close calls and actual detentions. These experiences are part of what it means to live as an "illegal alien."

Contact with immigration agents can happen suddenly, often when it is least expected. María Delgado lives south of downtown San Diego. The small house she rents is on a busy street in an area where mostly Mexican Americans and Latino immigrants live. She is a single mother and lives with her two children, Natalia, a ninth grader, and Marco, an eleventh grader. She works cleaning homes and has learned enough English to communicate with her employers. Although she has had a number of close calls, María had never been stopped by the INS until the summer before I interviewed her in 1987. María and her daughter had backed the car out of the alley behind the house and brought the car to the front of the house, along the busy street. Across the street from their house was an INS van, parked in front of a restaurant. As María told the story,

> I told my daughter not to look because immigration was over there. She asked me why I was afraid. I told her I wasn't afraid because they weren't going to do anything to us. My son came out of the house and he didn't notice either. He got into the car and I told him not to look, that immigration was back there. At that moment the immigration officers ran and got into their van.

María slowly drove away from in front of her house. The immigration officers followed her for three blocks and then turned on their red lights. María stopped her car.

> An immigration officer got off running, another one did too from the other side. So I asked the officers, "Now what did I do wrong?" in English. Then he asked, "Are you a U.S. citizen? What's your citizenship?" I said, "U.S." He asked, "May I question your passengers?" I said, "Yes, why not? Go ahead." Each officer questioned one of them, and they were interrogating them.

Fortunately, María and her children had practiced for such a day. Marco listed the elementary and junior high schools he supposedly attended and the high school he was presently attending. As for Natalia, "They asked me where I was born. And I said Mercy Hospital." According to María, the officers appeared satisfied with the answers. "He said, 'That's all, you can go.' When they said that we could go I was shaking."

For undocumented immigrants, any unsuspecting moment can turn into a dangerous confrontation with the authorities. The sudden appearance of immigration agents shatters their normal routine. When they escape detection it is attributed to luck. The lucky ones have yet to be fingered by fate. They avoid detection for years, or when stopped, they are able to slip through the net, like María and her children did. Others are not so lucky. They have been stopped and apprehended, after which their lives then revolve around the implications of their apprehension.

IMPLICATIONS OF BEING APPREHENDED

When undocumented immigrants are apprehended, they are offered two alternatives: They can sign a voluntary departure, after which they are escorted out of the country, or they can exercise their right to a hearing in front of an immigration judge to argue for a suspension of deportation. Recent migrants typically sign the voluntary departure form and return to their native country. The advantage of this alternative is that a voluntary departure is not considered a formal deportation. It is not held against the individual at a later date should they try to become a legal immigrant. Oftentimes, temporary migrants take a voluntary departure and then attempt to recross the border as soon as possible.

Undocumented immigrants who have been in the United States many years, especially more than 7 years, are less willing to sign a voluntary departure form. For undocumented immigrants who desire to legalize their status in the United States, taking a voluntary departure has some negative consequences. At the time I conducted fieldwork undocumented immigrants with 7 years of U.S. residence could attempt to "adjust" their status, that is, ask an immigration judge to "suspend," or stop, their deportation and grant them legal residence. Should an undocumented immigrant sign a voluntary departure and leave the country, the amount of time they have been in the United States, in essence, becomes erased, and the clock begins again when they return. This is an important reason for undocumented immigrants not to take the voluntary departure option if they have already lived in the United States for a number of years.

Asking for a formal hearing, however, is a risky strategy. One of the major criteria undocumented immigrants must be able to show an immigration judge is that he or she would suffer a "noneconomic hardship."[2] Although this is somewhat vague, it means, as far as I can understand it, that a suspension of deportation is not granted because immigrants will lose their job and their income or because they might lose any assets, such as a home or car or seniority at the job. Not being able to earn a decent living in their native country would also not be sufficient grounds for winning a suspension of deportation. Other seemingly noneconomic hardships, such as separating family members, are also not suitable criteria. For example, deported parents must make the decision to take with them children, such as those born in the United States, or to leave them behind in the United States with a guardian. Possible separation of family members as a result of deportation is insufficient grounds for winning a suspension case. I happened to testify in a case that actually won a suspension of deportation. It involved a man with a quadraplegic son. The argument in this case was that the man's son would face a tremendous hardship without his father to help him obtain health services in this country, and

---

[2]The 1996 immigration law has made suspension of deportation even harder to get. New regulations include 10 years of U.S. residence, and a U.S. citizen must be adversely affected.

the boy would not find adequate health services should the father take his son with him to Mexico.

Given the somewhat ambiguous nature of the criteria for satisfying a "noneconomic hardship," suspension of deportation cases are difficult to win. Should the case be lost, the person is then formally deported from the country, which potentially ruins any future chance of becoming a legal immigrant to the United States. In practice, the decision can be appealed.

Undocumented immigrants can also request a hearing for political asylum. They typically have to prove their life would be endangered if they returned to their native country, a task that often requires supporting documents, such as an arrest record or proof of previous experiences of torture. Then again, politics also seems to play a role in that applicants from countries with governments that the United States has supported (friendly governments) have had a lesser chance of obtaining political asylum than those from unfriendly, especially Communist, governments (Pedraza-Bailey, 1985). For example, in the fiscal year 1988–89, few Salvadorans or Guatemalans were granted asylum (4.2 and 4.3%, respectively) compared to those from Cuba (15.8%), Nicaragua (26.8%), the Soviet Union (84.2%), or Romania (90.1%); (Soble, 1990).

Quite often, undocumented immigrants are unaware of the ins and outs of immigration law. They experience the trauma of being detained. If they have not been in the United States for much time, they typically depart voluntarily. But many of those who have stayed a number of years in the United States have sought information on the legalization process from attorneys or legal consultants. When they are apprehended, they are aware that they should not sign a voluntary departure. With this brief background in immigration procedures, let's examine how apprehension affects the lives of undocumented immigrants.

APPREHENSION EXPERIENCES

During Héctor Gómez's first few years working in San Diego, he recollects he must have been apprehended and sent back to Mexico at least 15 times. But when his wife, Felicia, and five children joined him on the avocado farm, he began to take apprehension more seriously. Life on the avocado farm for Héctor's family was difficult. Héctor's employer allowed the family to sleep in a small room in the garage used to store the ranch's truck and other maintenance materials.

The garage provided a place to sleep, but Felicia and the children could not stay in there during the day. The garage was used for work and was also located right next to the street. Immigration agents would often stop at the garage and look around for undocumented workers. According to Felicia, "When I came here I suffered a lot here, perhaps even more than he did. Immigration would arrive over at that large garage and they would snoop around. I would try to quiet the kids. As soon as the two older ones left for school, I would leave the garage."

As a consequence, Felicia spent most of the day amidst the avocado trees. She would wash clothes just as she had in the rural community she left behind. "I would wash on a rock, but it seemed easier because there was plenty of water." When it rained, Felicia and the children sought refuge under an overhanging rock. Looking back on that time, she said, "We slept in the garage, but I lived under the rocks."

Since Héctor was now the full-time supervisor of the avocado farm, his employer built a small house for him and his family a good distance from the road and virtually invisible behind the avocado trees. Unfortunately, this did not shield the family from apprehension. One day, immigration agents arrived at the farm and asked Héctor for his documents. They then went to the house and apprehended Felicia and the children. They then took the family to the school and took the older children out of class.

The Gómez's oldest child, Guadalupe, was about 10 years old at the time she and her brothers and sisters were taken out of school by INS agents. When I interviewed her she was a senior in high school and planned to attend San Diego State University the following year. But she remembered well the embarrassment she felt when pulled from class:

> It was embarrassing. It's very hard because you don't know what to do. Kids get embarrassed as easy as grown-ups do. . . . They just came in and took us and there wasn't any time for anybody to ask us anything. . . . Everybody is just making fun of you, or they just watch and it's embarrassing for you even if they don't make fun of you, because you're different from everybody else. At least I felt different at the time because nobody else gets taken like that. It was embarrassing and I had to live with it.

Héctor and his family signed voluntary departures and were taken to Tijuana. Héctor, Felicia, and their five young children went to the Soccer Field that night and attempted to recross the border.

> We walked all night through the hills. The little girl was a year and a half [old] and we all spent the night walking. That night we were crossing and while passing under a bridge, the migra was there in the dark. So they got us easily. They said, "Stop. All of you, hands on your head." They stopped us and frisked us and the officer said, "Let's go to Mexico." And they threw us out. The next day we crossed using a different way. I don't even know where. I'm not familiar with that area. We walked more than half the night. We spent the night there sleeping under the brush because the area was full of migra at that time. So we stayed to sleep under the brush until it got later, around dawn, and then walked again. That's how we struggled to get back.

Two years later, in 1980, Héctor and his family were going to the beach in Oceanside. As he turned into the parking area, a police officer ordered him to pull his car over. "I thought I had made a wrong turn. I looked for a stop sign or some kind of sign. But I didn't see anything." The police officer asked Héctor for his driver's license, which he kept, and then he called the immigration authorities. When the immigration officer arrived, Héctor told him "I have 8 or 9 years around here. My family has 3 years here." Héctor was perplexed as to why the police officer stopped him in the first place:

> I asked, "Why are you treating me like I am such a big criminal?" And they never told me if I had made an error there. Why didn't the police officer give me a ticket? I believe it was just a bad joke that the police officer had done to us to be cruel. I believe that he should never have intervened at all.

The officer then took Héctor and his family to the San Clemente checkpoint. Héctor had consulted an immigration attorney shortly before this incident. Based upon the lawyer's advice, Héctor refused to sign a voluntary departure, which began a long process of hearings, deportation dates, and appeals. Héctor successfully used the court system to delay his family's deportation and is still living in Escondido. The story of how the Gómez family was able to generate community support for their cause is taken up later.

Isela Díaz's husband, Jorge, was apprehended at work one day soon after they had arrived in San Diego. Their oldest son, Alberto, was almost 3 months old at the time. Isela and Jorge were living with another couple, also undocumented. At about 7 P.M., Isela received a call from the wife of one of Jorge's coworkers, telling her that Jorge had been apprehended. Jorge called her shortly thereafter, saying he would try and cross that night. When he didn't show up, Isela went to Tijuana. Since she had a local border-crossing permit, she was able to cross the border without any problem. She took Jorge some fresh clothes, which he needed since he had tried to cross at the beach area, but was unsuccessful, and all wet. For Isela, Jorge's apprehension proved to be an important lesson. She would also have to work outside the home.

> It was very difficult for me because at that time I didn't work either. I was worried that he couldn't return to the United States and we [still] had to pay back the money we owed to the hospital. That's what worried me the most. It was that night when he returned that he decided that I too had to start working in order to quickly pay the money back and not have any problems.

Jorge's sudden apprehension made him and his wife realize how important it was for both of them to work, so that they could remove themselves from debt. Both of them working would also ensure that they would continue to have income should one of them be apprehended. Rather than making them think it was time to leave the United States and return home, apprehension forced them to take precautions against the setbacks caused by apprehension.

When undocumented immigrants are apprehended, they often experience a great deal of pressure to sign a voluntary departure form. When a person becomes defiant, as did Beatriz Valenzuela, the pressure can mount. Beatriz's experience reveals both the tragedy and the comedy of the situation.

Beatriz's greatest fear, for almost 18 years, had been that she would be apprehended while riding the bus to work in La Jolla. On July 9, 1986, that fear became a reality. During that week, the immigration authorities were boarding most of the buses entering La Jolla in search of "illegal aliens" who worked in the beach community's restaurants, hotels, and private homes. On that day, Beatriz's bus arrived on La Jolla Boulevard at about 6:40 A.M. With officers stationed at the doors in front and back of the bus to ensure no one could jump off, officers asked the occupants for their documents. Not having any, Beatriz was asked to get off the bus. Because they were interested in legalizing their status, Beatriz and Enrique had consulted a lawyer whose advice was not to sign a voluntary departure, but to ask for a court hearing. Armed with this knowledge, Beatriz was ready when the immigration agent suggested signing a voluntary departure.

He took out a piece of paper and told me that we were going to fill it out right now, so you can sign it, so that you can go to Tijuana. I told him that I was not going to sign anything. Why should I? He said, "You aren't going to sign?" I said, "No." He said, "Do you know how many years await you in jail?" I said, "No." He said, "You can expect 2 or 3 years in jail." I said, "Really." He said, "Yes, really, and all because you don't want to sign this document. If you sign it right now, you'll be taken to Tijuana. But if you don't sign it, it will go real bad for you." I said, "Well, too bad. If you're going to feed me in jail and I don't have to work, then that's a vacation for me!"

The immigration agents took Beatriz to a detention center near the border, where she stayed for 3 days. Beatriz remembers it well, since one of those days was her birthday. Three days later Beatriz was released, after Enrique posted a $2,000 bond to guarantee that she would appear at a court hearing.

Carolina, Beatriz's oldest child, was 13 when her mother was pulled off the bus and detained. Carolina's reactions to the news of her mother's arrest reflects the confused fears of a young child and her lack of experience with life in Mexico, the country of her birth. She said,

I was worried that we were going to be sent back to Mexico, that we had to go back and live like those people, without any homes. They have to sleep in the streets, sell anything, like gum. There was going to be no food. Maybe I couldn't go to school because my parents needed money. . . . We were going to lose everything we had here. . . . I was afraid that maybe my brother [age 11] had to stay here, and we had to go, because he's an American citizen. And maybe the government would send him to some kind of shelter for kids that don't have homes or anything. Maybe he was going to miss his parents and me.

Carolina's fears pictured the worst-case scenario, much of which was based on stereotypes of the poverty that exists in Tijuana. But even given that her depiction of possible events may not have been realistic, it was a vivid image in her mind. She suddenly found the future security of her home and family in doubt. She was caught up in events over which she had no control and little understanding. The only thing she knew at the time was that her life had the possibility of being turned upside-down, changing from one of hope to one of despair. Carolina's fears of her brother's separation from the family because of his different status—born in the United States and therefore a U.S. citizen—reflects the types of stress found in binational families.

Undocumented immigrants such as Beatriz often use public transportation to get to work. Knowing this, immigration agents target buses for inspection. But not only adults use the buses. Schoolchildren sometimes use public transportation to get to and from school. I sat one December afternoon in 1986 with Alicia Herrera in front of her lawyer's office in downtown San Diego. Alicia had taken part of the day off (which meant a considerable loss of income to this single mother) to come in from Encinitas and visit her lawyer because her two sons were apprehended while waiting for a bus after school. When they had not arrived home from school by early evening, Alicia became worried something had happened to them. Then she received the dreaded phone call:

They run in school, and when they were done running and practicing I didn't have time to pick them up. They decided to go on the bus. They were waiting for the bus when the immigration officials arrived . . . They took both of them, my older boy [age 17] and this son of 14. I was worried when the phone rang and my son told me that the [immigration] official would not let him go.

Alicia's sons believed that they were somewhat insulated from being apprehended. They had been in the United States for about 6 years, spoke English, and knew enough to provide a seemingly reasonable history of schooling in the local area. But all of this helped them little when the moment arrived, as Alicia's 14-year-old son, Aurelio's, description of events illustrates:

We were standing waiting for the bus. Then an immigration official came and started asking us questions. We were answering the questions in English. Later, after we answered correctly every question he asked, the immigration official got mad. The bus arrived that goes by my house and I was going to get on it. The official said, "No," that I should wait. So I waited with my brother. He asked us more questions and we answered them. Then the official made us board the van. Then later he asked how long we had been here. We told him that since '80. He said that if we didn't tell the truth that my older brother would go to jail for a year. We told him that we were telling the truth. So he said he was going to take us to Tijuana. They took us to Chula Vista and my brother called my mother.

The question of how long the boys had been in San Diego gets at the issue of the voluntary departure. Their mother asked friends for the name of an immigration attorney, who advised her to request a court hearing for her sons and for her to attempt to legalize her status under the legalization program of the 1986 Immigration Law. But even with the prospect of legalization, Alicia found apprehension cost her emotionally, not to mention the financial strain caused by days of lost work.

The disruption caused by apprehension can sometimes be severe, with a jail term a possibility. Federico found himself in what seemed to him a bizarre situation shortly after leaving his job at the electronic equipment store in 1982. He found work as a taxi driver, which he did for 10 to 12 hours a day and for which he earned about $65 a day. Federico liked to work the downtown area and the airport. One day, a fare asked him to take him to the border. After dropping off the fare, Federico collected a couple of passengers who asked to be taken to Chula Vista. Before he could drop them off, Federico was stopped by the police, who said he was going too fast. The police officer then told Federico he would have to wait because he suspected the passengers were "illegal."

The police officer radioed for assistance from the Border Patrol, which soon arrived on the scene. Federico described the drama that then took place:

The Border Patrol came and took them out of the car. He asked one of the people I was taking, who was fair-skinned, he looked white, "Are you American?" He answered "Yes." [The officer] said, "Where were you born?" He answered, "I was born in Chicago," but with a pretty bad accent. He mispronounced it because he said "Chacago." [The officer] said, "You son of a . . . come over here," and grabbed him by the jacket.

By then he had my license. He asked me, "Are you American?" I said, "Yes, sir." He said, "You know that it's illegal to carry those kinds of people?" I said, "I'm sorry, but that's not my job." He said, "What's your name?" I said, "Officer, you have my license." I don't know what he did. Maybe he called by radio to ask who I was. He said, "Are you sure you're an American?" Then I told him that I wasn't going to answer any more questions. "Go ahead and arrest me if you don't think I'm an American." He said, "OK. Let's find out."

So he started to dig. "Where were you born?" I said, "San Diego." And we started to converse all in English. "Here it says you were born in Mexico. You want to hear it?" Well, what could I do then? "You lied to me." He then called me a very dirty name. He said, "You're a fucking wetback, man." I said, "Well, maybe I am, man, but I try to do the best I can to live, you know." He said, "I don't give a shit. You just come with me." And they took me to the San Ysidro checkpoint.

Federico was not offered the voluntary departure form. Instead, he found himself prosecuted for smuggling aliens in his taxi and for his own illegal entry to the United States. Federico found this incredible and told his court-appointed attorney, the prosecutor, the judge, and anyone else who would listen, "I'm not an immigration officer, or an officer of any kind, to ask anybody boarding my taxi for papers." A plea bargain was finally reached and the charge of smuggling aliens was dropped. Federico was sentenced to 45 days in jail for illegal entry. Patricia, Federico's wife was aghast. She said,

I knew about three people [in San Diego]. It was something that destroyed me. My daughter was just a baby then. A baby daughter, without money, without anything, and with the sadness to see my husband detained, he who had never in his life set foot in a place like that [jail] or been charged with anything. It was very difficult for me.

Patricia managed to scrape by for the 45 days Federico spent in the Metropolitan Correctional Center, located in downtown San Diego. After Federico was escorted to the border and deported he soon made his way back to San Diego. Now that he had been formally deported, however, Federico's time clock had stopped. His residency, for legalization purposes, now began in 1982, rather than 1979. Dates, although a minor point to some, are very important as far as the law is concerned. To qualify for the general legalization program established under the 1986 immigration law, undocumented immigrants had to have been in the United States prior to January 1, 1982. Thus when I interviewed Federico in December 1986, his arrest for driving a taxi with undocumented immigrants was causing him no end of anxiety, and he cursed his bad luck.

FEAR AND BEHAVIOR

Undocumented immigrants often do things to try to minimize their chances of being apprehended. For example, Jorge Díaz did not want to return to Mexico to visit his parents because that would mean he would have to recross the border clandestinely. So his parents came to Tijuana. Jorge went to Imperial Beach, which is on the U.S. side of the border, and his parents went to Playas, on the Mexican side. They visited there, on the beach, each careful not to cross over to the other side lest they arouse the interest of the Border Patrol agent watching from the hill above. Jorge also believes that how one presents oneself is important. His work in construction causes him to drive throughout the San Diego area and even to other parts of southern California. To reduce his risk of being apprehended, he is careful how he appears to immigration agents:

> I imagine that how you present yourself counts a lot; if you're nervous or how you dress. In terms of the car, too. I've noticed that sometimes any Mexican that is in a dirty, poorly cared for car, they stop him immediately. Sometimes I go around sloppily dressed, but I always keep the truck clean at work.

Jorge believes his strategy is effective. He frequently passes through the San Clemente and Temecula checkpoints with little problem. Once, at the San Clemente checkpoint, an immigration agent stopped him because his car rode suspiciously low in the rear, as if he were carrying people in the trunk. When the agent saw the cement and other work material, he let Jorge go after a few simple questions. Jorge points with pride at his ability to escape detection, noting that he has even put in a patio for an immigration agent.

Because of their fear of detection, undocumented immigrants sometimes behave in ways that carry with them negative implications. For example, Angelina Ortega chose to deliver her son at home rather than risk being apprehended at a hospital. The year was 1979 and she was in Los Angeles at the time she became pregnant. She went to a major hospital serving low-income patients in the South-Central Los Angeles area because she had heard that the hospital charged reasonable rates and accepted payments from patients without medical insurance. In Mexico, she had not sought prenatal care for her two previous pregnancies, believing that since she was not sick she did not need to see a doctor. In Los Angeles, however, she did seek prenatal care. On her second visit, she saw a sign that caused her not to return:

> They told me that I had one week to go [until delivery]. So I got down [from the examining table]. When I got down, I saw a sign that said that immigration was around and that they were only going to serve people with green cards [immigration papers]. So I got scared.

Rather than return to the hospital, Angelina asked her mother and sister to come up from San Diego and help her deliver the baby. Her mother had been helping other women deliver their babies in Guanajuato since she became a widow a few years earlier. Conveniently, she was visiting Angelina's sister at the time.

After her son was born, Angelina made several appointments for him to see a doctor but never kept those appointments. As she said, "At that time we were told that if we said we had a child from here that they would throw us out. So the boy never received medical attention of any kind." Even though she intended to keep those appointments, the fear that INS agents would find her at the hospital kept her away. Even when her son was 2 years old and having convulsions from an extremely high fever, Angelina chose to care for him at home with cold baths and Tylenol. In her mind, seeking medical care could lead to deportation, and "Because actually you could live better here and we were working, well, I couldn't but think that I didn't want to have to go back [to Mexico]."

Angelina's fear of delivering in the hospital and of taking her son to see a doctor after the delivery has had important consequences. Her son does not have a birth certificate. He has no proof that he was born in the United States. Without such proof, he is not an American citizen. Since he was born in the United States, without a birth certificate, he also does not have status as a Mexican citizen. In essence, he is a child without a country.

Angelina found that when it came time to enroll her son in school, his lack of a birth certificate presented problems. "They didn't keep him in kindergarten. He only had a half of a year of kindergarten, then they took him out. I went to talk to the teachers and they told me as long as my son didn't have a birth certificate, he could not attend school." Angelina's solution was to purchase a fake birth certificate for her son so that he could attend school. She later tried to obtain a legitimate birth certificate with the help of a social service agency but was unsuccessful, primarily because a medical doctor had not seen her son as an infant.

SEEKING THE SECURITY OF DOCUMENTATION

Fake documents are a way for undocumented immigrants to get around some of the legal requirements that restrict their behavior. Not only birth certificates, but social security cards and green cards (which identify the bearer as a legal immigrant resident) are also readily available. One fellow had been using a forged green card and social security card, which he had purchased for $120, since 1979. Like many other undocumented immigrants with fake social security cards, he had even filed income tax forms under the number and had not had any problems. The employer sanctions provisions of the 1986 immigration law gave an unintended boost to counterfeiting such documents. The law established that all job applicants had to show identification that establishes their citizenship or legal residency. As a result, counterfeit social security cards and green cards are now readily available in the southern California black market for $45 a set, sometimes even cheaper. As Jorge Díaz anticipated, "The Mexican is very clever. As soon as the law [becomes effective] they are going to create documents, the way they have with green cards and social security cards. The faked things will continue to go on."

Buying fake documents is a way to get around certain types of requirements that undocumented immigrants encounter. But undocumented immigrants also turn to lawyers and legal consultants for assistance *(ampararse)* when they get apprehended. Oftentimes, they do this merely because they know the lawyer will be able to buy them time by filing legal papers. In the meantime, they are able to work until their case is finally decided by a judge. As Jorge Díaz said, "Many illegals are being caught now. The lawyers take $2,000 or $3,000 deposit [to take the case] and help them to stay. But sometimes you lose the money that the lawyer makes for not doing anything."

Undocumented immigrants who have been in the United States many years often desire to become legalized, which makes them easy targets for unscrupulous lawyers or by individuals who are not lawyers but operate as "immigration consultants." Often these consultants are notary publics, which causes some confusion in the minds of Mexican immigrants. In Mexico, notary publics are lawyers, whereas here they usually are not. Consequently, many undocumented immigrants assume the notary public they see advertising as an immigration consultant is also a lawyer.

Because of their desire to legalize their status, undocumented immigrants seek out lawyers and immigration consultants, sometimes with disastrous consequences, as with Enrique and Beatriz Valenzuela.

In 1976, after their son José was born in San Diego, Enrique and Beatriz sought legal advice on legalizing their status. They had heard that a U.S. citizen child could apply to have his or her parents enter the country as legal immigrants. Unfortunately, the law had changed so that a child must be 21 years old before being able to assist his or her parents to immigrate legally.

The "lawyer" they sought out had been recommended by a friend. As Enrique said, since the law had changed, "The lawyer, who said he was a lawyer, said he couldn't do anything more. The only thing was to wait for amnesty." For amnesty for Enrique, Beatriz, and their daughter Carolina, the "lawyer" charged them $700, with half due immediately, and the rest after the case was completed. According to Enrique, "From 1977 to 1980–81, he couldn't do anything. Amnesty wasn't getting here."

Enrique then asked him if there was any other way to legalize his family's status. "He said that there was another way, but it was expensive. He said that it came to about $5,000. I asked if it was a sure way. He said that in 90% of the cases it was. He said that we had been here a long time and it would be possible. I told him that we had some money saved, but it was all that we had."

Enrique gave the "lawyer" $1,000 that day. He then arranged to pay $200 a month until he paid $2,500. The other half would be due when the case was over. However, there arose additional expenses in the case for which the "lawyer" needed more money. "He said if you don't pay more then that's the end of everything, and you lose all you've put into it [the case]." Enrique and Beatriz believed that something was wrong, since the initial agreement was to only pay half of the total cost before the case was settled. But they paid nonetheless. The reason: fear. As Enrique noted,

> The man didn't threaten me, but we were afraid. When he required the second half from me, after I had paid him the first, we were very afraid. So we continued paying. Not so much for ourselves, because we knew he was cheating us, but because if we didn't finish paying he would denounce us [to the immigration authorities].

Two years later, Enrique confronted the "lawyer." Enrique was angry because nothing had been done and he had paid everything requested of him. The man's response, according to Enrique, was that "It was a matter for the courts, they should be calling us."

As it turned out, Enrique soon found out that the "lawyer" had a partner, another lawyer, who was also involved in the case. When this second lawyer died shortly after Enrique's confrontation with his original "lawyer," he found his case had been taken over by yet another lawyer. At this point the original "lawyer" directed Enrique to see the new lawyer about his case. "He now didn't have any more to do with my case."

Enrique went to the new lawyer and found out something surprising and disturbing. Virtually nothing had been done on his case. There were no legal papers filed (so the court would not be "calling"). Moreover, "We thought he was a lawyer, but later when he told us that he couldn't continue our case any longer and sent us to another lawyer, it was the other lawyer who told us that he wasn't a lawyer. He was a notary public." The real lawyer, who had died, was actually the lawyer of record on the case.

As we sat in his living room, the center of the only island of security he had in San Diego, Enrique just shook his head in disbelief. He had sought to increase his security and instead became a victim of those who prey on the misfortunes of others. As he said, "It's not fair that they steal from us in this way without doing anything. We earn our money as quickly as we can and it is not much that we can save. It's easy for them to take it away quickly." Beatriz was clearly angry when she reflected on the years they were involved with this person and the money they spent:

> In order to meet his installments we had to cut back and deny ourselves other things that we needed, for us and our children. We had to pay $200 every month, every month. It made me sick to think that over here we had to limit ourselves a lot because of him, and it's not fair.

Unfortunately, Enrique and Beatriz's experience is not uncommon. Undocumented immigrants who have lived in the United States for many years, have families, and fear that detection and apprehension will destroy everything they have worked for provide easy targets for schemers who dangle the dream of security that comes with documentation. Enrique and Beatriz's experience was just one of the many, sometimes bitter, lessons undocumented immigrants encounter as they learn to live in the United States.

10 / Incorporation

Juan Rios lives on his employer's property in El Cajon, a community east of downtown San Diego. In 1984, Juan's employer brought Juan to San Diego specifically to take care of fighting cocks. This was the same person for whom Juan had worked in the rural Mexican community of El Colorado in Nayarit. Juan left behind his wife and four children, to whom he sends most of his earnings. Juan has had little opportunity to interact with the larger society and will return to his family in Mexico after about another year, when "my boss finds someone to leave in my place."

Leonor Guerrero has worked as a live-in maid for the same employer since she arrived in San Diego 3 years earlier. She left her three young children in Jalisco after being abandoned by her husband. At this point, Leonor intends to go back. "My life is in Mexico, next to my parents and children." As for her interactions with the larger society in San Diego: "I live isolated from all its [society's] ways of living and the memory of my Mexico doesn't leave me." Over the years, the greatest difficulty Leonor has had to overcome has been loneliness.

Esperanza González's husband, a farmworker, had been picked up by immigration officials just 3 days before I interviewed her. She had no idea of his whereabouts. She was frightened, alone with her 3-month-old daughter, without legal immigration documents, and with little money. She had been in San Diego for 2 years. Although her husband was opposed to the idea, Esperanza desired to return to her hometown of Guzman, Jalisco. She has found the loneliness, her lack of English, and now the apprehension of her husband too much to bear. "It is very sad to be illegal. One suffers a lot. It is better to be in Mexico, safe and tranquil."

These examples reflect one end of a continuum of the incorporation of undocumented immigrants into American society. Outside of work, the above individuals interact little with the larger society. Yet we have also seen those undocumented immigrants who have settled in San Diego. They are at the other end of the continuum: They have learned to work in the U.S. labor market. They have established relationships with employers. They have achieved some fluency in English. They have formed social networks of friends and family.

In this final chapter, I want to move the focus away from the lives of relatively recent arrivals (such as those presented in the examples above) and examine more closely the incorporation of settled undocumented immigrants into the local community. To do this, it is useful to examine various facets, or modes, of incorporation: economic, social, linguistic, cultural, and personal. Although I will discuss these modes of incorporation separately, in reality they are as interwoven as the various threads in a rope. Each aspect of incorporation influences the other modes.

ECONOMIC INCORPORATION

It is easy to see how undocumented immigrants are incorporated into the local economy. Indeed, every chapter in this book includes examples of the work performed by undocumented immigrants. Work affects almost all other aspects of the undocumented immigrants' lives, including their plans for migrating and settling in San Diego, as we saw in chapter 8.

Undocumented immigrants who are able to develop relationships with employers and find relatively secure employment have established important economic links to American society. These ties are important considerations for undocumented immigrants who are considering staying in San Diego. Indeed, they are so important that the 1986 immigration law tried to discourage their formation by making it illegal to hire undocumented workers. The employer-sanctions provisions in the law require employers to check the identification of all workers to ensure they can legally work in the United States. Employers who hire undocumented immigrants face possible fines and even time in jail. In this way, the larger society discourages the economic integration of undocumented immigrants in an attempt to undermine an important incentive that undocumented immigrants might have for staying and becoming settlers in the United States.

SOCIAL INCORPORATION

Undocumented Mexicans who have formed a family in the United States, I find, are less likely to want to return to Mexico. Their desire to settle in the United States does not necessarily occur immediately after other family members are brought over, but it does become more prevalent after living in San Diego a few years. As we saw in chapter 7, undocumented immigrants tend to experience an increase in family and friends over time as a result of having children, family reunification, and increasing social contacts with coworkers and neighbors. Social networks, in turn, lead to increased incorporation into the local community, even though in many cases this community may consist mostly of other undocumented and legal immigrants.

The formation of a family in San Diego is a major influence on settlement patterns. When a migrant's most immediate family is in Mexico, then he or she is tied to that family emotionally, socially, and economically (sending most of his or her money home, for example). Forming a family in San Diego, however, causes a reorientation to take place. The migrant's center of gravity shifts from the family "back home" to the family that is now in San Diego. This is not always a sudden change, but more typically one that occurs gradually as children are raised in the local culture and the number of friends and family members increases in the area. Children grow up and marry (and their spouses are often U.S. citizens or legal residents). Stays become extended and migrants become settlers as family life becomes centered in San Diego. The comments of Ester Portero, whose parents and siblings all moved to San Diego, reflects this shift in orientation: "Return to Mexico? For what? I don't have anything in Mexico. The important things are here, which is my family."

Enrique Valenzuela reflected on how he originally came to earn some money and go back home. But slowly he changed his mind about returning, as he gained experience working and formed a family:

> I came with the intention of making money to open my own business [in Mexico]; buy some machinery and work on my own. Once I was here, I saw that the system here, of this country, of this government, was very good. So little by little I started to think that I would never return again. . . . You see, we're people who want to live here. We didn't come like many others of our countrymen, who a year later go back two or three times. Their family is back there. And well, we don't think that way. We want to reside here and our roots are here.

To settle in the United States does not mean that a person will not return to Mexico someday. As Héctor Gómez said, "When you can't work anymore you can't do anything, and it's better, I think, to return to Mexico, to go and die in one's land." Undocumented Mexicans, like many immigrants, often express a desire to return to their native country. But returning becomes more difficult the longer a person stays. Children, then grandchildren, other family members, and friends act as roots in this new land, roots that become increasingly hard to cut.

Children and Incorporation   Children raised in the United States link their undocumented parents to the larger society and make it difficult for them to simply pack up and return to Mexico. This relates to the complex process of growing up, going to school, acquiring an identity, and identifying with a place called "home." In addition, parents desire to avoid severe disruptions in their children's lives and have a concern for their future.

When children are brought to the United States while still young, they often have few memories of Mexico. In many cases they may not even be aware that they are undocumented immigrants. This can pose a dilemma for their parents. Federico Romero's son was an infant when he arrived in San Diego. Later, Federico's daughter was born in San Diego, making her a U.S. citizen. He realizes that his children have a different experience from his, which complicates all their lives. When we began to discuss his children, Federico lowered his voice to say that his son [then 8 years old] came as a baby and that he did not know he was "illegal." Federico then said:

> Look, I have Mexican roots. I am a Mexican. You see that [American] flag over there [up on the wall]? He asked me to buy it for him because he likes it; it's his American flag. He said, "Dad, I would like an American flag. I want my flag." If I were to take my son to Mexico someday he would see a different world. He doesn't even know Tijuana. So I see him in a different world. Like the story of the lioness of two worlds. They left the lioness in a different place where she didn't know how to defend herself. It would be like that; he doesn't know anything. [As for my daughter], this is her country. She was born here.

I found that it was quite common for children to have been raised in the United States virtually all their lives. Since their parents came as young adults, their children were often infants (chapter 7). Or, in some cases, mothers already in San Diego returned to Mexico (often Tijuana) to give birth because they feared delivering a baby in a U.S. hospital might lead to apprehension by the INS. Or they believed they would not be admitted to the hospital because of their lack of money and medical insurance. Often these recently arrived undocumented immigrants later did give birth to children in the United States. Beatriz and Enrique Valenzuela's experience, and that of their daughter Carolina, was typical of this pattern.

Carolina Valenzuela had been born in Tijuana but was raised in San Diego since a few days after birth. Although she and her friends, some of them recently arrived from Mexico, rarely discuss their immigration status openly, she is certain that all her friends believe she is a U.S. citizen.

> I've told everybody I'm an American citizen, that I was born here. On applications, I just put I was born in the U.S.A. So all my friends know I'm a U.S. citizen. But I just lie. . . . And I think I have friends that lie just like me. . . . I'd rather say I'm American born because I feel I have more rights. . . . I feel more comfortable saying I'm an American citizen, like I could go to any college. . . . I have more opportunities.

Carolina participates as a citizen in various school activities. When I first met her in 1986, she was in her first year of high school and a member of the campus Reserve Officer Training Corps (ROTC). The year before that, she had been 1 of 4 students (out of about 300) chosen to speak at her eighth-grade graduation ceremony. She was the only Latina so chosen, an honor she believes she would not have received had it been known she was an "illegal alien." Through their children's activities, such as Carolina's, undocumented parents are drawn into the larger society.

Isela Díaz also believes she has become more connected to the larger society as a result of her son's school and sports activities. Her son Alberto is an avid Little League baseball player. Isela actively supports Alberto's sports activities, which has meant interacting with the coaches and other parents. As a result,

> I also feel I'm part of [this community] because I talk with the other mothers and I feel. . . . as if I were American because we get along well together, without any problems. I've also noticed that Alberto is never excluded because he is Mexican. On the contrary, they include him because he loves sports and they see him as one of them. That's why I feel that through them [other parents] I feel a connection, support from the Americans.

Giving birth to children also creates a link to U.S. society. Children born in the United States are, of course, U.S. citizens no matter what their parents' immigration status. Having a baby can also lead to other links to U.S. society. For example, Jorge Díaz found that diligently making payments on his debt to the hospital where his two sons had been born—especially the $12,000 for his second son, who was born with medical complications—helped him to establish a credit rating, which in turn helped him to work as an independent construction contractor. As he explained it:

> My credit began when my son was born. I paid the hospital earlier than I expected to. When I solicited credit to purchase a car, they asked me if I had credit. I told them only at the hospital. Then they asked me for my income tax report. They saw that I could pay my taxes. After I had established that credit account, I paid my car earlier than the expected date. Then Bank of America offered me the Visa, then Mastercard and American

Express, and it developed from that. For example, I have credit lines at the places where I purchase the materials that I work with.

Children and Return Migration   Most parents I interviewed said their children did not want to return to Mexico or Central America.[1] This perception of their children's attitudes helps anchor parents in the United States. As Alicia Herrera, a single mother, commented, "If my kids don't want to go to Mexico to live, what business do I have there?"

Tension can arise between parents who long to return to their native land and children who resist such a move. This is a central theme in "The Gilded Cage" ("Jaula de Oro") played on those radio stations to which many Mexican immigrants listen. The song states:

Tengo mi esposa y mis hijos que me los traje muy chicos, y se han olvidado ya de mi Mexico querido, del que nunca me olvido, y no puedo regresar.

I have my wife and children whom I brought at a very young age. They no longer remember my beloved Mexico, that I never forget and to which I can never return.

"Escúchame hijo, te gustaría que regresáramos a vivir en Mexico?" "What you talkin' about Dad? I don't wanna go back to Mexico. No way, Dad."

[SPOKEN] "Son, would you like to return to live in Mexico?" "What you talkin', about, Dad? I don't wanna go back to Mexico. No way, Dad."

Mis hijos no hablan conmigo. Otro idioma han aprendido y olvidado el español. Piensan como americanos niegan que son mexicanos aunque tengan mi color.

My children don't speak to me. They have learned another language and forgotten Spanish. They think like Americans. They deny that they are Mexicans even though they have my complexion.

An important moment in the song occurs when the father asks his son in Spanish if he would like to return to Mexico. The son responds, in English, "No way, Dad." The song reflects the tension between the parent's culture and desires and the culture and desires of their children who have been raised in the United States. This theme is an important one for Mexicans, Central Americans, and indeed, most other immigrant groups. The theme is also seen in many movies made in Mexico and shown in downtown San Diego, Los Angeles, and other cities where Mexican immigrants live. These movies—including one based on the song "The Gilded Cage"—dramatize the life of undocumented immigrants caught between two cultures.

CULTURAL INCORPORATION

The children of undocumented immigrants are subject to the great socializing influences of American television and school. As a consequence, children are much

---

[1]Out of 55 Mexican parents I surveyed in 1986, 80% believed their children did not want to return to their parents' native country. Similarly, Of the 61 Central American parents, 82.4% believed their children did not want to return.

quicker than their parents to learn local culture and the English language. But they also learn the culture of their parents. The result is often a hybrid of beliefs and behaviors, part American and part Mexican (or Salvadoran, or whatever nationality). These changes are noticed by parents and become part of the parents' own changing set of perceptions about goals for the future, especially their children's educational and economic opportunities. All of this begins to obscure old goals and notions of returning to the native country.

Children and English   Parents speak Spanish to their children at home. But children learn English and often speak among themselves in both English and Spanish.[2] Parents typically wanted their children to learn English because it would help them in school and in future jobs. At the same time, they wanted them to retain Spanish. Héctor Gómez said of his five children:

> They always talk to each other in English. And they speak to us in Spanish because we've never lent ourselves to practicing English with them. They know we don't like to speak English with them, apart from not knowing how.

For Héctor Gómez, speaking English to his children would place him at a distinct disadvantage. He did not want to sound childish in front of his children, since his English was rudimentary. I believe he feared that his lack of verbal competency would undermine his authority within the family.

When children come to this country young, or are born here, their English fluency is often greater than their competency in Spanish. Spanish is learned at home, while English is learned from television and friends and at school. For Felicia Gómez, her children's proficiency in English, acquired over the 9 years they had been in the United States, would be an obstacle to returning to Mexico:

> They [her five children] have studied since they were little here. They have never studied in anything else but English. They know how to speak and understand what [Spanish] we have taught them at home. But they have not formally studied Spanish. . . .
> Since they speak nothing but English among themselves, people [in Mexico] would laugh at them.

English and Incorporation   For adults, acquiring English proficiency is a slow process. And even though many undocumented immigrants take an English-as-a-Second-Language (ESL) class after arriving in the United States, they often have little opportunity to practice English, since they work at jobs where their coworkers are typically also Spanish speakers (see chapter 8).[3] Those who would like to have their children teach them English often find they are too tired after a day's work to practice consistently.

Despite the difficulty learning English poses, the ability to speak English is a key to better jobs and more money. Not speaking English is also considered by

---

[2]In my 1986 survey, 48.3% of the 58 Mexican parents (and 34% of 74 Central Americans) said their children speak to each other in English and Spanish.

[3]57.8% of the Mexicans and 61.4% of the Central Americans surveyed in 1986 had taken an ESL class.

many undocumented immigrants as a major obstacle to becoming incorporated into the larger society. Not knowing English is associated with an "outsider" status, as Ester Portero relates. She came to San Diego with her family when she was 17 years old, and attended 1 year of U.S. high school:

> In my class there were only about five people who spoke Spanish, that I knew spoke Spanish. But I didn't dare speak to them for fear that they would say "I don't speak Spanish!" . . . Generally, for the person who just came from Mexico, those who speak Spanish avoid you. They avoid you because they are afraid of what others will say about them hanging around a polla.

Lack of English fluency poses a very real obstacle to cultural incorporation into the larger society. However, the presence of children, other family members, and friends offsets a lack of English proficiency in the short term. As a consequence, feelings of social integration were sometimes quite high among undocumented settlers despite limited English proficiency.

Children and Customs Undocumented parents realize their children acquire American customs *(costumbres),* or cultural beliefs and behaviors, as a result of living in the United States. This is viewed as different from the way adults pick up some cultural behaviors, which occurs in a more conscious fashion. Jorge Díaz noted, "I think that the customs here are useful. But one's roots are never forgotten because you carry the customs in your blood. You can't change that."

In contrast, children unconsciously learn American culture, as well as some of their parents' culture, but lack extensive experience in their parents' native land. This difference is both apparent and important to parents who realize that their children are not exact cultural reproductions of themselves. Isela Díaz, Jorge's wife, reflected on her two U.S.-born sons, ages 10 and 5:

> Their habits are from here [San Diego]. Their whole life is here. They have a few Mexican customs because I continue to have them. . . . They know they are Americans because they were born here, but they realize that their parents are Mexican and that they too are Mexican, and that they should be able to speak their language.

Alberto, the Díaz's 10-year-old son, also perceived himself as being between two cultures:

> I consider myself American and sometimes I consider myself Mexican. I consider myself American when I'm in school and I consider myself Mexican when I'm out of school. [At home], I feel like I'm Mexican. I'm talking Spanish all the time, eating Mexican food.

Their children's acquisition of American culture is an important consideration for future planning. Jorge Díaz weighed the situation very seriously:

> My children are attending school here. They already have the customs. I believe that they have 65% out of 100% of customs which are of the United States. If I took them to Mexico it would be a great problem. They would have to begin again, and considering the many problems in Mexico, this would be terrible.

Children and Memories of Mexico   Their children's lack of familiarity with Mexico adds to their parents' reluctance to take children back to Mexico after a number of years in the United States. Children who migrated at an early age have at most faint memories of Mexico. They know Mexico principally from news reports or from what they learn in school. Some have visited family in Mexico, but for only brief periods. This lack of experience with Mexico is a concern for some parents. For example, Héctor Gómez's children have lived on an avocado ranch in Escondido since they migrated to the United States in 1978. Now, Héctor believes his children are

> more like the United States than Mexico. They aren't familiar with Mexico, not even the customs. They haven't experienced Mexico, what it's like to be in the rural areas. They don't know how we lived. They don't know what hunger is. They have everything right here. There [Mexico] they rode burros. I don't think they remember that. There you go everywhere on foot because having a car is not as easy as it is here.

For Héctor's wife, Felicia, that her children have grown up in San Diego means that they have no friends in Mexico. She believes that taking them back to Mexico at this point, without childhood friends, would place them in a sad situation. "It is better for them here than in Mexico because if they were to return to Mexico, they wouldn't know anyone."

Beatriz Valenzuela echoed this sentiment. Her 14-year-old daughter had been raised in San Diego since infancy and her 10-year-old son had been born in the city. When considering taking her children back to Mexico to live, she said, "You can only imagine the brutal change they would face. First of all, our children would lose their friendships, school, customs, food, manner of dress. For them, it would be terrible." Beatriz likened such an experience to a plant being pulled out of the ground by its roots. "The roots are here and it's like ripping a tree out of the ground and taking it over there. Can you imagine those roots? By the time they got there, they would be practically dead."

Children, Education, and the Future   The undocumented settlers I met had a clear set of values, hopes, and desires for their children's future that form part of the immigrant dream and also influence incorporation and return migration. Undocumented immigrants hope their children will be better educated and find better, less menial jobs than they. For some, the life they must endure as "illegal aliens" is part of the sacrifice they are willing to make for the next generation. This set of beliefs gets mixed up with all their other reasons for wanting to stay in the United States.

For example, both family and work have contributed to Federico Romero's intention to stay in the United States and legalize his immigration status. "Right now my ideas are very firm in that this country will be mine. In this country I will have what I have wanted most, that my children study, that my children become educated."

Felicia Gómez would also like to see her children go to college, a major step up from her own grade-school education. Her oldest daughter, Guadalupe, was a senior in high school when I interviewed her in 1986, and she wanted to attend San Diego State University the following year. Felicia's concern was that her undocumented status would pose a problem: "At college, they require a green card to enter. It's not as easy as entering high school."

Enrique and Beatriz Valenzuela also see more opportunities for their children in the United States. They view education as an important key to mobility, as Beatriz noted:

> I think that our children do have more opportunities here for an education, to study, to have what I didn't have. I didn't get an education in Mexico, but we worked and worked so that they would have more opportunities than we had. And that's why I want them to study and study hard so that they won't have to work as hard as we did.

Unfortunately, life does not always proceed as desired. Three years after this interview, the Valenzuela's daughter, Carolina, became pregnant, dropped out of high school, and moved in with her boyfriend. Given that she was a very good student, her parents hold onto the hope that she will eventually finish her education. Isela and Jorge Díaz want to stay in San Diego for a number of reasons, including their work. But their sons' education has given them, especially Isela, a major incentive for staying. Alberto, her oldest son, was born in San Diego and was 10 years old in 1986. His school had placed him in a program for gifted children, and she believed her younger son would also prove very intelligent. Isela believed she had a much greater chance of helping her sons reach their full potential in San Diego than in Mexico. "Although it is our Mexico and we love it very much, we don't have the means to educate them [her sons] there. It is easier here because you don't have to have a lot of money like you do in Mexico."

The value Isela Díaz placed on her sons' education came out strongly when she discussed the time they went to court to try to legalize their immigration status. Unfortunately, the judge denied their request. Despite being ordered to leave the country, Isela and Jorge stayed. Isela argued,

> Like I told [the judge], I can take [Alberto] to Mexico, but what's going to happen to him? He's going to be like me, maybe he finishes fourth or fifth grade; he'll forget about his education and get to work like everybody else does. What good is his intelligence going to be? I imagine that even [then-President] Reagan and everybody needs people who have greater abilities. Like Alberto tells me, "Mommy, I can be whatever you want me to be because to me nothing is impossible." I tell him that he has to do what he wants to do.

Isela and Jorge continue to live in San Diego. They were both eventually legalized under the 1986 immigration law. However, had they not been legalized, I believe they would have continued to live in San Diego anyway. Their work, their children's educational future, and their children's U.S. citizenship linked them to the local area. Jorge said about the future, before becoming legalized,

> What I want to see in the future is my children grown up in this country, see them with a career, so they can take care of themselves, so they will not be a burden to this country. [I want to see them] finish their education in order to be worth something to this country because this is where they were born. No matter if their parents are Latinos, their citizenship belongs to the United States.

PERSONAL INCORPORATION

With more time in the United States and the increasing ties to the larger society created through work and family, many undocumented immigrants begin to consider themselves part of the local community. Others, however, do not imagine themselves as part of the community. Such contradictory attitudes are sometimes held by the same person, which underscores the complexity of this issue.

The undocumented immigrants I interviewed had many reasons why they did not feel themselves part of the local community. Some, like the cases given at the beginning of this chapter, mentioned that their family remained back in Mexico or Central America. Others found cultural differences hard to transcend; their beliefs, behaviors, and language kept them apart. Still others lived isolated from the larger society, and so they believed they were not a part of it. Overall, however, the single most important reason why undocumented immigrants felt themselves to be outside the local community was their legal status. Héctor Gómez commented,

> There's lots of discrimination against the illegal. That's one of the major things, because no matter where you are they call you "illegal" or "wetback." Wherever you go, at times you are humiliated because you are not legal. In all things you come last. Even our own race humiliates us.

I also found, however, that many undocumented settlers believed they were part of the local community. They spoke of adapting to local life and becoming interested in local events, as did this Mexican immigrant: "I have adapted to the society. I'm concerned about the community. I'm interested in things that happen in this city, this country." For a Nicaraguan woman, it was only a matter of time: "With time, I have become accustomed to the way of life and to the people." Feeling part of the community appears to be related to how well they have overcome feelings of isolation, developed a network of family and friends in the local community, acquired some English fluency and local cultural knowledge, and reconciled themselves to the possible threat of deportation.

Once again, Héctor Gómez serves as a good example of someone who became involved in community activities despite his undocumented status. He, his wife Felicia, and their children all attend church services regularly and participate in many church-related social groups. I joined them on one occasion, when their oldest daughter Guadalupe was a princess in a church procession through downtown San Diego. Héctor has also taken many continuing education classes—for example, training to be an electrician. Over time, he has learned to be more open and not let his status hinder him in these pursuits. In the process, he has gone, in his own estimation, from being a rather timid rural person to someone who is not afraid to express himself, even with English-only speakers. Héctor and his family find participating in various activities helps them to escape the isolation of the avocado farm. Moreover, these activities have given them a sense of community, as Héctor notes:

> There's a lot of work to be done in the community. That's how the community grows. I like to participate a lot. We hardly ever miss a meeting. We go every month, as sick or tired as we are we must go. So, I think I have a lot of help because I am conscientious and I'm constantly at our meetings, and that's what helps us. The doors are never closed to us. We have help when we need it and that's the advantage. Participate in whatever is in your community, work hard, and that's the point, so that we can have everything, friends, acquaintances, and there's the salvation.

The friends Héctor and his family made through their community involvement proved instrumental in their long battle to stay in the United States. After being apprehended a second time in 1980, Héctor and his family faced a series of deportation deadlines. Each time a deadline arrived, they received a reprieve as a result of the letters and petitions of friends and church officials to the immigration authorities. After years of stalling deportation, the Gómezes were finally legalized under the 1986 immigration law.

Some undocumented immigrants felt they had earned the right to feel part of the community; they had paid their dues in one form or another. As a fellow from Mexico said, "Since I have been here I have contributed to the community by paying taxes and so I am part of the community." A Salvadoran echoed this sentiment: "I pay taxes, I shop in the stores, I eat in restaurants. I am part of the community." A Salvadoran woman went even further when she said, "Because of all the abuse I have suffered since I arrived, I feel I am of this community." Jorge Díaz adds yet another perspective that helps us to understand why undocumented immigrants might feel part of the community:

> I feel like part of the community. Of course, why shouldn't I? As Latinos we form a community within the United States. . . . Because of our roots, because there are Latinos who are legal, we communicate whether we are legal or illegal. Even among the Americans, we communicate with them at work and in the environment that we all live in.

The long history of Mexicans in the U.S. Southwest and the presence of legal immigrants provide Jorge with a sense of community. And for Jorge, interacting with those around him helps him feel like he belongs.

Beatriz Valenzuela feels part of the community because she receives notices about community events. This makes her feel accounted for and considered by the community:

> I do feel part of the community because when there are meetings here in the neighborhood, they send me a notice or an invitation, so that I will be able to attend those meetings. They always send me information on whatever programs there are. That's why I feel like part of the community.

Enrique, Beatriz's husband, also likes the U.S. government's general respect for the law. At the same time, both Beatriz and Enrique realize that feeling part of the community is somewhat illusory and their situation could change dramatically if deported. "You may have something, but you have a lot of fear, too, because the whole time you think that they might take it away from us because we are not here legally in this country. So for us the [immigration] papers are the most important thing." The Valenzuelas were also legalized under the 1986 immigration law.

Federico Romero emphasized the importance of friends in giving him a sense of community:

> I've always felt like part of the community since I arrived in 1979, because I've had friends and relationships with a lot of people. I've always felt part of the community despite the fact that I have that fear that doesn't allow me to go out and develop in the way that I would like, that doesn't even permit me to take my children to Disneyland.

Although Federico feels part of the community, he, like many others, also recognizes that his undocumented status ultimately serves to undermine those personal feelings of incorporation. Undocumented immigrants are drawn into, or increasingly incorporated into American society and culture through work, learning English, raising children who attend U.S. schools and acquire American culture, and by developing friendship networks. These experiences can lead to increasing feelings of personal incorporation, of feeling part of the local community. But even if they do imagine themselves as community members, their full incorporation into the larger society depends not on their own beliefs or actions alone, but ultimately on the larger society's perception of undocumented immigrants. Federico Romero perceptively made this point:

> To be treading on land that is not ours [is a problem], and we say that because at one time it was [ours], but that's past history. Now, legally, we are treading on territory that is not ours. Many people may believe we [Mexicans] are people without education and that we don't have an ability to develop better things, [but] we want, and hope, for an opportunity to show them that we can make it and that we don't need to depend on government aid in order to subsist and achieve what we want.

In sum, despite lacking a guarantee of full incorporation, over time undocumented immigrants develop the kinds of ties to the local economy and society that result in their staying and settling in U.S. communities. Experiences such as finding a job, maintaining steady employment, acquiring job responsibility, learning English, forming a family, giving birth to children in the United States, having them attend U.S. schools and acquire American culture, learning to navigate in the larger society, and, ultimately, legalizing their immigration status incorporate undocumented immigrants into the new society. Moreover, establishing a network of friends and relatives, some of whom may be from the same home community, increases solidarity with the new society. These factors begin to counterbalance the forces encouraging return to the country of origin and are the reason why many undocumented immigrants assert their intention to stay and become a part of the local community despite their legal status. Through such desires and behaviors they are, in essence, refuting the larger society's characterization of them as transient and rootless aliens.[4]

INCORPORATION AND THE LARGER SOCIETY

Undocumented settlers are tied to a society that continually questions their right to remain. Should undocumented immigrants be rounded up and deported? Should they be allowed medical services? Should they be allowed to live in public housing? Should their children be allowed into public schools? Should their children be allowed to participate in school lunch programs?[5] Such questions constantly underscore the undocumented immigrants' tenuous foothold in this society.

---

[4]This is not surprising since the commonsense view of undocumented immigrants discussed in chapter 1 under the concept of hegemony suffers from a limitation of that concept. Scott (1985, p. 317) argues that "Hegemony ignores the extent to which most subordinate classes are able, on the basis of their daily material experience, to penetrate and demystify the prevailing ideology."

[5]I have examined some of these public policy issues in various articles. See, for example, Chavez, 1986, 1988; and Chavez, Flores, & Lopez-Garza, 1990.

Because these questions are far from settled, undocumented immigrants and their families encounter a barrage of confusing public policies that affect their lives. Such questions do not have easy answers. For example, advocates for undocumented immigrants argue that most work and pay taxes and therefore deserve public services such as health care. The counter argument is that county governments should not be responsible for the cost of their health care since undocumented immigrants are not legal residents of the state of California. The question of legal residency in a state such as California complicates the picture because state residency is not necessarily determined by federal immigration status. Living in California for a specific amount of time is often enough to establish residency. What constitutes a legal resident of California, then, is a matter of interpretation that even the courts have not resolved definitively.

Questions about residency are important because they point to the basic assumption that "outsiders" should not enjoy the same societal benefits as "insiders," or citizens. As a consequence, the larger society excludes, or attempts to exclude, undocumented immigrants from public goods such as taxpayer-financed health care, education, housing, and so on. But in the long run, it is unclear how far such exclusions should extend. For example, removing undocumented immigrants from public housing may sound reasonable to some, but what about their U.S.-born children? As citizens, are they not as entitled as anyone to such benefits?

In education, the U.S. Supreme Court decided that it was not in society's interest to exclude the children of undocumented immigrants from public elementary and secondary schools. The court argued that all children should be allowed the opportunity to achieve educationally so that they might make their maximum contribution to the welfare of the larger society (Alien Children Education Litigation, 1980). In California, the focus has shifted to higher education. Should public colleges and universities charge undocumented students foreign student tuition, which amounts to thousands of dollars more than a resident of California pays? Once again, this may seem reasonable at first glance, if we think of undocumented students as recent arrivals. But as we have seen here, many of the children of undocumented immigrants have lived virtually all their lives in the United States. Moreover, to be eligible to attend state colleges and universities, they must have satisfied the requirements just like other California students. This policy places a major financial obstacle to higher education for students from families with low incomes, or most of the families I have interviewed.

Policies often give mixed signals. For instance, we allow the children of undocumented immigrants to attend public schools. Some go on to public colleges and universities. On the other hand, the 1986 immigration law made it illegal to hire undocumented immigrants. When undocumented students graduate, therefore, they cannot be hired. The education society provides them at public expense is short-circuited by the employer-sanctions law. To work, these students must find a way to become legal immigrants or purchase fake documents, which is a criminal offense.

As these few examples suggest, policies designed to control undocumented immigration have unintended consequences. As yet, we don't know the long-term effects such policies will have on immigrants and their families or on society at large. One thing is clear, however. Policies designed to stem the flow of undocumented workers have not worked well. The Border Patrol reported a sharp increase in arrests of undocumented immigrants along the U.S.–Mexico border in November and December 1990 (McDonnell, 1990b).[6] The forces that draw undocumented immigrants to the United States continue to operate. Mexicans come for jobs, family, adventure, and many other reasons. Political conflict still makes life difficult in Central America.

The stories I heard are not unique. I am sure similar stories can be told everywhere undocumented immigrants live and work. And, as recent trends suggest, they will be repeated again by those crossing the border today. Undocumented immigrants will arrive as outsiders. But some will, over time, develop economic, social, linguistic, cultural, and personal ties to the communities in which they live. And yet, the larger society does not readily recognize this process. Contrary to Anderson's (1983, p. 16) assertion that the nation is always a "deep horizontal comradeship," the larger society in San Diego does not readily perceive undocumented immigrants as part of the community. As a result, the territorial passage that undocumented immigrants begin when they leave home does not come to an end; many find full incorporation into the new society difficult to achieve. Until the larger society imagines undocumented immigrants as part of the community, they will continue to live as "outsiders" inside American society.

[6]Border Patrol agents in San Diego recorded 33,687 arrests in November, an increase of 22% over November 1989, eclipsing the previous November record set in 1985, the year before Congress passed legislation to curb undocumented immigration (McDonnell, 1990b).

EPILOGUE

Since the publication of *Shadowed Lives,* the mood of the country has turned decidedly less hospitable toward immigrants. Many of the issues I discussed in the last chapter of the book under incorporation and the larger society have come to the forefront of the public debate over the place of immigrants in American society (McDonnell, 1995a).

An important watershed moment in the public debate over immigration was the 1994 election in California. On November 8 the voters of California overwhelmingly passed Proposition 187, which was to, in the words of its supporters, "Save Our State" by denying "illegal aliens health care, education, and other publicly funded benefits" (Chavez, 1996; Martin, 1995). Following California's lead, politicians in other states, congressional representatives, and presidential candidates took up the anti-"illegal alien" rhetoric, but in the process broadened the focus to include legal immigrants. Immigration reform soon became a rallying cry that would, in theory, eliminate or reduce the source of "problems" facing citizens, such as problems in the economy, education system, health care, and even the relations of local governments with the federal government (McDonnell 1995a).

Following the assumption put forward by proponents of Proposition 187, that social services (rather than jobs) are the magnet drawing undocumented immigrants to the United States, national immigration reform proposals began to target aid to immigrants, both documented and undocumented (Johnson, 1995). For example, Representative E. Clay Shaw, Jr. (a Republican from Florida), proposed that only citizens be provided benefits such as Aid to Families with Dependent Children, food stamps, and Medicaid. Denying these benefits to legal immigrants, would, according to Representative Shaw, take away the attraction to come to this country, that is, welfare and the social safety net (Shogren, 1994). In all, the Republican legislative program for immigration reform that was brought to the U.S. House of Representatives in Proposition 187's wake would have denied 60 kinds of federal assistance to millions of legal immigrants, including health programs, Social Security, Supplementary Security Income, disability payments, housing assistance, childhood immunizations, subsidized school lunches, job training, and aid to the homeless (Epstein, 1994, p. A1). On March 24, 1995, the House of Representatives passed the Personal Responsibility Act, which included many of these proposals to limit social services to legal immigrants (Shogren, 1995a).

The U.S. Senate followed the House's example when it passed on September 19, 1995, its own bill on welfare policy. The Senate's bill cut fewer benefits for legal immigrants than the House's bill, but also restricted benefits for naturalized citizens who immigrate after the bill's enactment (Shogren, 1995b). If enacted, this would have been the first time in U.S. history that government benefits were denied naturalized citizens because they were not born in the United States, thus establishing a two-tiered or segmented structure for citizenship. Although this version of the welfare reform bill was vetoed by President Bill Clinton and was later dropped in the final version of the bill, it indicates the willingness of policy makers to treat naturalized citizens differently than U.S.-born citizens.

On August 22, 1996, President Clinton signed into law a major welfare reform bill (Shogren, 1996). The law ends the federal government's 61-year commitment to provide cash assistance to every eligible poor family with children. The law is expected to save the government $54 billion over the following 6 years. About half of those savings, or $24 billion, will come from restricting legal immigrants' eligibility for food stamps, Supplemental Security Income, and aid for low-income elderly, the blind and disabled. Undocumented immigrants, who already were denied virtually all federal assistance, continue to be barred from assistance except for short-term disaster relief and emergency medical care (Shogren, 1996).

In addition to the welfare bills, the U.S. Congress also considered immigration reform in 1996. Although the congressional debates targeted legal immigration as well as illegal immigration, the bills passed by the House of Representatives (in March 1996) and Senate (in May 1996) dealt principally with illegal immigration. However, the Senate bill would have drastically cut public assistance to legal immigrants, including English classes, job training classes, and child care, and would make the use of such services grounds for deporting legal immigrants (Schmitt, 1996). The House's immigration bill contained a provision that would have allowed states to deny undocumented children access to education (kindergarten through 12th grade) in public schools. The Senate's bill did not contain this provision. The final bill coming out of Congress in September 1996, and quickly signed into law by President Clinton, dropped some of these more controversial proposals, including giving states the right to deny undocumented children a public education and making the provision that would have allowed deportation of legal immigrants who received welfare for a total of 12 months over seven years (Grimaldi, 1996).

In addition, the U.S. Congress has questioned the practice of conferring automatic citizenship to children born in the United States whose parents are undocumented immigrants. In June 1995, a House task force chaired by Representative Elton Gallegly (Republican from Simi Valley) recommended an amendment to the U.S. Constitution to end automatic citizenship for U.S.-born children whose parents are undocumented immigrants (Lacey, 1995). Representative Gallegly was an early proponent of this policy. (Gallegly 1991a, b). Representative Brian Bilbray of San Diego has proposed a measure that "fine tunes" the 14th Amendment to the U.S. Constitution, thus avoiding a battle over amending the Constitution. Representative Bilbray's measure would change the 14th Amendment to specify that children born in the United States must have parents who are U.S. citizens or legal residents in order to receive citizenship.

IMMIGRATION AND THE NATION

This brief overview of the public policy debate over immigration reflects the American public's growing unease with both undocumented and documented immigration. Tension appears to be growing over issues related to the way we think of ourselves as a nation and as a people. Indeed, the proponents of restricting immigration view today's immigrants as a threat to the "nation" that is conceived of as a singular, predominantly Euro-American, English-speaking culture. The "new" immigrants—the *trans*nationalists—threaten this singular vision of the "nation" because they allegedly bring "multiculturalism" and not assimilation (Martinez & McDonnell, 1994). This was clearly part of U.S. Representative Newt Gingrich's intended message when, shortly after passage of Proposition 187, he promised that as Speaker of the House he would preside over a freewheeling congressional debate about the "cultural meanings of being American" (Healy, 1994a, p. A1).

The question of who is an "American" and anti-immigrant sentiments can become entangled in revealing ways. For instance, on October 18, 1994, California State Senator William Craven, a Republican from Oceanside, was quoted as saying "that the [California] state legislature should explore requiring all people of Hispanic descent to carry an identification card that would be used to verify legal residence" (Hunt, 1994, p. A1). By targeting "all Hispanics," citizens, legal residents, and undocumented immigrants, Senator Craven defines all Hispanics as belonging to a suspect class.

Why Senator Craven focuses only on Hispanics is not clear. After all, California's ethnic diversity includes many other ethnic groups, including undocumented Canadians and Europeans who overstay their visas. Perhaps the reason Senator Craven appears more concerned with Latinos than Euro-immigrants has to do with the assumptions about social evolution and progress implicit in the way people sometimes talk about immigration. Senator Craven expressed these assumptions when addressing a senate hearing on migrant workers held in San Diego in February 1993; he said that "migrant workers were on a lower scale of humanity" (Hunt, 1994, p. A1). Of course, "lower scale of humanity" refers to discredited nineteenth-century scientific notions about social evolution that continue to underlie thinking about the order of countries in the world. According to this thinking, Euro-Americans and Europeans sit at the top of a hierarchical ordering of civilized societies ("developed" and "technologically advanced" being common metaphors for this hierarchy) in contrast to less civilized societies ("less developed" and "technologically backward").

Gifts to charitable organizations provide another example of how anti-immigrant sentiments distinguish between "deserving" and "undeserving" members of the community. In Orange County, California, donors to charities are increasingly stipulating that those who receive their gifts not be illegal aliens. In some cases, the donors specifically state that the recipients should be English speaking or even non-Latinos to ensure their citizenship status. As one director of a charitable agency said, "I had to find someone white and English speaking" to receive the donations (Berkman, 1994).

Perhaps one of the clearest statements about the threat of immigration to the "complexion" of American society comes from Pat Buchanan, a presidential candidate during the 1992 and 1996 elections. Buchanan said: "A nonwhite majority is envisioned if today's immigration continues." Buchanan would like a moratorium on all immigration to the United States, not merely closing the borders to undocumented immigrants (Buchanan, 1994; Graham, 1994). The question of who is "American," as defined by complexion and phenotype, is clearly at issue here.

More recently, Peter Brimelow (1995), himself an immigrant from Great Britain, has painted a dark picture for a future of continued immigration. America's problems, according to Brimelow, are due to immigrants who lack the cultural background of earlier European, especially British, immigrants. He argues that America needs a "time out" from immigration. Failure to restrict immigration, Brimelow warns, will lead America on the road to becoming an "alien nation."

THE NEW NATIVISM AND MEXICAN IMMIGRATION

Discourse surrounding Proposition 187 and subsequent immigration and welfare reform proposals relied heavily on the use of war metaphors and characterized the immigrant, especially Mexicans, as the "enemy." In his classic book, *Strangers in the Land,* John Higham (1985[1955], p. 4) defined nativism as "intense opposition to an internal minority on the ground of its foreign (i.e., 'un-American') connections." Higham argued that nativism gets much of its energy from modern nationalism, and that "nativism translates broader cultural antipathies and ethnocentric judgments into a zeal to destroy the enemies of a distinctively American way of life."

Proponents of immigration reform often target immigrants as the new threat to national security and the national identity, filling the void left by the loss of the old enemies after the collapse of the Soviet Union and the end of the Cold War. Immigrants as foreigners who threaten the American way of life was a central part of the pro-Proposition 187 campaign in California. Proponents of Proposition 187 banked on the widely held perception that an "invasion" of undocumented immigrants, especially from Mexico, was the cause of California's economic problems and eroding the lifestyles of U.S. citizens to the point of reducing the United States to a "Third World" country (Martinez & McDonnell, 1994). The "Third World" serves here as a metaphorical allusion to social evolution and the threat of immigration leading to the devolution of "American civilization."

U.S. Representative Dana Rohrabacher (a Republican from Huntington Beach, California), in arguing for passage of Proposition 187 shortly before the election, carried the war metaphor even further when he said, "Unlawful immigrants represent the liberal/left foot soldiers in the next decade" (Martinez & McDonnell, 1994).

Another proponent of Proposition 187, Ruth Coffey, the director of Stop Immigration Now, frequently raised the specter of "multiculturalism," commenting that "I have no intention of being the object of 'conquest,' peaceful or otherwise, by Latinos, Asians, Blacks, Arabs or any other groups of individuals who have claimed my country" (Martinez & McDonnell, 1994).

Ronald Prince, one of the cofounders of the Save Our State (SOS) initiative, speaking to a gathering in Orange County, explained how Proposition 187 would stop undocumented immigration by using a metaphor that harkened back to images of frontier justice, when Mexicans were routinely hanged by vigilante mobs: "You are the posse and SOS is the rope" (McDonnell, 1994a).

Glenn Spencer, founder of the Voice of Citizens Together, a San Fernando Valley-based group that was a principal grassroots backer of Proposition 187, also put his views into a war metaphor framework. Before the November elections in California, he argued for passage of Proposition 187 because illegal immigration is "part of a reconquest of the American Southwest by foreign Hispanics. Someone is going to be leaving the state. It will either be them or us" (Martinez & McDonnell, 1994).

After passage of Proposition 187, Spencer spoke at a rally to deny public education to illegal immigrants and the Clinton Administration's proposed $40-billion aid package to Mexico. Spencer said, "It boils down to this: Do we want to retain control of the Southwest more than the Mexicans want to take it from us?" Spencer went on to compare "the conflict" to the Vietnam war: "It's a struggle between two groups of people for territory" (McDonnell, 1995b). Even when confronted with academic research that suggests immigrants generally assimilate and improve their economic well-being, Spencer's comment was that "What we have in Southern California is not assimilation—it's annexation by Mexico" (McDonnell, 1995b).

Central to the war metaphors applied to immigration, especially from Mexico, is the characterization of transnational migrants as people who do not respect traditional borders and the sovereignty of nation-states and thus pose a threat to the national security, sovereignty, and control of U.S. territory. As Bette Hammond, the head of S.T.O.P.I.T. (Stop The Out-of-control Problems of Immigration Today), a Marin County-based group that was an early and key organizer on behalf of Proposition 187, put it: "We've got to take back our country" (McDonnell, 1994a, p. A24). Representative Newt Gingrich, speaking about immigration reform, also raised the sovereignty issue: "If they're illegal, why aren't they gone? Whatever law we have to pass to be able to protect American sovereignty and to be able to say we're not going to have illegal people in the United States, we should pass" (Healy, 1994b, p. A34).

According to Linda B. Hayes, the Proposition 187 media director for southern California, the loss of U.S. territory can occur as a result of the rapid demographic shifts caused by Mexican immigration. As she wrote in a letter to the *New York Times:*

> By flooding the state with 2 million illegal aliens to date, and increasing that figure each of the following 10 years, Mexicans in California would number 15 million to 20 million by 2004. During those 10 years about 5 million to 8 million Californians would have emigrated to other states. If these trends continued, a Mexico-controlled California could vote to establish Spanish as the sole language of California, 10 million more English-speaking Californians could flee, and there could be a statewide vote to leave the Union and annex California to Mexico. (Hayes, 1994)

Why people who left a country in search of economic opportunity and a better life would vote to return the state to the country they left is not explained by Ms. Hayes. Nor is it clear why, in the year 2004, the children and grandchildren of immigrants—all U.S. citizens who did not grow up in Mexico and who will not have the same nostalgia for Mexico as their parents or grandparents—would vote to annex California to Mexico. Of course, such questions may be beside the point since nativist arguments rely more on emotional resonance than the marshaling of empirical evidence and support found in academic treatises.

REPRODUCTION VERSUS PRODUCTION

Anthropologists often find it is useful to differentiate between production and reproduction when discussing immigrants (Meillassioux, 1975). Proposition 187, and most of the immigration and welfare reform proposals that followed it, targeted health care, education, and other social services as the principal attractions for immigrants, both legal and undocumented. This approach to the control of immigration, however, targets women and children, or the reproduction of the immigrant family, rather than targeting the labor of the immigrant worker (both male and female). Since immigrant women and children are more likely than immigrant men to use health care, educational services, and other social services, denying immigrants these social services would, supposedly, reduce the incentives for family formation (i.e., reproduction), and thus fewer spouses and children of immigrant workers would decide to come to the United States (Chavez et al., 1992; Chavez, 1988; Chavez et al., 1985, 1986). Immigrants, especially women and children, already in the United States would decide to go "back home." California's Governor Pete Wilson emphasized this point when, shortly after President Clinton's signing of the welfare reform into law, he ordered state agencies to stop providing prenatal care services to undocumented women. Prenatal services are, according to Wilson, a "magnetic lure" that causes women to come to the United States illegally (Lesher & McDonnell, 1996).

This is not to suggest that some proposals do not advocate increased funding for the Border Patrol (which are basic provisions of both the House and Senate immigration bills) and that the Justice Department does not occasionally "get tough" on employers because both statements are true (Bornemeier, 1995; Hook, 1995a). Rather, the point I am trying to make is that denying immigrants social services would clearly make immigrant families' lives more difficult. But if the families of immigrant workers decide to return to Mexico or other family members back home stay put, then we will have reduced the costs associated with immigrant labor while maintaining, and even increasing, the profits of that labor. It is certainly true that immigrant families have reproductive costs, some of which are subsidized by society, such as education and health care. Immigrant workers, on the other hand, have many benefits for production, since they cost society little to produce (the costs of raising and educating them were borne by their families and home societies), are often willing to perform low-wage work, are typically young and relatively healthy, and are often afraid to pursue, or are unaware of, their rights as workers. By targeting reproduction, immigration reform does little to undermine the lucrative and highly profitable relationship between employers and workers.

Proposition 187, welfare reform, and most of the immigration reform proposals discussed above do not target production, or the immigrant worker. For example, Proposition 187 did not advocate more funds for ensuring fair labor standards and practices and thus reducing the incentive for hiring immigrant, especially undocumented, labor. As Labor Secretary Robert B. Reich noted: "One reason that employers in the United States are willing to risk employer sanctions right now and hire illegal immigrants is because they can get those illegal immigrants at less than the minimum wage, put them in squalid working conditions, and they know that those illegal immigrants are unlikely to complain" (Bornemeier, 1995). Nor did the proposition propose increased enforcement of employer sanctions. Congressional immigration reform included pilot-testing systems to verify worker status, but employer participation is voluntary (Lacey, 1996). The implicit message is that we are going after the reproduction of the undocumented worker's family but not the laborer or the employer.

This impression is further enhanced by revelations in the press that California's Governor Pete Wilson, one of the most vociferous proponents of denying health care and education to undocumented immigrants, often encouraged the immigration commissioner to stop raids on California companies, arguing that sweeping up undocumented workers caused unnecessary disruptions to business (Jacobs, 1995). Such actions stand in marked contrast to anti-immigrant discourse, suggesting that production must be safeguarded but reproduction of the worker's family must be stopped.

This relationship between production (positive) and reproduction (negative) is revealed most clearly in the proposals for a guest-worker program. At the same time that proponents of immigration reform appear to be clamoring for an end or reduction in immigration, there are serious proposals to bring foreign workers to the United States on a temporary basis to work in agriculture and highly competitive high-technology companies. Shortly after the November 1994 elections in California, Governor Wilson was in Washington promoting a new *bracero* or guest-worker program (Brownstein, 1994). An advocate of providing California agribusiness low-cost seasonal labor (guest-workers) when he was a U.S. senator, Wilson again made his plea for a guest-worker program on November 18, 1994, in an address to the Heritage Foundation. Wilson justified a guest-worker program as a way "to alleviate the pressure for illegal immigration created by Mexico's inability to produce enough jobs for its people." Wilson clearly stated his vision of a return to a use of primarily Mexican male labor that would exclude the workers' families: "It makes sense—it has in the past, it may well continue to do so in the future—to have some sort of guest-worker program. But not the kind of thing we have been seeing where there has been massive illegal immigration, where whole families have come and where they are...requiring services that are paid for by state taxpayers" (Brownstein, 1994, p. A28). Harold Ezell, a coauthor of Proposition 187 and a past official of the INS, has also suggested a guest-worker program as a means of meeting labor shortages that cannot be filled by U.S. workers (Olmo, 1995). Even Representative Gallegly, who is adamant about denying citizenship to children born in the United States if their parents are not legal residents, acknowledged that there may be a need for immigrants to work in temporary jobs in the United States (Lacey, 1995a).

This would be the next logical step since a guest-worker (bracero) program institutionalizes the perfect cost-benefit ratio for immigrant labor: Foreign workers produced at no cost to the American public. Since they would be forbidden to bring their families, there would be minimal reproductive costs (i.e., health care and education). In essence, production without reproduction, workers without families, sojourners not settlers.

To a certain extent we have come full circle in the debate over immigration, especially immigration from Mexico. We may be on the verge of a return to institutionalizing the migration of single male and female workers who will be allowed to work on a temporary basis—without their families accompanying them. Ultimately, however, even some temporary workers manage to bring their families to join them and they find a way to become settlers. As Doris Meissner, Commissioner of the INS has observed, "History shows that every contract-worker program falls victim to the inexorable goal of workers who wish to reunite with their families or to become members of the community in which they work" (Meissner, 1995).

As the lives examined in this book testify to, even undocumented workers, our unofficial guest-workers, and their families have a remarkable capacity to develop a feeling of belonging to a community in the United States (Hondagneu-Sotelo, 1994; Chavez, 1994). Although they may have come originally as temporary migrants, over time they marry or bring their spouses and children to join them in the United States, have children born here, have other relatives and friends living near them, and have important networks in the job market. These social and familial developments increase the likelihood of settlement in the United States.

THE BORDER AS POLITICAL THEATER

San Diego's southern border with Mexico has changed quite a bit. I toured the area in Spring 1994 with Grupo Beta, a special task force of Mexican police whose job it is to protect migrants from criminal activity. The Soccer Field that I described in chapter 3 has a new political geography. A corrugated steel fence now stands on the border. Migrants no longer wait anxiously for the cover of night on U.S. territory. Instead, they wait just as anxiously on the Mexican side of the fence. At one spot an enterprising entrepreneur had dug a hole under the fence and charged each migrant a fee to use the hole. At other places along the border migrants simply climb up and over the metal fence, which is easy given that the ridges in the fence serve as a natural ladder.

The new metal fence along the U.S.-Mexico border.

The fence at the Soccer Field was part of a 14-mile fence completed in 1993 in preparation for Operation Gatekeeper, which was launched by the U.S. Department of Justice on October 1, 1994 (U.S. Immigration and Naturalization Service, 1995). Two-and-a-half miles of high-intensity lighting were also installed on the border, institutionalizing the ad hoc "light up the border" initiative of San Diegans against illegal border crossings.

Operation Gatekeeper has meant much greater presence of Border Patrol agents on the border. From September 1993 to October 1995, the number of Border Patrol agents in the San Diego sector increased 45%, from 992 to 1,434 agents. Operation Gatekeeper also improved the night-vision equipment and radio communications. The efforts of Operation Gatekeeper were aided by new laws that made illegal reentry to the United States a felony with a statutory federal prison sentence ranging from 5 to 20 years. Smugglers (coyotes) also face expanded prosecution guidelines. The concerted effort of Operation Gatekeeper resulted in increased apprehensions of border crossers (U.S. Immigration and Naturalization Service, 1995).

As Operation Gatekeeper clamped down on the Imperial Beach area of the border, people wishing to cross the border clandestinely were forced to try their luck more toward the east, along more difficult terrain. Areas once bypassed by border crossers have become new sites of entry. Apprehension rates in remote areas have risen dramatically. For example, in January 1995, 246% more apprehensions occurred than in the same month 1994. In El Centro, which is across the border from Tecate, Mexico, apprehensions were up 1,661% between February and July 1995 compared to the same period the previous year. One month, June 1995, experienced a 3,599% increase in apprehensions in the El Centro area (U.S. Immigration and Naturalization Service, 1995, p. 19).

Although apprehension rates are an imprecise guide to the numbers of actual border crossers, they do indicate that rather than stopping the flow of border crossers, Operation Gatekeeper appears to have succeeded in redirecting it. This shift in migration patterns has raised the ire of Americans living in what were once out of the way rural areas (O'Conner, 1996a).

The Immigration and Naturalization Service has touted Operation Gatekeeper as a major success. As they noted in their publication *Operation Gatekeeper: Landmark Progress at the Border,* "Today, the progress is clear. New resources are shifting illegal traffic, toughening enforcement at the ports of entry, disrupting smuggling operations, and prosecuting a record number of illegal crossers" (Immigration and Naturalization Service, 1995, p. 1). However, critics have questioned the effectiveness of the operation, arguing that moving border crossers farther east is not much of an accomplishment for the amount of resources expended (O'Conner, 1996b). In addition, the head of the Immigration and Naturalization Service, Commissioner Doris Meissner, has ordered an investigation into allegations that supervisors for the U.S. Border Patrol falsified arrest reports in order to show Operation Gatekeeper as a success (Granberry, 1996).

Although the border has changed in some ways, it still remains a place where the debate over immigration is dramatically played out. People are still drawn to the United States by jobs and dreams of a "better life." Some of these immigrants continue to find shelter in migrant camps similar to the ones I described in chapters 4,

5, and 6. The growth and destruction of these camps seems to be an enduring story in northern San Diego County.

THE CONTINUING SAGA OF MIGRANT CAMPS

The temporary shelters and campsites that I encountered during my fieldwork among rural farmworkers and suburban day workers in the 1980s continue to be found today. In 1994, there were still about 200 campsites with about 15,000 migrants throughout San Diego County (Carr, 1994). Many of the people living in these camps were employed in the area's $800-million agricultural industry.

The largest of the camps was in McGonigle Canyon. The residents of the camp called it Rancho de los Diablos (Village of the Devils). The camp meanders for about a mile along a creek bed between Rancho Peñasquitos and Del Mar.

Men have been living in McGonigle Canyon for more than 20 years. At its peak in the late 1970s, the campsite had as many as 2,000 inhabitants (Carr, 1994). In 1975, César Chavez, the leader of the United Farm Workers, visited the canyon and attempted to unionize the workers living there. After seeing the conditions the workers lived in, Chavez said, "I've seen a lot. But these conditions [were] among the worst. Disgusting. Inhuman" (Carr, 1994, p. 25).

Similar to events in Green Valley (chapters 5 and 6), demolition of the camp became a high priority for city officials in Rancho Peñasquitos. The camp began to draw a lot of attention from local homeowners in 1993, when the camp had about 300 structures and about 750 inhabitants, including women and children, most of them legal immigrants (Sherman, 1993). Because the camp was so large, life went on just as it might in any village community. Ceremonies marked special occasions, such as baptisms, First Communions, quinciañeras (the coming out party for a girl's 15th birthday), weddings, and deaths (Carr, 1994). After the ceremonies, parties were held at one of the restaurants in the canyon.

In May 1993, camp residents received notice that abatement proceedings had begun, and that their homes would soon be demolished (Sherman, 1993). Residents of the camp began to leave voluntarily. By October 1993, the number of buildings was reduced to about 240 and the population was down to about 520, including 44 women and nearly 100 children. The first demolition of some of the buildings began Monday, October 5, 1993 (Sherman, 1993).

By May 1994, the number of residents had been cut in half, but there were still 50 families and 250 single adults living there (Sherman, 1994a, b). On May 26, 1994, 40 more homes and other buildings were razed in an attempt to reduce the number of people living in the camp. The rest of the camp was set to be demolished in October 1994.

The camp's impending destruction received considerable media attention. To help camp residents relocate to apartments, a private nonprofit corporation called Esperanza ("hope" in Spanish) received $518,000 in federal funds. Esperanza assisted qualifying residents with first and last month's rent for an apartment. Some residents, especially families with children, sought out Esperanza's help. Single

Young girls walking to their quinciañera (15th birthday) party in the McGonigle Canyon campsite.

males often took their chances without help, looking to other less visible canyons for shelter (Carr, 1994).

By the first week of November 1994, the bulldozers had finished their work. They had cleared away 401 shacks, a medical clinic, six restaurants, two soccer fields, four basketball courts, a volleyball court, the communal bathhouse, and a general store (Carr, 1994). Men from the freshly razed camp had already begun constructing a new camp less than a mile away.

And so the cycle continues. The demand for labor in northern San Diego County keeps attracting immigrant workers, some with families. Pay is minimum wage and regular housing is costly. Makeshift encampments provide an alternative for workers who wish to live near available work. When a campsite becomes too large, demands for its destruction begin. Camp dwellers relocate, many to other canyons and hillsides, at least for a while, until the furor over their presence grows.

Of course, some workers and their families break out of the cycle and manage to find steady employment and earn enough money for regular housing. Others find another way out. In chapters 5 and 6, I described a restaurant in the Green Valley camp run by a woman I called Gloria Martinez. Gloria had her two young sons living with her at the time, Robert (age 7) and Alejandro (age 11). Gloria died from a terminal disease a couple of years after *Shadowed Lives* was published. Her two sons found themselves in foster care. They eventually were taken in by a family in northern San Diego County. Don Bartletti, whose photographs of life in Green Valley are in this book, has been following their lives. Alejandro, who used to leave the Green Valley camp every morning to attend elementary school, has now graduated from high school, speaks perfect English, and is planning to attend college. According to Don, he is a fine young man who dreams of being a successful businessman. He has shown an amazing resiliency to the adversity he has faced in his short life. Growing up in the makeshift shacks in Green Valley and suffering the sudden loss of his mother has not caused Alejandro to give up on his mother's dream of a "better life" for her family in the United States.

BIBLIOGRAPHY

Alien Children Education Litigation. (1980). Brief for the Appellants. Case Nos. 80-1538 and 80-1934. Washington, DC: Supreme Court of the United States.

Aliens said preying on school kids. (1986, September 19). *San Diego Union*, p. A1.

Alvarez, R. R. (1985). *Familia: Migration and adaptation in Baja and Alta California, 1800-1975*. Berkeley: University of California Press.

Anderson, B. (1983). *Imagined communities*. London: Verso.

Ardener, E. (1975). Belief and the problem of women. In S. Ardener (Ed.), *Perceiving women* (pp.1-7). London: Dent.

Bailey, E. (1988, December 18). Breaking camp. *Los Angeles Times*, p. B1.

Bailey, E. (1989, March 1). Judge clears way for removal of Encinitas migrant camp. *Los Angeles Times*, Sec.2, p. 1.

Bailey, E., & Reza, H. G. (1988, June 5). An alien presence. *Los Angeles Times*, Sec. 1, p. 36.

Barfield, C. (1989, October 12). Migrants shot by youths using paint-pellet rifles. *San Diego Union*, p. B1.

Basch, L., Schiller, N. G., & Blanc, C. S. (1994). *Nations unbound: Transnational projects, postcolonial predicaments, and deterritorialized nation-states*. Amsterdam: Gordon and Breach.

Balibar, E. (1991). Is there a "Neo-Racism"? In E. Balibar & I. Wallerstein (Eds.), *Race, nation, class: Ambiguous identities* (pp. 17-28). New York: Verso.

Bean, F. D., Edmonston, B., & Passel, J. S. (1990). *Undocumented migration to the United States*. Washington, DC: The Urban Institute Press.

Beckland, L. & Taylor, R. (1980, April 27). Pesticide use in Mexico, a grim harvest. *Los Angeles Times*, p. B1.

Berkman, L. (1994, November 24). Some attach strings to the spirit of giving. *Los Angeles Times* (Orange County edition), p. B1.

Biernacki, R., & Waldorf, D. (1981). Snowball sampling. *Sociological Methods and Research, 10*, 141-163.

Borjas, G. J., & Tienda, M. (1993). The employment and wages of legalized immigrants. *International Migration Review, 27*, 712-747.

Bornemeier, J. (1995, February 8). Clinton moves to curb illegal immigration. *Los Angeles Times*, p. A3.

Bowman, S. (1979, August 8). Illegals' camp burns, arsonist sought. *Coast Dispatch*, p. A1.

Brimelow, P. (1995, June 22). *Alien nation: Common sense about America's immigration disaster*. New York: Random House.

Brimelow, P. (1992, June 22). Time to rethink immigration? *National Review*, pp. 30-46.

Brownstein, R. (1994, November 19). Wilson proposes U.S. version of Prop. 187. *Los Angeles Times*, p. A1.

Buchanan, P. J. (1994, October 28). What will America be in 2050? *Los Angeles Times*, p. B11.

Bustamante, J. A. (1983). The Mexicans are coming. *International Migration Review, 17*, 323-441.

California Ballot Pamphlet: General Election Nov. 8, 1994. (1994). Proposition 187. Sacramento: State of California.

Cardoso, L. (1980). *Mexican emigration to the United States, 1897-1931*. Tucson: University of Arizona Press.

Carr, E. (1994, November 27). The last days of Rancho de Los Diablos. *Los Angeles Times Magazine,* pp. 20-56.

Chavez, L. R. (1985). Households, migration, and labor market participation: The adaptation of Mexicans to life in the United States. *Urban Anthropology, 14,* 301-346.

Chavez, L. R. (1986). Mexican immigration and health care: A political economy perspective. *Human Organization, 45,* 344-352.

Chavez, L. R. (1988). Settlers and sojourners: The case of Mexicans in the United States. *Human Organization, 47,* 95-108.

Chavez, L. R. (1990). Coresidence and resistance: Strategies for survival among undocumented Mexicans and Central Americans in the United States. *Urban Anthropology, 19,* 31-61.

Chavez, L. R. (1991). Outside the imagined community: Undocumented settlers and experiences of incorporation. *American Ethnologist, 18,* 257-278.

Chavez, L. R. (1994). The power of the imagined community: The settlement of undocumented Mexicans and Central Americans in the United States. *American Anthropologist, 96,* 52-73.

Chavez, L. R. (1997). Immigration reform and nativism: The nationalist response to the transnationalist challenge. In J. Perea (Ed.), *Immigrants out!: The new nativism and the anti-immigrant impulse in the United States.* New York: New York University Press.

Chavez, L. R., & Flores, E. T. (1988). Undocumented Mexicans and Central Americans and the Immigration Control and Reform Act of 1986: A reflection based on empirical data. In L. F. Tomasi (Ed.), *Defense of the alien Vol. 10* (pp. 137-156). Staten Island: Center for Migration Studies of New York.

Chavez, L. R., Flores, E. T., & Lopez-Garza, M. (1989). Migrants and settlers: A comparison of undocumented Mexicans and Central Americans in the United States. *Frontera Norte, 1,* 49-75.

Chavez, L. R., Flores, E. T., & Lopez-Garza, M. (1990). Here today, gone tomorrow? Undocumented settlers and immigration reform. *Human Organization, 49,* 193-205.

Chavez, L. R., Flores, E. T., & Lopez-Garza, M. (1992). Undocumented Latin American immigrants and U.S. health services: An approach to a political economy of utilization. *Medical Anthropology Quarterly, 6,* 6-26.

Chavez, L. R., Hubbell, F. A., Mishra, S. I., & Valdez, R. B. (1997). Undocumented Latina immigrants in Orange County, California: A comparative analysis. *International Migration Review, 31,* 88-107.

Chavez, L. R., Cornelius, W. A., & Jones, O. W. (1985). Mexican immigrants and the utilization of health services. *Social Science & Medicine, 21,* 93-102.

Chavez, L. R., Cornelius, W. A., & Jones, O. W. (1986). Utilization of health services by Mexican women in San Diego. *Women and Health, 11,* 3-20.

Chavira, R. (1983, January 1). Desperation is daily fare for Oaxacan migrants in Tijuana, North County. *San Diego Union,* p. A1.

Chavira, R. (1990, November 19). Hatred, fear and vigilance. *Time,* pp. 12-20.

Congress moves on immigration reform. (1995, October). *Migration News, 2*(10), p. 1.

Cornelius, W. A. (1978). Mexican migration to the United States: Causes, consequences, and U.S. responses. *Migration and Development Monograph C/78-9.* Cambridge, MA: MIT Center for International Studies.

Cornelius, W. A. (1980). *America in the era of limits.* Working Paper No. 3. La Jolla, CA: Center for U.S.-Mexican Studies, University of California, San Diego.

Cornelius, W. A. (1981). *The future of Mexican immigrants in California: A new perspective for public policy.* Working Paper No. 6. La Jolla, CA: Center for U.S.-Mexican Studies, University of California, San Diego.

Cornelius, W. A. (1982). Interviewing undocumented immigrants: Methodological reflections based on fieldwork in Mexico and the United States. *International Migration Review, 16,* 378-411.

Cornelius, W. A. (1988, June). The persistence of immigrant-dominated firms and industries in the United States: The case of California. Paper presented at the Conference on Comparative Migration Studies, Paris, France.

Cornelius, W. A., Chavez, L. R., & Castro, J. (1982). *Mexican immigrants in Southern California: A summary of current knowledge.* Working Paper No. 36. La Jolla, CA: Center for U.S.-Mexican Studies, University of California, San Diego.

Cornelius, W. A., Martin, P. L., & Hollifield, J. F. (1994). *Controlling immigration: A global perspective.* Stanford: Stanford University Press.

Craig, R. B. (1971). *The Bracero Program: Interest groups and foreign policy.* Austin: University of Texas Press.

Curry, B. (1980, November 21). Pesticide clouds lives of 60. *Los Angeles Times,* p. B1.

Curry, B. (1986, June 16). Hunt for better life leads aliens to "Season of Death." *Los Angeles Times,* Sec. 1, p. 1.

Davis, D. (1989, March 7). Judge won't block sweep of campsite. *San Diego Union,* p. B1.

Dawsey, D. (1988, August 8). Malaria outbreak in San Diego County: Tests indicate 11 cases of the disease in migrant workers' camp. *Los Angeles Times,* Sec. 2, p. 10.

De Leon, A. (1983). *They called them greasers.* Austin: University of Texas Press.

Dennis, G. (1979, July 25). Curb urges for alien work permit. *Del Mar Surfcomber,* p. A1.

Donato, K. M. (1993). Current trends and patterns of female migration: Evidence from Mexico. *International Migration Review, 27,* 748-771.

Epstein, A. (1994, December 27). GOP targets legal noncitizens. *Orange County Register,* p. A1.

Feldman, P., & Connell, R. (1994, November 10). Wilson acts to enforce parts of Prop. 187; 8 lawsuits filed. *Los Angeles Times,* p. A1.

Foucault, M. (1970). *The order of things.* New York: Vintage Books.

Foucault, M. (1979). *Discipline and punishment.* New York: Vintage Books.

Frank, G. (1979, June 8). U.S., Baja officials to act on border strife. *Los Angeles Times,* Sec. 2, p. 1.

Freedman, J. (1990, February 19). In an area growing too fast, anger is taken out on the weak. *Los Angeles Times,* p. B11.

Friedlander, J. (1975). *Being Indian in Hueyapan.* New York: St. Martin's Press.

Fulwood, S. III. (1990, November 18). New bill may pave path for Irish aliens. *Los Angeles Times,* p. A32.

Gallegly, E. (1991a, October 22). Gallegly seeks to end automatic citizenship for illegal alien children. Washington, DC: Press release from the Office of Congressman Elton Gallegly.

Gallegly, E. (1991b, October 22). Time to amend our birthright citizenship laws. Speech presented by Rep. Gallegly in the House of Representatives. Copy in first author's files.

Gandelman, J. (1986, April 6). Wilson would back Marines on border if reform move fails. *San Diego Union,* p. A3.

Gandelman, J. (1989a, February 9). Meetings on migrants' camp set. *San Diego Union,* p. B1.

Gandelman, J. (1989b, February 14). Encinitas migrant workers to be evicted. *San Diego Union,* p. B1.

Gandelman, J. (1989c, February 28). Migrants' eviction delayed by lawsuit. *San Diego Union,* p. B1.

Geertz, C. (1973). *The interpretation of cultures.* New York: Basic Books.

Glionna, J. M. (1990, April 12). Encinitas hires firm to clear migrant camps. *Los Angeles Times,* p. A3.

Gorman, T. (1986, February 17). Rising illegal alien crime a touchy issue. *Los Angeles Times,* Sec. 2, p. 1.

Gould, S. J. (1981). *The Mismeasure of man.* New York: W. W. Norton & Company.

Graham, J. L. (1994, November 27). Xenophobic fears about a "nonwhite majority" are nonsense. *Los Angeles Times* (Orange County edition), p. B17.

Granberry, M. (1996, July 6). INS investigates Border Patrol's arrest statistics. *Los Angeles Times,* p. A1.

Greer, E. (1982). Antonio Gramsci and Legal Hegemony. In D. Kairys (Ed.), *The politics of law: A progressive critique* (pp. 304-309). New York: Pantheon.

Grimaldi, J. V. (1996, September 29). Immigration reforms pass in the House. *Orange County Register,* p. 1.

Hayes, L. B. (1994, October 15). California's Prop. 187 [Letter to the Editor]. *New York Times,* p. 18.

Healy, M. (1994a, November 12). Gingrich lays out rigid GOP agenda. *Los Angeles Times,* p. A1.

Healy, M. (1994b, November 13). House GOP charts California agenda. *Los Angeles Times,* p. A1.

Herrera-Sobek, M. (1979). *The bracero experience.* Los Angeles: UCLA Latin American Center Publications.

Higham, J. (1985). *Strangers in the land.* New York: Antheneum.

Himmelspach, D. (1989, February 24). Encinitas orders migrants out of their new camp by March 6. *San Diego Union,* p. A1.

Hoffman, A. (1974). *Unwanted Americans: Mexican Americans in the Great Depression, repatriation pressures, 1929-1939.* Tucson: University of Arizona Press.

Hondagneu-Sotelo, P. (1994). *Gendered transitions: Mexican experiences of immigration.* Berkeley: University of California Press.

Hook, J. (1995a, May 7). Clinton moves to speed deportations. *Los Angeles Times,* p. A1.

Hook, J. (1995b, June 8). Immigration cutback urged by U.S. Panel. *Los Angeles Times,* p. A1.

Housing badly needed for county's migrants. (1988, December 25). *San Diego Union,* Sec, 2, p. 2.

Hunt, M. C. (1994, October 18). Craven says all Hispanics should carry I.D. cards. *San Diego Union-Tribune,* p. A1.

An illegal alien jumped into swiftly flowing Santa Paula Creek. (1982, April 2). *Los Angeles Times,* Sec. 1, p. 2.

Intersection of cars and bad policy. (1990, August 11). *Los Angeles Times,* p. B10.

Jackson, P. (1989). *Maps and meaning.* London: Unwin Hyman.

Jacobs, P. (1995, September 25). Wilson often battled INS, letters show. *Los Angeles Times,* p. A3.

Johnson, K. R. (1995). Public benefits and immigration: The intersection of immigration status, ethnicity, gender, and class. *UCLA Law Review,* 42(6), 1509-1575.

Kearney, M. (1986). Integration of the Mixteca and the Western U.S.-Mexico border region via migratory wage labor. In I. Rosenthal-Urey (Ed.), *Regional impacts of U.S.-Mexican relations.* La Jolla: Center for U.S.-Mexican Studies, University of California, Monograph Series.

Kearney, M. (1991). Borders and boundaries of state and self at the end of empire. *Journal of Historical Sociology, 4*(1), 52-74.

King, C. (1995, September 21). Too narrow a view of who's American. *Los Angeles Times*

(Orange County edition), p. B11.

Kozub, L., & Valencia, C. (1989, February 15). If camp shut, migrants will find new canyon. *San Diego Union,* Sec. 2, p. 1.

La Ganga, M. L. (1985, May 2). Officer not charged in shooting at border. *Los Angeles Times,* Sec. 2, p. 1.

Lacey, M. (1995a, March 16). New task force targets illegal immigration. *Los Angeles Times,* p. A3.

Lacey, M. (1995b, June 29). Illegal immigration report to House urges stiff curbs. *Los Angeles Times,* p. A1.

Lacey, M. (1995c, June 30). Immigration report gains key support. *Los Angeles Times,* p. A34.

Lacey, M. (1996, September 29). Toned-down immigration bill passes in House. *Los Angeles Times,* p. A27.

Lamm, R. D., & Imhoff, G. (1985). *The immigration time bomb.* New York: Truman Talley Books.

Lesher, D. (1995, August 29). Wilson kicks off campaign to protests. *Los Angeles Times,* p. A3.

Lesher, D., & McDonnell, P. (1996, August 28). Wilson calls halt to much of aid for illegal immigrants. *Los Angeles Times,* p. A1.

Maggio, M. (1980, July 13). Shifting sands of U.S. immigration policy trap Salvadoran refugees. *Los Angeles Times,* Sec. 5, p. 1.

Mann, J. (1995, September 24). GOP candidates warm to anti-foreign policy. *Los Angeles Times,* p. A3.

Marcus, G. E., & Fischer, M. M. J. (1986). *Anthropology as cultural critique.* Chicago: University of Chicago Press.

Martin, E. (1987). *The woman in the body.* Boston: Beacon Press.

Martin, P. (1995). Proposition 187 in California. *International Migration Review, 24,* 255-263.

Martinez, G. & McDonnell, P. J. (1994, October 30). Prop. 187 forces rely on messsage—not strategy. *Los Angeles Times,* p. A1.

Massey, D. S., Alarcon, R., Durand, J., & Gonzalez, H. (1987). *Return to Aztlan.* Berkeley: University of California Press.

McDonnell, P. J. (1986, June 24). Hunter asks for National Guardsmen along border. *Los Angeles Times,* Sec. 2, p. 3.

McDonnell, P. J. (1987, August 17). North County's farm worker camps: Third World squalor amid affluence. *Los Angeles Times,* Sec. 2, p. 1.

McDonnell, P. J. (1989a, October 22). Priest wishes diocese would care more. *Los Angeles Times,* Sec. B, p. 1.

McDonnell, P. J. (1989b, October 23). A private raid. *Los Angeles Times,* Sec. B, p. 1.

McDonnell, P. J. (1989c, October 30). Minority migrants. *Los Angeles Times,* Sec. B, p. 1.

McDonnell, P. J. (1990a, December 13). U.S. citizen charged in May killings of immigrant boy. *Los Angeles Times,* Sec. B, p. 5.

McDonnell, P. J. (1990b, December 29). Border Patrol reports record arrests for illegal immigration. *Los Angeles Times,* Sec. B, p. 6.

McDonnell, P. J. (1994a, August 10). Prop. 187 heats up debate over immigration. *Los Angeles Times,* p. A1.

McDonnell, P. J. (1994b, November 10). Prop. 187 win spotlights voting disparity. *Los Angeles Times,* p. A3.

McDonnell, P. J. (1995a, January 28). Is Prop. 187 just the beginning? *Los Angeles Times,* p. A1.

McDonnell, P. J. (1995b, November 3). Study disputes immigrant stereotypes, cites gains. *Los Angeles Times,* p. A1.

Meillassoux, C. (1975). *Maidens, meal and money: Capitalism and the domestic community.* Cambridge: Cambridge University Press.

Meissner, D. (1995, January 30). Contract workers: Human exploitation. *Los Angeles Times* (Orange County edition), p. B9.

Meyer, J. S. (1986, April 6). Sheriff urges posting Marines along border. *San Diego Union,* p. A3.

Migrants linked to crime rise. (1986, August 28). *San Diego Union,* p. A1.

Miller, J. (1995, September 13). Ezell urges new limits for legal immigration. *Orange County Register,* Metro, p. 7.

Miller, M., & McDonnell, P. (1990, December 9). Rise in violence along border brings call for action. *Los Angeles Times,* p. A4.

Mitchell, A. (1995, September 5). President rebuts some G.O.P. themes on economic woes. *New York Times,* p. A1.

Montemayor, R. (1980, October 5). Canyon of the damned. *Los Angeles Times,* Sec. 1, p. 1.

Montes Mozo, S., & Garcia Vasquez, J. J. (1988). Salvadoran migration to the United States: An exploratory study. Washington, DC: Center for Immigration Policy and Refugee Assistance, Georgetown University.

Moore, H. L. (1988). *Feminism and anthropology.* Minneapolis: University of Minnesota Press.

Nagengast, C., Kearney, M., & Stavenhagen, R. (1989). Human rights and indigenous workers: The Mixtecs in Mexico and the United States. Mimeo in author's files.

Nogy, S. (1989, October 11). Guatemalans converge in Encinitas. *Blade-Citizen,* p. B1.

O'Conner, A.-M. (1996a, July 26). Border crackdown turns ranchers into irate activists. *Los Angeles Times,* p. A3.

O'Conner, A.-M. (1996b, August 15). Beyond GOP rhetoric, border crossers keep coming. *Los Angeles Times,* p. A22.

Olmo, F. del (1995, January 31). Open the door to Mexican workers. *Los Angeles Times* (Orange County edition), p. B9.

Owens, H. (1988a, December 7). Migrants are victim of burglary. *Carlsbad Journal,* p. 1.

Owens, H. (1988b, December 23). Camp demolition delayed, permit may be required. *Carlsbad Journal,* p. A1.

Owens, H. (1989a, January 20). Migrant camp: Opposition to temporary site builds. *Carlsbad Journal,* p. A2.

Owens, H. (1989b, January 27). Five more families receive housing assistance. *Carlsbad Journal,* p. A1.

Passel, J. S. (1985, August 16). Estimates of undocumented aliens in the 1980 census for SMSAs. Memorandum to Roger Herriot, Chief, Population Division, Bureau of the Census. MS, files of the author.

Passel, J. S., & Woodrow, K. A. (1984). Geographic distribution of undocumented aliens counted in the 1980 census by state. *International Migration Review, 18,* 642-671.

Pedraza-Bailey, S. (1985). *Political and economic migrants in America, Cubans and Mexicans.* Austin: University of Texas Press.

Pierce, E. (1988a, December 10). Migrant families left with no place to call their own. *San Diego Union,* p. A1.

Pierce, E. (1988b, December 13). Vigil in N. County stresses plight of homeless migrants. *San Diego Union,* p. B1.

Piore, M. J. (1979). *Birds of passage: Migrant labor and industrial societies.* London: Cambridge University Press.

Piore, M. J. (1986). The shifting grounds for immigration. *Annals of the American Academy of Political and Social Science, 485,* 23-33.

Portes, A., & Bach, R. L. (1985). *Latin journey: Cuban and Mexican immigrants in the United States.* Berkeley: University of California Press.

Rangel, J. (1983, April 30). Mitchell asks raids on undocumented workers in district. *San Diego Union,* p. B1.

Redfern, J. (1979, June 11). Blazing gunfire turns fear into reality along border. *San Diego Tribune,* p. A1.

Reimers, D. (1985). *Still the golden door.* New York: Columbia University Press.

Reyes, D. (1990, September 24). Alien killed on freeway south of checkpoint. *Los Angeles Times,* p. B1.

Reza, H.G. (1986a, May 13). Golding wants U.S. to pick up alien tab. *Los Angeles Times,* Sec. 2, p. 1.

Reza, H.G. (1986b, November 22). Three teens held in sniper attack on aliens. *Los Angeles Times,* Sec. 2, p. 1.

Reza, H.G. (1988a, July 17). Home cooking among the hooches of La Costa. *Los Angeles Times,* p. B1.

Reza, H.G. (1988b, November 26). Migrant camp in Encinitas will be razed. *Los Angeles Times,* Sec. 1, p. 26.

Reza, H.G. (1989a, January 19). No place like home—anyplace. *Los Angeles Times,* Sec. 2, p. 1.

Reza, H.G. (1989b, February 2). Valle Verde migrants join ranks of homeless as makeshift camp closes. *Los Angeles Times,* Sec. 2, p. 1.

Reza, H.G. (1989c, March 2). Three migrant families go from hooches to jacuzzi. *Los Angeles Times,* Sec. 2, p. 1.

Reza, H.G. (1989d, February 4). Border Patrol to investigate allegation that agent harassed legal alien. *Los Angeles Times,* Sec. 2, p. 1.

Reza, H.G. (1989e, February 10). Encinitas, county chase migrants from new site. *Los Angeles Times,* Sec. 2, p. 1.

Richwine, L. (1995, January 14). Packard vows to bar illegal immigrants from flood aid. *Los Angeles Times* (Orange County edition), p. B1.

Rodgers, T. (1988, December 22). Nobody's children. *La Costan,* p. A1.

Romo, R. (1983). *East Los Angeles: History of a barrio.* Austin: University of Texas Press.

Rouse, R. (1991). Mexican migration and the social space of postmodernism, *Diaspora,* 1, 8-23.

Rumbaut, R., Chavez, L. R., Moser, R., Pickwell, S., & Wishik, S. (1988). The politics of migrant health care: A comparative study of Mexican immigrants and Indochinese refugees in San Diego. *Research in the Sociology of Medicine Vol. 7* (pp. 143-202). Greenwich, CT: JAI Press.

Rural California Report. (1990, January). *Farm labor: Overview of 1989.* Davis, CA: Working Group on Farm Labor and Rural Poverty, California Institute for Rural Studies.

Said, E. (1978). *Orientalism.* New York: Vintage Books.

Scott, J. (1985). *Weapons of the weak: Everyday forms of peasant resistance.* New Haven: Yale University Press.

Serrano, R. A. (1989, October 12). Judge's ruling prompts teen to admit killing of two migrants. *Los Angeles Times,* p. B1.

Sherman, L. (1989, February 8). Border Patrol to probe claim agent tore up refugee's papers. *San Diego Tribune,* p. B1.

Sherman, L. (1993, October 5). Family homeless as canyon shacks are razed. *The San Diego Union-Tribune,* p. B1.

Sherman, L. (1994a, May 27). Bulldozers raze 40 camp homes. *The San Diego Union-Tribune,* p. B1.

Sherman, L. (1994b, July 16). 8 more families to swap shacks for bright, clean housing today. *The San Diego Union-Tribune,* p. B1.

Shogren, E. (1994, November 21). Plans to cut safety net leave legal immigrants dangling. *Los Angeles Times,* p. A1.

Shogren, E. (1995a, March 25). House OKs welfare overhaul that cuts off aid guarantees. *Los Angeles Times,* p. A1.

Shogren, E. (1995b, September 20). Senate approves shifting control of welfare to states. *Los Angeles Times,* p. A1.

Shogren, E. (1996, August 23). Clinton's signature launches historical overhaul of welfare. *Los Angeles Times,* p. A1.

Simon, R. J. (1985). *Public opinion and the media.* Lexington, MA: Lexington Books.

Smollar, D. (1984, April 14). Four Marines to stand trial in raids on illegal aliens. *Los Angeles Times,* Sec. 2, p. 1.

Soble, R. L. (1990, November 25). Alien's fate rests with obscure court. *Los Angeles Times,* p. A3.

Steinberg, S. (1981). *The ethnic myth: Race, ethnicity, and class in America.* New York: Atheneum.

Stevens, J. (1979, March 31). High school mulls violence on the campus. *Coast Dispatcher,* p. A11.

Stolcke, V. (1995). Talking culture: New boundaries, new rhetorics of exclusion in Europe. *Current Anthropology, 36,* 1-24.

Suarez-Orozco, C., & Suarez-Orozco, M. (1995). *Transformations: Immigration, family life, and achievement motivation among Latino adolescents.* Stanford: Stanford University Press.

Sumner, B. (1988, December 16). Let well enough alone. *Carlsbad Journal,* p. A4.

Takaki, R. (1989). *Strangers from a different shore: A history of Asian Americans.* Boston: Little, Brown.

Taylor, R. B., & Montemayor, R. (1980, December 15). Legal pleas seek to assist workers in avocado groves. *Los Angeles Times,* Sec. 1, p. 1.

Three in North County charged in slaying of alien, robberies. (1980, December 10). *Los Angeles Times,* Part 1, p. 3.

Turner, V. (1974). *Dramas, fields and metaphors.* Ithaca, NY: Cornell University Press.

U.S. Bureau of the Census. (1984). *Money, income and poverty status of families in the United States: 1983.* Series P-60, No. 145. Washington, DC: U.S. Government Printing Office.

U.S. House of Representatives. (1986). *Immigration Reform and Control Act of 1986.* Conference Report. 99th Congress, 2d Session. Report 99-1000. Washington, DC: U.S. Government Printing Office.

U.S. Immigration and Naturalization Service. (1995, October). *Operation Gatekeeper: Landmark progress at the border.* Washington, DC: Author.

van Gennep, A. (1960). *The rites of passage.* Chicago: University of Chicago Press.

Walbert, C. (1981, June 7). All hope of U.S. dollars vanished in blazing hut. *San Diego Tribune,* p. A1.

Walker, S. L. (1988a, December 20). Migration a matter of survival for entire Mexican villages. *San Diego Union,* p. A1.

Walker, S. L. (1988b, December 21). Some days, the work is only for 2 hours. San Diego Union, p. A1.

Walker, S. L. (1989a, January 19). County officials to target migrant housing. *San Diego*

Union, p. B1.

Walker, S. L. (1989b, February 2). Migrants set up camp at old landfill. *San Diego Union,* p. B1.

Walker, S. L. (1989c, February 3). Migrants at new site threatened by methane. *San Diego Union,* p. B1.

Weintraub, D. M. (1984, February 29). Two sentenced in farm workers' murders. *Los Angeles Times,* Sec. 2, p. 1.

Weintraub, D. M. (1986, October 15). Telegram on illegal aliens by Romney is condemned. *Los Angeles Times,* Sec. 2, p. 1.

Wolf, E. R. (1982). *Europe and the people without history.* Berkeley: University of California Press.

Wolf, D. H. (1987). *Alarm and sensibility: Demystifying undocumented alien crime in San Diego.* [Monograph No. 29.] La Jolla: Center For U.S.-Mexican Studies, University of California, San Diego.

Wolf, L. (1989, July 31). A harvest of charges, countercharges. *Los Angeles Times,* Sec. 2, p. 1.

Woodrow, K.A., & Passel, J.S. (1990). Post-IRCA undocumented immigration to the United States: An assessment based on the June 1988 CPS. In F. D. Bean, B. Edmonston, J. S. Passel (Eds.), *Undocumented migration to the United States* (pp. 33-75). Washington, DC: The Urban Institute Press.

Zola, I. (1978). Medicine as an institution of social control. In J. Ehrenreich (Ed.), *The cultural crisis of modern medicine* (pp. 80-100). New York: Monthly Review Press.

Glossary

Amigo de confianza: A trusted friend.

Ampararse: To enjoy protection, favor, or assistance.

Barrio: Neighborhood or local district.

Bracero: A hired hand or laborer for hire. Also refers to the Bracero Program, a U.S. governmental program that ran from 1942 to 1964 and allowed American employers to contract out work to Mexican laborers for short periods, usually a few months at a time.

Cantina: Drinking establishment or bar.

Cantón: A makeshift house or shelter, or a group of such shelters.

Cholo: A Mexican American gang member.

Colonia: A neighborhood or settlement, as in *colonia obrera,* a workers' settlement.

Costumbre: Custom, habit, or tradition. Here, the term *costumbres* often refers to traditions of Mexican or Latino origin carried on in the United States.

Corrido: A popular or sentimental ballad of Hispanic origin.

Coyote: A guide-for-hire for Mexican or Latino workers wishing to cross illegally into the United States. Some *coyotes* have become notorious for accepting money and then abandoning their charges in difficult or dangerous situations.

Fayuquero: A peddler of food or other items. A fayuquero may sell items at exorbitant prices to illegal workers living in camps, taking advantage of their fear of going out to legitimate stores.

Gabacho: An "Anglo," or non-Hispanic American; a derogatory term. The term broadly connotes foreignness; in Spain, it refers to the French.

Ilegale: An illegal, or undocumented, resident.

Indocumentado: An undocumented resident.

Maquiladora: A Mexico-based factory for the assembly (only) of parts, manufactured elsewhere, into goods for sale outside the country. Such assembly plants were set up under a program established by the Mexican government in 1965 to encourage foreign investment; and such companies pay only a small tax on the value added to the parts by their assembly when exporting to the United States.

Mejorar economicamente: To better oneself economically.

Mejor vida: "A better life," the goal of most undocumented workers.

Migra: Slang term for the U.S. Immigration and Naturalization Service (INS) or its agents.

Mojado: An undocumented worker. The term derives from the Spanish verb *mojar* (to get wet, soak, or dip in water) and is the Spanish counterpart to the English term *wetback* (an undocumented worker who has crossed into the United States by, e.g., swimming the Rio Grande); the term is used by the workers themselves.

El monte: "The hills." Here, the unpopulated wilderness around the U.S.– Mexico border.

El otro lado: "The other side"; that is, the U.S. side of the United States–Mexico border.

Paisano: Countryman; a rural dweller or peasant *(campesino).* Often refers to persons who have come from the same region of Mexico and prefer one another's company in the United States.

Parientes: Relatives, kinfolk.

Patrón: A boss, host, landlord, or other figure of authority.

Pocho: A person of Mexican ancestry born in the United States; derogatory.

Pollo: Literally, a chicken; *caldo de pollo,* chicken soup or stew. Figuratively, an undocumented worker, connoting the worker as a pursued, preyed-upon figure. Compare the figurative implications of the term *coyote.*

Progresar: To make progress, to advance economically.

Rancho: A cattle ranch or a small, agriculture-based settlement.

Sacadolares: Those who take money *(dolares)* out of Mexico for protection in foreign banks, or did so during the country's economic crisis and peso devaluation in the 1980s *(la Crisis)*. Derogatory; compare the terms *sacadineros* (swindler), *sacamuelas* (quack dentist), and *sacaperras* (slot machine)—all connoting the term *sacar,* or "extraction."

Subir: To rise, to come up.

Superarse: To surpass one's current situation; to set one's goals higher.

Vecino: Neighbor; from *vecindad,* vicinity or neighborhood.

APPENDIX / FILMS ON UNDOCUMENTED IMMIGRANTS

Many documentaries have been made on undocumented immigration and the U.S.–Mexico border area. Some deal specifically with Mexican immigrants in the San Diego area and thus are particularly useful companions to this book. They are listed below.

"In the Shadow of the Law." 60 minutes. The author was assistant producer and coauthor of this documentary on the lives of four families living for many years as undocumented immigrants in the United States. Explores the daily fears, work experiences, family life, and adjustments made by families who have settled in U.S. communities. The film can be purchased or rented from:

University of California
Extension Media Center
2176 Shattuck Avenue
Berkeley, CA 94704

"Uneasy Neighbors." 30 minutes. Dramatically illustrates how conflict arises when recent immigrants set up camps of makeshift housing in the midst of a relatively affluent community. It tells the story of the Green Valley camp, the subject of chapters 5 and 6. Topics examined include life in Green Valley, the attitudes of the larger society toward migrant workers, and workers' attitudes toward their lives and work. The author participated in the production of this documentary as well, and many of the people mentioned in this book are profiled. The film can be purchased or rented from:

University of California
Extension Media Center
2176 Shattuck Avenue
Berkeley, CA 94704

"The Ballad of an Unsung Hero: Pedro J. Gonzalez." Tells the story of Pedro J. Gonzalez, who fought in the Mexican revolution and then immigrated to Los Angeles in the 1920s. He eventually became a major musical recording star and radio personality in Spanish. At the height of his popularity he was falsely accused of a crime and sent to San Quentin prison. The film can be purchased or rented from:

The Cinema Guild
1697 Broadway
New York, NY 10019

"The Lemon Grove Incident." Tells in docudrama form how, in the early 1930s, Mexican parents in a small community in the San Diego area resisted the local school board's efforts to put their children into a separate school. They courageously took the school board to court and won, stopping overt segregation in their local school system. It was the first successful legal challenge to segregation in the United States. The film can be purchased or rented from:

The Cinema Guild
1697 Broadway
New York, NY 10019

INDEX

Permissions

N.I.M.B.Y.

Paper Due Next Friday

Sep pt1
Arturo Xuncax
Guatamala

Trans pt2
El Coyote
Mexico

Incorporation pt3
El Norte
L.A.